Music and Performance in the Book of Hours

This study uncovers the musical foundations and performance suggestions in books of hours, guides to prayer that were the most popular and widespread books of the late Middle Ages.

Exploring a variety of musical genres and sections of books of hours with musical implications, this book presents a richly textured sound world gleaned from dozens of extant manuscript sources from fifteenth-century France. It offers the first overview of the musical content of these handbooks to liturgy and devotional prayer, together with cues that show scribal awareness for the articulation of sacred plainchants. Although books of hours lack musical notation, this survey elucidates the full range of musical genres and styles suggested both within and beyond the liturgical offices prescribed in these books. Privileging sound and ritual enactment in the experience of the hours, the survey complements studies of visual imagery that have dominated the category.

The book's interdisciplinary approach within a musical context, and beautiful full-color illustrations, will attract not only specialists in musicology, liturgy, and late medieval studies but also those more broadly interested in the history of the book, memory, performance studies, and art history.

Michael Alan Anderson is Associate Professor of Musicology at the Eastman School of Music, University of Rochester. He specializes in European sacred music from the fourteenth to the sixteenth century, with emphasis on lay devotion and saints.

Routledge Research in Music Series

Researching Secular Music and Dance in the Early United States
Extending the Legacy of Kate Van Winkle Keller
Edited by Laura Lohman

Orpheus in the Academy
Monteverdi's First Opera and the Accademia degli Invaghiti
Joel Schwindt

Sound in the Ecstatic-Materialist Perspective on Experimental Music
Riccardo D. Wanke

Sound Heritage
Making Music Matter in Historic Houses
Edited by Jeanice Brooks; Matthew Stephens and Wiebke Thormählen

West Side Story, Gypsy, and the Art of Broadway Orchestration
Paul R. Laird

Modes of Communication in Stravinsky's Works
Sign and Expression
Per Dahl

Music by Subscription
Composers and their Networks in the British Music-Publishing Trade, 1676–1820
Edited by Simon D.I. Fleming and Martin Perkins

Early English Composers and the Credo
Emphasis as Interpretation in Sixteenth-Century Music
Wendy J. Porter

Music and Performance in the Book of Hours
Michael Alan Anderson

For more information about this series, please visit: www.routledge.com/Routledge-Research-in-Music/book-series/RRM

Music and Performance in the Book of Hours

Michael Alan Anderson

LONDON AND NEW YORK

First published 2022
by Routledge
4 Park Square, Milton Park, Abingdon, Oxon OX14 4RN

and by Routledge
605 Third Avenue, New York, NY 10158

Routledge is an imprint of the Taylor & Francis Group, an informa business

© 2022 Michael Alan Anderson

The right of Michael Alan Anderson to be identified as author of this work has been asserted in accordance with sections 77 and 78 of the Copyright, Designs and Patents Act 1988.

With the exception of Chapter 2, no part of this book may be reprinted or reproduced or utilised in any form or by any electronic, mechanical, or other means, now known or hereafter invented, including photocopying and recording, or in any information storage or retrieval system, without permission in writing from the publishers.

Chapter 2 of this book is available for free in PDF format as Open Access from the individual product page at www.routledge.com. It has been made available under a Creative Commons Attribution-Non Commercial-No Derivatives 4.0 license

Trademark notice: Product or corporate names may be trademarks or registered trademarks, and are used only for identification and explanation without intent to infringe.

British Library Cataloguing-in-Publication Data
A catalogue record for this book is available from the British Library

Library of Congress Cataloging-in-Publication Data
Names: Anderson, Michael Alan, 1975– author.
Title: Music and performance in the Book of hours / Michael Alan Anderson.
Description: New York : Routledge, 2022. | Series: Routledge research in
   music | Includes bibliographical references and index.
Identifiers: LCCN 2021058337 (print) | LCCN 2021058338 (ebook) |
   ISBN 9780367691325 (hardback) | ISBN 9780367691387 (paperback) |
   ISBN 9781003140511 (ebook)
Subjects: LCSH: Divine office (Music)—France—15th century—History and
   criticism. | Gregorian chants—France—15th century—History and
   criticism. | Books of hours—France—History—15th century. |
   Sound—Religious aspects—Christianity.
Classification: LCC ML3027.2 .A53 2022 (print) | LCC ML3027.2 (ebook) |
   DDC 781.71/2009440902—dc23
LC record available at https://lccn.loc.gov/2021058337
LC ebook record available at https://lccn.loc.gov/2021058338

ISBN: 978-0-367-69132-5 (hbk)
ISBN: 978-0-367-69138-7 (pbk)
ISBN: 978-1-003-14051-1 (ebk)

DOI: 10.4324/9781003140511

Typeset in Times New Roman
by Apex CoVantage, LLC

Contents

List of figures	vi
List of music examples	viii
List of tables	x
Acknowledgments	xi
List of abbreviations	xiii
Introduction	1

PART I
Music of the Offices   15

1 Psalms   17
2 Antiphons   36
3 Hymns   64
4 Responsories   86
5 Dialogues   105

PART II
Music beyond the Offices   119

6 The Seven Penitential Psalms   121
7 The Litany   141
8 Suffrages   162
9 Mass for the Virgin   193

Sources and bibliography	215
Index	226

Figures

1.1	Psalm 18	21
1.2	Psalm 8	23
1.3	Psalm 24	26
1.4	Psalm 18	28
1.5	Magnificat	30
2.1a/b	Antiphon, *In loco pascue* with Psalm 22 (beginning and end)	42
2.2a/b	Antiphon for the Benedictus at Lauds, *Beata dei genetrix* (beginning and end)	45
2.3	Vespers Antiphons in the Office of the Virgin	47
2.4	Invitatory antiphon, *Ave Maria gratia plena* with Psalm 94	50
2.5	Invitatory antiphon, *Regem cui omnia vivunt* with Psalm 94	54
2.6	*Salve regina*	57
3.1	Hymn, *Quem terra pontus aethera*	67
3.2	Hymn, *Patris sapientia veritas divina*	75
3.3	Hymn, *Nobis sancti spiritus*	78
3.4	Te Deum (excerpt)	82
4.1	Responsory, *Sancta et immaculata virginitas*	94
4.2	Responsory, *Credo quod redemptor*	95
4.3	Responsory, *Peccantem me quotidie*	97
4.4	Responsory, *Libera me Domine* (II)	102
5.1	Opening of Matins in the Office of the Virgin with versicle, *Domine labia mea aperies*	108
5.2	Pater noster	115
6.1	Seven Penitential Psalms opening with David in prayer	124
6.2	Seven Penitential Psalms opening with David in prayer	125
6.3	Seven Penitential Psalms opening with David and Bathsheba	126
6.4	Seven Penitential Psalms opening with David and Bathsheba	128
6.5	Penitential Psalms 50 and 101 (partial)	131
6.6	Antiphon, *Ne reminiscaris Domine*	133
6.7	Antiphon, *Ne reminiscaris Domine*	134
6.8	Antiphon, *Ne reminiscaris Domine*	136
6.9	Antiphon, *Ne reminiscaris Domine*	137
7.1a–g	The Litany (excerpts)	143
7.2	The Litany (excerpt)	158
8.1	Suffrage for St. Apollonia	166
8.2	Suffrage for St. Barbara	170

8.3	Sequence, *Stabat mater*	176
8.4	Suffrage for St. Michael	182
8.5	Memorial for All Saints	184
8.6	Memorial for the Trinity	186
9.1	Two Alleluias, Mass for the Virgin	198
9.2	Introit, Kyrie, and Gloria from the Mass for the Virgin	202
9.3	Kyrie and Gloria from the Mass for the Virgin	204
9.4	Mass for the Virgin Mary (excerpt)	206
9.5	Mass for Christmas Day (opening)	211
9.6	Sequence, *Lauda Sion salvatorem* (beginning)	212

Music examples

1.1	Magnificat, Mode 2 tone	33
2.1	Antiphons from the Office of the Virgin	39
2.2	Mode 7 Antiphons MA4–MA6 from the Office of the Virgin	40
2.3	Antiphon, *In loco pascue*	44
2.4	(a) Invitatory, *Ave Maria gratia plena*, CAO 1041; (b) Antiphon, *Ave Maria gratia plena*, CAO 1539	49
2.5	Invitatory antiphon, *Regem cui omnia vivunt*	52
2.6	Antiphon, *Salve regina*	56
2.7	Antiphon, *Adoramus te*	59
2.8	Antiphon, *Veni Sancte Spiritus*	60
3.1	Two versions of the hymn *Quem terra pontus aethera*	66
3.2	First verses of the hymns *Memento salutis auctor*, *Quem terra pontus aethera*, and *O gloriosa domina*, set to Stäblein melody 16	70
3.3	Tenor from anonymous Gloria "O patris sapientia"	73
3.4	*Patris sapientia veritas divina* (tenor)	74
3.5	Melodic formulas of the Te Deum	80
4.1	Responsory, *Sancta et immaculata virginitas*	88
4.2	Responsory, *Beata es Maria*	90
4.3	Responsory, *Felix namque es*	91
4.4	Responsory, *Libera me Domine* (I), CAO 7092	99
4.5	Responsory, *Libera me Domine* (II), CAO 7091	101
5.1	Versicle, *Diffusa est gratia*	112
5.2	Versicle and response, *Deus in adiutorium* and doxology	112
5.3	Pater noster	114
6.1	Antiphon, *Ne reminiscaris Domine*	132
7.1	Opening of the Litany	153
7.2	Excerpts from the "Ab/A" and "Per" series in the Litany	154
7.3	Select "Ut" petitions from the Litany	155
7.4	Concluding items from the Litany	156
8.1	Antiphons: (a) *Te invocamus, te adoramus* for the Trinity; (b) *Inter natos mulierum* for John the Baptist; (c) *Petrus apostolus* for Peter and Paul	165
8.2	Sequence, *Gaude Barbara beata*, set to select verses of *Laudes crucis attolamus* (1A, 2A, 4A)	172
8.3	Versicle for St. Martin	179

8.4	Versicle and response for John the Baptist	180
9.1	Introit, *Salve sancta parens*	194
9.2	Gradual, *Benedicta et venerabilis*	195
9.3	Offertory, *Felix namque es*	197
9.4	Communion, *Beata viscera*	197

Tables

1.1	Psalms in the Office of the Virgin	19
1.2	Psalms in the Office of the Dead	19
2.1	Antiphons for the Office of the Virgin	38
2.2	Antiphons for the Office of the Dead	41
4.1	Matins responsories for the Office of the Dead	92
8.1	Common antiphons in the suffrages	163
8.2	Common versicle-response pairings in the suffrages	178
9.1	Masses in Paris, BnF, Ars. Ms-616 réserve, with their Introits	209

Acknowledgments

Writing this book has been like putting together a puzzle: there are seemingly innumerable pieces to fit together, but one must also keep an eye on the whole. While my overall vision has remained steady for this project, I cannot take credit for fitting many of the little pieces together to form the mosaic of this undertaking. The work to create this book has truly been a team effort. Profound scholarship laid the foundation for this monograph, but countless individuals have given generously of their time and expertise to ensure that this endeavor advanced from its earliest stages.

I would first like to acknowledge those colleagues who supplied me with bits of knowledge over the past seven years to help this montage come together. Their expertise came not always with books of hours per se; their talents span general medieval studies to music typesetting. This group includes Benjamin Baker, Ilya Dines, Roger Freitas, Nicholas Gresens, Nancy Norwood, Michael Peppard, Ellen Rentz, and Anne Yardley. Further, an ensemble of expert and efficient librarians made my work less daunting than it could have been. I extend special gratitude to Justina Elmore and Stephanie Frontz at the River Campus Libraries, as well as to Katie Papas and Anna Siebach-Larsen at the Rossell Hope Robbins Library of the University of Rochester. Finally, hats off to a triumvirate of librarians at the Sibley Music Library at the Eastman School of Music, my home away from home. Jim Farrington, Robert Iannapollo, and Rick McRae have been patient, resourceful, and creative with my countless requests to aid this project over the years. Thank you for your tireless work.

A large group of seasoned researchers provided me with sage counsel where my training and experience fell short. My sincere gratitude goes to Terence Bailey, Rebecca Baltzer, Susan Boynton, Mitchell Brauner, Joseph Dyer, Margot Fassler, Edward Foley, Barbara Haggh-Huglo, David Hiley, Leofranc Holford-Strevens, Peter Jeffery, Debra Lacoste, Patrick Macey, William Mahrt, Yossi Maurey, Honey Meconi, Emerson Morgan, William Prizer, Virginia Reinburg, Catherine Saucier, and Emily Thelen. Their collective contributions to this book have strengthened the final product. Above all, I must salute Roger Wieck from the Morgan Library & Museum in New York, an authority on books of hours. In 2012, he generously prepared slides and in-concert remarks for a program, "Music of the Hours," performed in Chicago by Schola Antiqua under my direction. We reprised this program in New York at the Morgan in 2014 in connection with Wieck's beautifully curated exhibit *Miracles in Miniature: The Art of the Master of Claude de France*. I kept in touch with him about my work on books of hours and am ever grateful that he read the full manuscript with care and gave helpful suggestions to improve it.

Genevieve Aoki, music editor at Routledge, has been cheering the prospect of this book since we met in 2017. She moreover has worked to ensure that the monograph could be delivered in color and in a larger format than typical scholarly publications. Calvin Bower and Anne Robertson have remained mentors to me for more than two decades; my instincts as a researcher in many ways trace to the wisdom they have imparted to me over the years. My mother, Virginia Anderson, continues to be a big supporter of my work and a helping hand with the Latin language. Finally, my wife Laura has understood the unreasonable amount of time required to finish this book and has responded with patience, kindness, and love. I owe her greatly for all that she has contributed so that this project could reach its end.

*

This book has received the Weiss-Brown Publication Subvention Award from the Newberry Library. The award supports the publication of outstanding works of scholarship that cover European civilization before 1700 in the areas of music, theater, French or Italian literature, or cultural studies. It is made to commemorate the career of Howard Mayer Brown. Professional development funding from the Eastman School of Music further provided generous support for publication expenses.

Abbreviations

Bibliographic abbreviations

AH *Analecta hymnica medii aevi.* 55 vols. Ed. Henry Marriott Bannister, Clemens Blume, and Guido Maria Dreves. Leipzig, 1886–1992.

CAO *Corpus antiphonalium officii.* 6 vols. Ed. René-Jean Hesbert. Rerum Ecclesiasticarum Documenta, Series maior, Fontes 7–12. Rome, 1963–79.

CE *The Catholic Encyclopedia: An International Work of Reference on the Constitution, Doctrine, Discipline, and History of the Catholic Church.* 17 vols. Ed. Charles George Herbermann, Edward A. Pace, et al. New York: Robert Appleton Company, 1907–1912.

DACL *Dictionnaire d'archéologie chrétienne et de liturgie.* 15 vols. Ed. Fernand Cabrol and Henri Leclercq. Paris, 1907–1953.

GR *Graduale Sacrosanctae Romanae Ecclesiae De Tempore et De Sancti.* Sablé sur Sarthe, 1974.

LU *The Liber Usualis: with Introduction and Rubrics in English.* Tournai and New York, 1961.

NCE Catholic University of America. *New Catholic Encyclopedia.* 15 vols. Detroit, 2003.

NG *The New Grove Dictionary of Music and Musicians.* Second edition. 27 vols. Ed. Stanley Sadie. New York, 2001.

PL *Patrologiae cursus completus: series latina.* 221 vols. Ed. J. P. Migne. Paris, 1844–79.

Abbreviations used to designate libraries and manuscripts

BnF, Ars. Bibliothèque nationale de France, Bibliothèque de l'Arsenal
BnF, fr.   Bibliothèque nationale de France, Département des Manuscrits, français
BnF, lat. Bibliothèque nationale de France, Département des Manuscrits, latin
BnF, n.a.l. Bibliothèque nationale de France, Département des Manuscrits, nouvelles acquisitions latines
LBL London, British Library

Conventions

All scriptural references use the Septuagint/Vulgate numbering, most notably the Psalms. The gamut of pitches takes *F* as its lower boundary note (F2 in scientific pitch notation) and uses italicized capitals through that octave. Lowercase italicized letters (beginning with *f* for F3) consume the adjacent octave above, and a prime symbol added to this letter (beginning *f′* for F4) distinguishes the next octave. No notes exceed that range in this study of vocal music. Positions of liturgical items in the Divine Office use the nomenclature developed in Andrew Hughes, *Late Medieval Liturgical Offices: Sources and Chants* and continued in the Cantus Index online.

Introduction

Salve regina, mater misericordiae,
Vita, dulcedo, et spes nostra, salve.
Ad te clamamus exsules filii Evae.
Ad te suspiramus, gementes et flentes in hac lacrimarum valle.
Eia, ergo, advocata nostra, illos tuos misericordes oculos ad nos converte;
Et Iesum, benedictum fructum ventris tui, nobis post hoc exilium ostende.
O clemens, O pia, O dulcis Virgo Maria.

Hail Queen, Mother of mercy;
Our life, our sweetness, and our hope, hail.
To you we cry, poor banished children of Eve.
To you we sigh, mourning and weeping in this valley of tears.
Turn then, O most gracious advocate, those merciful eyes toward us;
And after this exile, show us the blessed fruit of your womb, Jesus.
O clement, O loving, O sweet Virgin Mary.

In the fifteenth century, the venerable *Salve regina* was on the lips of European sailors roughing the high seas. On many ships, the affective Marian text was delivered not as a spoken prayer, but rather in song, echoing the melody that had become etched in the Christian memory since its introduction into the liturgy three centuries earlier. In monastic settings, this plainchant traditionally resounded after the service of Compline, marking the end of each liturgical day for about half of the year.[1] More than one account reveals that seafarers mimicked religious communities, not just closing their days in prayer with the *Salve regina* but also observing other pauses for devotion during their time on board. In his late fifteenth-century travel diaries, the Dominican Felix Fabri from Ulm chronicled three daily commemorations, which included the sailors singing the *Salve regina* at sundown, a ritual known from the fourteenth century.[2] The custom of keeping hallowed hours for prayer and devotional song was not confined to monks, nuns, and mariners; lay Christians across late medieval Europe were well acquainted with the ceremonial practices of the Divine Office and able to imitate them each day. Personal devotional manuals known as books of hours ensured that the faithful at large could keep the church's distinguished rituals close at hand.

Books of hours (*horae*) offered guides to prayer that captured the experience of the daily Liturgy of the Hours in a compact, portable form. Sometimes lavishly decorated for wealthy owners, these books are one of the more familiar vestiges of late medieval and early modern European culture, earning the oft-repeated "best-seller" status among extant artifacts of these periods. Indeed, for more than 300 years, ownership of books of hours outpaced that of every other kind of book, including the Bible. In 1571, Pope Pius V banned the use of existing books of hours, but their widespread circulation and use took decades to decline.

Books of hours trace their heritage through psalters. Members of the clergy and monastic communities had long owned books of psalms for their private use, but by the eleventh century, the Christian laity joined in the possession of psalters. The best known of all biblical texts, the psalms formed the core of the daily liturgies practiced in monasteries, convents, and cathedrals, where all 150 psalms were organized into a weekly cursus for recitation.[3] Psalters became more than a prescriptive textbook for the private enactment of the ritual hours; they also functioned as a pathway to learning Latin and absorbing Christian teaching. As ownership of psalters expanded, new devotional content crept in. Abbreviated office liturgies appeared in psalters, giving rise to the phenomenon of a hybrid psalter-hours. Among the offices, the "Little Office" for the Virgin Mary was the most common, but the number and length of these liturgies grew until another genre emerged when the two separated.[4] The condensed offices plus ancillary devotions shed their connection to the psalters altogether and became stand-alone books of hours from the mid-thirteenth century onward.[5] Production of books of hours was concentrated in French and Flemish scriptoria, but circulation grew across western Europe as printed copies commodified the genre by the early sixteenth century. As compilations with local variations, books of hours escaped the oversight of the church while still retaining many of the eminent texts and august rituals of ecclesiastical practice that the laity held dear.

Books of hours feature an array of devotional possibilities. They usually open with calendars to situate daily observances and could include gospel readings, the Litany of the Saints, the Seven Penitential Psalms, prayers to the Virgin Mary and the saints, and of course material associated with liturgical offices, the veritable work of God (*opus Dei*). An office for Mary remained central to books of hours but was paired with the Office of the Dead, which became the book's second anchor. Psalms saturated both liturgies, along with readings, responses, and other genres that mirrored formal liturgical exercises. Each office contained different types of utterances one would encounter liturgically, from prayers in silence to communal speech and song.

Developed in monastic circles by the tenth century, the Office of the Virgin Mary must be viewed as part of the growth in Marian devotion that blossomed through the late Middle Ages. This "Little Office" (*Officium Parvum Beatae Mariae Virginis*) was sung in the choir alongside the daily prescribed liturgies, most notably at the Cathedral of Notre Dame of Paris.[6] Fastened to each of the eight canonical hours, the texts of the Office of the Virgin must have been deeply ingrained in the minds of clerics, performed far more often than the once-per-year feasts at the main altar. Small wonder that the Office of the Virgin spun out in an isolated form and eventually in books of hours. The services in this office began with the celebration of Matins (sometimes condensed, which explains the modifier "Little") and cycled through more modest observances of Lauds, the four minor hours (Prime, Terce, Sext, None), Vespers, and Compline. In illuminated *horae*, artistic cycles of images preceding each service reinforce that each of the eight hours marked a significant event in Mary's life, from the Annunciation to her coronation as Queen of Heaven.

The Office of the Dead, the other liturgical pillar of a book of hours, unfolded in three services (Vespers, Matins, and Lauds) and reflected Christians' perpetual concern about the prospect of death. This office was also a near-daily occurrence in monastic institutions, given the exhaustive list of the departed, from brothers and sisters of religious communities to local leaders and benefactors. Testators often specified that the Office of the Dead—the primary funeral liturgy—be sung for a period of time after burial, as the soul was considered to be in an especially fragile state in the immediate days after death.[7] This office for the deceased, an event sometimes followed by a Requiem Mass, was not infrequently open to public mourners. In some English books of hours, musical notation accompanied the Office of the Dead, a sign of both luxury and the role that singing must have played among lay attendees.[8] In a mid-fifteenth-century book of hours from the Provence region, the Office of the Dead opens with a miniature of monks gathered around two books performing the funereal rite, one of the books visibly bearing notated music.[9] This office was by no means designed only for public use; Christians could recite it in private using their books of hours as a way to remember their ancestors or to prepare for their own death and judgment in a structured, ritualized way.

From sights to sounds

Surviving in the tens of thousands and scattered among libraries, museums, and private collections around the world, books of hours have been the subject of scholarly interest for more than a century and have arguably become the best-known relic of late medieval and early modern culture. Investigations have scarcely concerned the two offices that consume most of the book's contents; rather, the intricate color miniatures, ornate borders, and other visual splendor have long attracted historians to books of hours as *objets d'art*. Since the late nineteenth century, art historians have tended to dominate major studies of books of hours, what might be called "general" studies of the genre.[10] Still today, catalogs of books of hours, in print and online, may be indexed by their illuminations, which often signal new sections. Collectors too have foremost gravitated to books of hours for their exquisite imagery, less concerned with the revered texts contained in these devotional guides. Iconography, however, was a means to assist with the experience of prayer: studies of the alluring images and borders in books of hours should not diminish the esteem the faithful had for the powerful words of the rite. One scholar of the genre, Gregory Clark, has noticed an inclination in the field to study the art first and text second, likening it to enjoying dessert before eating one's broccoli.[11] Rachel Fulton has also criticized scholars for dismissing the experience of devotion through formulaic prayer: "it is not the artifacts (books, exercises, formulas) that are at fault but, rather, ourselves."[12] Recurring recitation and habit-forming rehearsal of venerable texts lie at the center of Christians' daily encounters with books of hours and demand attention to balance study of the genre.[13]

In the early fifteenth-century *Book of the Three Virtues*, French court poet and author Christine de Pizan counsels a princess about her responsibilities to her young daughter, explaining that the latter must know "her religious offices and the mass" before receiving books of devotion and of good behavior.[14] Fluency in the liturgy evidently preceded the development of literacy, a gesture as much to the ear as to the eye, a point that guides the study ahead. As the aristocracy began to lose its exclusive grip on books of hours in the fifteenth century, near mass production and the dawn of the print age resulted in widening circulation of these books among a more modest social class, which included traders, lawyers, judges, teachers, and secretaries. If a household was lucky enough to own a single book, that book was likely a book of hours—some owned several copies.[15] Though these books were cherished family heirlooms, the centrality of the liturgical hours remained. Hubert Meurier, a sixteenth-century canon of Reims Cathedral, wrote that the laity, notably women and small children, "knew most of the office of the sacrament as if they had been brought up from the start among ecclesiastics."[16]

Scholars used to assume low levels of literacy from the Christian laity, which in part may explain the lure of visual artistry for historians of books of hours as much as their owners.

But the reality was that many books of hours had few or no illustrations; this suggests that users hungered for the stipulated liturgical texts, psalms, and prayers that ordered public life.[17] Investigations of prayer texts and the nature of reading steadily emerged from literary scholars and others attentive to lay interaction with the content of books of hours. It is by now accepted that owners of all stripes had much more familiarity with the Latin prayer texts than was traditionally credited to them. As with learning to read, acquaintance with psalms, hymns, and other omnipresent devotions must have been made through a combination of hearing texts and sounding out the phonemes from a young age from a primer or book of hours.

Beyond the subject of literacy, historians of the book and material culture have probed experiences with books of hours more deeply, further rebalancing the attention that had been given to pictorial artistry. Sandra Penketh, Virginia Reinburg, and others have pursued the topic of female ownership and involvement with books of hours, whether from the nobility or lower social ranks.[18] This topic has led the way to ethnographic studies and social histories of books of hours. Studies have looked to these intimate prayer guides to discover the identities of their owners and their family histories, traced through customizing elements and annotations that unveil personalization of the artifact. Combining some of these elements in a large-scale study of English books of hours, Eamon Duffy deliberately avoided an art-historical perspective and instead provided a "tribute to scribbles," or marginal writings, in books of hours, which can evince "clues to the beliefs and devotional habits of medieval people—not least to the innermost thoughts of women, who formed a large proportion of the medieval market for such books."[19] At the same time, the work of Duffy and others has tended to bypass the central texts of books of hours, focused instead on personal touches and marginalia as objects of study.[20]

While no one will admit that charming miniatures and ornate marginalia of some books could not distract the eye in an experience with prayer books, the liturgies and prayer texts were the foundational substance for handwritten books of hours and had a "look" of their own that is not shown often enough in studies. Although these durable texts for modern observers may not hold the immediate visual grandeur of, say, a detailed miniature of the Annunciation, the words of the liturgy, the arrangement of time-honored rites, and the presence of potent prayer texts seem to have prompted an experience that was just as enticing as any illumination for its owner. Hallowed and vibrant for devotees, the written word crackled with familiar sounds, inextricable from the ancient texts that flooded the pages of books of hours.

Concerned with manuscript reception studies in general, Pamela Sheingorn reminds us that a "full encounter" with the open book represents a multisensory, embodied experience.[21] Other studies of medieval cultures have also emphasized the somatic aspects of texts.[22] Human interaction with text necessarily involves sight, but the sense of hearing and the recollection of sound prompted by texts invite consideration for those interested in recovering the phenomenology of books of hours. These precious prayer books were more than an archive of sacred texts; for many, the words of the liturgy and extraliturgical devotion cued an experience with a network of assorted sounds—not ephemeral noises, but melodic echoes that were recognizable because they simultaneously recalled performance and were performable by nature.

As has often been repeated in studies of books of hours, the lay experience with these prayer manuals foremost constituted the act of emulation of monastic practice. The *horae* allowed Christians to move beyond the role of spectator into one of active participation through the structure and patterns of the liturgy. The offices in a book of hours, which account for the majority of its contents, establish a ritualized rhythm for the faithful, summoning the unceasing liturgical exercises of monks, nuns, and secular clergy, no small part of it delivered musically. Virginia Reinburg has highlighted that the liturgies and other devotional items in books of hours reflected religious "speech,"[23] but the varied kinds of speech in turn embed sounds, imagined or performed by the user of a book of hours. Many of the utterances in books of hours are in fact recoverable melodies.

Musicologists are no strangers to books of hours. A natural outgrowth of art-historical studies, surveys of organological iconography constitute music specialists' early engagement with the genre. In the mid-1970s, Edmund Bowles's "checklists" of musical instruments in illuminated manuscripts in part addressed those drawn in books of hours.[24] Margareth Owens's dissertation focused exclusively on books of hours and musical iconography (instruments and musicians), including what they can teach us about late medieval practice.[25] Apart from these early studies centered on the familiar territory of images and marginalia, musicologists have noticeably remained at an arm's length from these popular devotional books.

Extant psalters occasionally reveal musical notation for antiphons, but in books of hours notation was rare, a seeming dead end for music historians.[26] Since the 1990s, however, musicologists have alluded to books of hours in a selective and peripheral way. Mentions of the genre in music-oriented studies tend to occur in connection with investigations of sixteenth-century choral polyphony. Howard Mayer Brown's study of early printed music highlighted the predominance of devotional texts that reflected those found in books of hours.[27] Bonnie Blackburn, David Rothenberg, Julie Cumming, Geneviève Bazinet, Patrick Macey, John Constant, and David Crook have each independently discovered similar links between texts in books of hours and those set in polyphony, especially by early sixteenth-century composers.[28] Kate van Orden's illuminating study of literacy, music, and sixteenth-century print culture further traced connections between repertoire, aural memory, and lay devotion as expressed in primers and prayer books including books of hours.[29] The ties to the Renaissance musical canon are undeniably many and there are doubtless more to discover, but musicologists have avoided mapping the sounding phenomena within books of hours themselves.

Encoded sounds

Through the genre of books of hours, Paul Saenger identified a cultural shift in the fifteenth century from reading aloud to silent absorption of texts.[30] "Silence" must be qualified, though. More recent strands of scholarship have underscored the user's sound experience of prayer books with attention to the "inner ear." Intent to remedy manuscript studies that omit sound from discussion, Beth Williamson identified musical notation and depictions of music-making in prayer manuscripts, which she interpreted as appeals to the interior senses rather than to physically sounding music.[31] Similarly, in a detailed analysis of images from the late fifteenth-century "Gualenghi-d'Este Hours," Tim Shephard, Laura Ştefănescu, and Serenella Sessini further explored the inner sensorium through suggestive depictions of music-making, introducing the concept of "silent music." They argue that silent music is preferable to physical sounds and especially efficacious in prayer. This is an exceptional kind of music that a devotee could recall, hear, and create "with the heart," taking a cue from the words of St. Paul (Ephesians 5:19 and 1 Corinthians 14:15).[32] Both studies lean on patristic writings to confirm the inner senses as a means of drawing one closer to God. In the *Confessions*, Augustine famously described Ambros achieving a state of meditative contemplation with an active form of reading done in silence.[33] This silent but lively type of engagement could help explain how some users of books of hours interacted with prayer texts, seeing the text to prompt the memory of pronounced and sung words.

The early medieval encyclopedist Isidore of Seville wrote about song and the voice: "Their sound, because it is something perceived by the senses, vanishes as the moment passes and is imprinted in the memory . . . for unless sounds are held by the memory of man, they perish, because they cannot be written down."[34] Historians typically cite this passage to confirm that a formal notation of sound did not exist in the early seventh century. Texts had long preserved sound before musical notation could independently harness melodies. Books of organized chant texts pre-date our earliest surviving notated manuscripts by more than two centuries.[35] Even in the ninth century, Notker of St. Gall set poetry to long melodies of liturgical sequences so that the individual notes could remain tethered in his memory.[36] If words themselves could tie down the elusive nature of the sonic realm, it will be worthwhile to consider how texts in books of hours may awaken a sound bank in the user's memory, instead of being understood as prayers to be read and reread in abject silence.

As studies in music and literature have shown repeatedly, the rise of literacy in the late Middle Ages did not signal the death of orality in the reading and performance of texts. Oral processes complemented literary contexts, often reinforcing one another rather than standing in opposition.[37] This study of music and performance in books of hours attempts to answer Beth Williamson's call for an "aural turn" within medieval studies that admits sound, speech, and song into devotional practice.[38] From an "ear first" perspective, it seeks to identify not only signals for the sound-specific contents of books of hours—whether or not the sounds were realized by users—but also indications of performative action associated with the sound that these pages can offer. Emma Dillon proposes a "complex practice of sound in prayer," recognizing the book of hours in particular as inherently sonorous, even filled with its own brand of notation.[39]

Identification of genre is a simple but important task in the quest to unlock the sound world of books of hours. The offices in particular unveil a variety of liturgical items, all of which were performed vocally and perchance recollected as vocal performances. The genres ranged from poetry to prose and fluctuated from elaborately sung to murmured in silence. The textual and sonic gamut produced an array of unexplored vocal "textures" in the book of hours. It is hardly a mystery to recognize these textures, as scribes diligently provided rubrics and scripts of variable sizes to distinguish liturgical genres. These conscious designs allow "saccadic" indexing for the eye to grasp major shifts on the page while moderating the pacing of text.[40] Although Katherine Zieman finds "little evidence that users of such books made practical variations in their private performances to signal the distinction," this positivistic view unnecessarily restricts the possibilities of realizing the material of the page.[41] Taking a more accommodating and imaginative approach, Pamela Sheingorn has suggested that calling attention to new sections of text "encourages the reader-viewer to 'hear' the new passage in a specific voice distinct from that of the passage that preceded."[42] As paratexts, rubrics announced the principal chants and prayers, and were reliable indicators of modifications in vocal tone that fit the text, whether it was a florid musical passage reserved for a soloist, a short communal response as part of a dialogue, or a simple prose oration uttered by a priest. Specifications of genre alert the owner of a book of hours to the kind of voice that may be imagined or even produced.

Performing the *horae*

One large task of this project is to identify the sounds referenced in books of hours, but another aim seeks to understand how texts might be internalized or performed. Scholars seem to have dismissed the texts of books of hours as frozen in time rather than laden with prompts for action. While the popular prayers "O Intemerata" and "Obsecro te" may strike one as streams of lengthy prose in the *horae*, many scribes elsewhere laid out folios and presented lines in a way that suggests the texts were echoes of a performance.[43] Instructions for reenactment are of course not divulged outright, but neither should the possibility of execution (or imagined execution) be excluded. The early thirteenth-century statutes for both lay and clerical workers at a hospital in Montdidier (northern France) required those who knew the Office of the Virgin to sing it (*decantet*), not recite it. If they knew only the Seven Penitential Psalms, they were to sing those instead as part of morning prayer.[44] From these widely adopted orders, one can rest assured that these texts, all found in books of hours, stirred some users to enact or express the musical sounds of prayer.

Hovering over the question of performance of the texts are thorny issues of public and private consumption of the book of hours. While standard definitions of the book of hours emphasize its use in private devotion in the home, it has already been intimated that usage of the *horae* in public was not an uncommon practice. With a flexible context in mind rather than an unconstructive binary opposition, one can imagine different types of performative interaction with the book of hours, generating a web of engagement possibilities. We know that "private" devotional activity was fostered in the public context of Mass, for instance.[45] Mass itself exhibited different levels of vocality and gesture to consider in the ritual act. Outward participation was also conventional for public funereal rites, but domestic contexts did not prevent these voices from reemerging on a similar embodied spectrum to produce a state of *meditatio*. Reinburg has described the exercises revealed in books of hours as "both individual and collective, public and private" all at once.[46] This study seeks to keep open these possibilities when journeying through the central texts of books of hours, particularly in light of signs of a performance-oriented *mise-en-page*. It further acknowledges the close connection of reading and sound, allowing for the presentation of texts to reveal their own "charisma," evoking voices of differing types and contrasting styles of performance.[47]

In a study of orality and the written word, Thomas Cohen and Lesley Twomey assert, "Script is . . . silent. But the reader's mind is loud, as is the writer's, and script must labour if it is to command that interior loudness by script-devices that coax or compel the reader's mind to align itself at least partly with the writer's interior voice."[48] The user's reaction to both texts and "script-devices" may take different forms in the experience of the *horae*. Whether listening to the mind's ear, murmuring, or outright singing, supplicants' responses to texts are necessarily variable and are all put on equal footing in the investigation ahead.[49] Notably, the chapters of this book avoid the term "reader" for the owner of a book of hours. Replacing this word with "user," "owner," "supplicant," and the like, this study reminds us of the performative potential of every opening in a manuscript, much of it filled with musical correlates from the liturgy presented without conventional staff notation.

Limits

Giacomo Baroffio recognized the performative experience one could have with a book of hours in the absence of music notation. His 2011 study established the heavy musical stamp on books of hours, cataloging the organization and transmission patterns of liturgical melodies in connection with Italian books of hours in manuscript form, mainly from the fifteenth century during their prime.[50] The survey ahead will likewise confine observations principally to fifteenth-century manuscript books of hours, but of French provenance. General studies of the genre have long centered on France, which dominated production of books of hours in the late Middle Ages. Artistic traditions in the circle of John, Duke of Berry (1340–1416) have attracted considerable attention, but workshops in the north, Paris especially, constituted a hub of book copying and illustrating.[51] The few inventories of manuscripts available in the aggregate indicate that extant books of hours in France account for more than half of the global count. In the age of print (outside the scope of this study), Parisian presses similarly controlled production of the *horae*, credited with 90 percent of all editions from 1470 to the end of the sixteenth century.[52]

Besides the temporal and geographic boundaries of this investigation, an additional restriction of liturgical "usage" will be placed on this exploration of musical sound in books of hours. The collation of items in the liturgy was by no means stable across Europe. The office liturgies recorded in books of hours either reflected local liturgical practice or—increasingly in the fifteenth century—offered the conventional "use" of Rome, a rite adopted in the thirteenth century by the Roman curia from the Franciscans and later standardized after the Council of Trent. Some cities, like Paris, Amiens, and Rouen, had their own emphases in the calendar and special assortment of liturgical items; scholars have consequently identified "use" as one of the basic properties of a book of hours. Various "tests" have been developed to determine usage, with focus not only on the local calendar but also on the Office of the Virgin, the Office of the Dead, and stipulated saints in the Litany.[53] By focusing primarily on the popular Roman usage in this study, sources can be compared more readily, and nuances in the *mise-en-page* can emerge more visibly as textual variants are kept to a minimum. (The liturgical specifications for Advent in the Office of the Virgin in most books of hours are beyond the scope of this study.) Even with the chronological, geographical, and ritual guardrails in place, variants within sources remain numerous. Digital access to well over 100 books of hours meeting these criteria—many from the Gallica website of the Bibliothèque nationale de France—has made the project manageable and allowed insights to surface more swiftly than could have been imagined even a few years ago.

Both the beauty and frustration of working with manuscript books of hours involves their individuality. Each copy must (rightly) be accepted as a customized document and often as a family treasure; this principle goes far to justify the preponderance of single-source studies.[54] The resulting paucity of general studies, though, creates an environment where broad observations and interpretations of the corpus may be left unsaid. Common traits in books of hours may go unnoticed if attention is largely fixed on individual peculiarities. Many sources brought out in this book would never attract individual study. Not only might they lack imagery, but their precise ownership and chronology may also be unidentified. Such books of hours find a home here, however, as universal lessons about content and signals of engagement within the texts of the *horae* can be learned without detailed knowledge of a source's full context. And while patterns and trends in the display of liturgical and devotional texts may be distilled from a high level, there is still room for exceptional cases to be explored among the dozens of sources.

*

There are different ways one could organize a study of the musical sounds and cues to performative action in books of hours. Since these prayer manuals contain a relatively conventional progression of sections, most of which have musical content, it would be possible to lead the reader through the various sections of books of hours from start to finish, noting sounds along the way. Such an approach would miss larger points common to these sections, however. One could also survey the genres of music encountered in books of hours, often rigorously rubricated. Prescriptions for plainchant and other utterances, ranging from simple responses to mellifluous melodies, abound in most extant sources. But an entire examination of genres may leave the reader untethered in the context of these highly sectionalized books. The investigation therefore attempts to integrate these approaches in its design, on one hand highlighting key genres within the major liturgical offices of books of hours, while on the other hand probing the kinds of sonic structures, vocal textures, and performative cues provided in some distinct sections of these devotional books.

The book overall divides into two formal parts: I. Music of the Offices and II. Music beyond the Offices. If the user experience with a book of hours was centered on the emulation of the liturgy, then an examination of the contents in the offices is of urgent importance. In his magisterial study of books of hours in the Bibliothèque nationale de France, Victor Leroquais rightly considered the Office of the Virgin and Office of the Dead to be essential elements of a book of hours, though he relegated the abbreviated Hours of the Cross and Hours of the Holy Spirit to secondary status.[55] In its first five chapters, this study considers the substance of all of these liturgies together, as they unveil similar genres, forming a core vocal repertoire for the book. Each of these chapters explores a category of liturgical song with discrete compositional characteristics: psalms, antiphons, hymns, responsories, and dialogues.

Psalms have long been taken for granted in studies of books of hours but will be restored here to their pride of place as the principal liturgical occupation of the Divine Office. As both pedagogical and exegetical texts, the Book of Psalms constitutes the heartbeat of the two chief offices in books of hours. Chapter 1 examines the nature of the psalms in the context of the office, not only reviewing the expected material content but connecting it with the practices of vocal alternation in psalmody and the realization of the *media distinctio*—the structural, devotional, and performative pause in the middle of a psalm verse, which is sometimes indicated in manuscript books of hours. The second chapter highlights the concise liturgical melodies known as antiphons. Antiphons frame the recitation of a psalm or group of psalms in the offices and form a dialogue between the Old Testament and nonscriptural sentences.[56] As short texted pieces of monophony with modest musical contour, antiphons have an idiosyncratic way of unfolding in books of hours, led by an incipit that reaches its plenitude only after the completion of the psalm. The performative tradition of interweaving the invitatory antiphon with Psalm 94 will be also examined, along with the role of the well-known Marian antiphons in the *horae*.

Chapter 3 concerns the genre of the hymn in the book of hours. Like psalms, hymns represented an important building block of one's elementary education. Scribes usually denoted both psalms and hymns in larger script, projecting an oversized presence among the items in the offices. Structurally, however, psalms and hymns diverge: whereas psalm recitation relies on a flexible musical prescription for execution, hymns consist of distinct melodies, some of which became the liturgy's most popular tunes. The rhythmical structure and characteristic rhyme of hymns made them ripe for memorization. This chapter traverses the central hymn texts of the main offices, as well as those of the Hours of the Cross and Hours of the Holy Spirit. Included in the survey is a close look at the Te Deum, the multipurpose "hymn" of the Christian faith, which has recitational characteristics of a psalm.

Flowing from the melody of hymns comes a chapter on responsories, the most elaborate type of song one could hear in a performance of the Divine Office. Dispatched in the service of Matins in both the Office of the Virgin and the Office of the Dead, responsories followed individual lections in practice and represented an ecstatic musical outpouring given in response to the word of God. Florid melodies infused responsories and their attendant verses, each part duly delineated in books of hours. The customary vocal repetitions (*repetenda*) in responsories are treated with care by scribes, fulfilling liturgical prescriptions while remaining attentive to the user experience with the page. Responsories occupy yet another "texture" in books of hours separate from the monotony of surrounding readings, one that was ornate and fit for a talented soloist. Among the responsories, *Libera me Domine* from the Office of the Dead will be scrutinized.

Versicles and their attendant responses—together known as dialogues—round out the examination of genre and execution in the Office repertoire. These liturgical items are scattered throughout the liturgies and function as linking devices between different genres or types of action. Structured in a call and response-type format, the dialogues notably introduce each canonical hour of a liturgical office, following a simple recitation formula. They are arguably the most familiar of musical items in the liturgy but have scarcely been recognized in the literature on books of hours as near-automatic vocal exchanges fixed in Christian consciousness. This chapter includes exploration of the Pater noster in office liturgies: while not properly a versicle and response, a brief dialogue occurs at its conclusion, sensitively marked for the eye and ear in many books of hours.

The second part of this study involves musical content and performative gesture outside of the liturgical offices; it highlights four discrete sections of the book of hours, three of them standard and one an infrequent occurrence, though rich with sonic potential. First, the Seven Penitential Psalms (numbered 6, 31, 37, 50, 101, 129, and 142) represent the venerable psalms of confession, indistinguishable in appearance from other psalms in the book of hours. In illustrated books, the set will open with a miniature featuring King David, the reputed author of the psalms. Musical sound figures into these miniatures as the scene routinely shows David with his characteristic harp. The variable role of the harp in the Davidic imagery will be examined, followed by a review of performance contexts for the Seven Penitential Psalms and close analysis of the antiphon *Ne reminiscaris Domine*, which frames all seven psalms in the *horae*. As we will see, a hitherto unrecognized supplement curiously attaches to *Ne reminiscaris Domine* in books of hours, presenting a sonic conundrum.

The Litany immediately trails the Seven Penitential Psalms in the book of hours and will likewise follow in this part of the book. The dialogic exchanges witnessed in Chapter 5 are taken to their extreme in the Litany, a hypnotic listing of saints whom the faithful begged to "pray for us" with the iterative intonation *ora pro nobis*. The recitation of the Litany is still practiced widely today, reserved for special occasions, and is always sung. Often performed in procession in the Middle Ages, the congregational responses were of the simplest sort and incessant in their repetition. The variety of requests from beyond the realm of saints (and their modest congregational responses), rarely discussed in the literature, receive further attention. Perhaps more than any section of the book of hours, the *mise-en-page* of the Litany communicates the spirit of a performance, separating the cantor's invocation from the corporate response, often with use of ornate line-fills. While the cues for performance and signals for engagement with the text remain evident, the artistic decoration and relentless text repetitions further argue against the traditional inclination to save space in manuscripts. A performance-oriented *mise-en-page* requires careful planning to apportion the proper amount of space needed to reflect the desired vocal sound, texture, and action.

The entreaties to saints from the Litany intensify in the section of a book of hours dedicated to suffrages, the subject of Chapter 8. Devotion to a roster of handpicked saints—much narrower than that found in the Litany—was a hallmark of medieval life. In the absence of relics for veneration, individuals could experience the power and intercession of the saints by reading about their lives (*vitae*) or reciting select mantric prayers, such as those found in suffrages. While office liturgies were highly conventional and followed standard liturgical usages, the suffrages represent one of the more personalized and variable sections in books of hours. Suffrages for provincial saints have further helped researchers localize source material and understand the patterns of devotion by individual supplicants. The structure of each saint's suffrage (also called a "memorial") consists of an antiphon, versicle, response, and prayer (*oratio*), meticulously labeled as such. All four items would have been intoned if encountered in a liturgical setting. The musical bedrock of prevalent antiphons will be outlined, as well as key dialogues found across the suffrages. The chapter takes an important detour by highlighting the occasional use of the liturgical sequence in place of a suffrage antiphon. Scribes recognized the rhymed and rhythmical profile of the sequence and brought these musico-poetic gems to life on the page for the active user.

The most contoured of melodies in the Christian liturgy are found in the celebration of the Mass. And while liturgical offices dominate books of hours, a Mass for the Virgin Mary will appear sporadically as an accessory section and will be treated in the final chapter of this book. The Lady Mass usually consists of texts for the Proper chants and lections, beginning with the elaborate Introit *Salve sancta parens*, which entered the repertoire in the eleventh century. Given the frequency that the laity requested and interacted with the votive Mass for the Virgin, it is hard to believe that owners of books of hours would not have heard or known these melodies. The chapter describes the sounds that were invoked in these crucial texts of the Marian Mass and how they were presented as scripts for envoicing. While the Mass was a relatively uncommon inclusion in fifteenth-century books of hours, especially rare strings of masses in select manuscripts will be exposed to conclude the study.

The sonic terrain of books of hours is vast and ripe for investigation. Through the lens of fifteenth-century French books of hours, this study endeavors to reclaim the devotional vademecum as a storage site of sound material with performative potential as revealed in various cues and layouts. Studies of books of hours have tended to focus on the periphery of these volumes—miniatures, marginalia, and subtle artistic clues to ownership. The survey ahead returns to the central premise of the book of hours—the emulation of the daily liturgical hours and recitation of ubiquitous devotional texts. By shifting attention almost entirely to the principal texts and key sections of books of hours, a latent sound world, though silent on the page, emerges in plain "sight." The presence of words prompts a range of well-known pieces of music, vocal interactions, and sound textures. Let us unleash the unsung voices and listen.

Notes

1 For key studies on the history and circulation of the text and melody, see Maier, *Studien zur Geschichte der Marienantiphon Salve Regina*, and Canal, *Salve regina misericordiae*, 27–125. The earliest extant manuscript to contain the *Salve regina* is the mid-twelfth-century Cistercian antiphoner BnF, n.a.l. 1412, associated with the abbey of Morimondo, southwest of Milan. The chant inspired the development of Marian *Salve* services in lay confraternities of northern Europe, providing another context for the prayer. On the development of *Salve* service, see Forney, "Music, Ritual, and Patronage."
2 Fabri, *The Wanderings*, 1: 140–50. On the practice, see Remensnyder, "Mary, Star of the Multi-Confessional Mediterranean," 315. The singing of the *Salve regina*, other liturgical staples, and observances of the traditional hours aboard the ships of Christopher Columbus is described in Hale, *The Life of Christopher Columbus*, 38; Grant, *The Last Crusader*, 25–26.
3 For a short history of the psalter, see Joseph Dyer, "Psalter, Liturgical," *NG* 20: 518–520.
4 The abbreviation of Matins to a single nocturn accounts for the use of the word "little" (*parvum*) in connection with the office; the office is otherwise a full complement of services and texts.
5 On the birth of books of hours from psalters, see Leroquais, *Les livres d'heures manuscrits*, 1: ix–xiv; Delaisse, "The Importance of Books of Hours," 204.

6   Baltzer, "The Little Office of the Virgin."
7   Gittings, *Death, Burial, and the Indivdual*, 162–163; Loades, "Rites of Passage," 209; Ottosen, *The Responsories and Versicles of the Latin Office of the Dead*, 44–49.
8   Schell, "The Office of the Dead in England," 189–227.
9   Philadelphia Museum of Art, Department of Prints, Drawings, and Photographs, MS 1945-65-8, fol. 77r.
10 Among the early art historical studies is Pollard, *The Illustrations in French Books of Hours*. Later landmark studies include Harthan, *Books of Hours and Their Owners;* Wieck, *Time Sanctified*; Avril et al., *Les petites heures de Jean, duc de Berry*; König, "Französische Buchmalerei um 1450"; Plotzek, *Andachtsbücher des Mittelalters aus Privatbesitz*; Smith, *Art, Identity and Devotion in Fourteenth-Century England*. Crucial inventories include Leroquais, *Les livres d'heures manuscrits* and Randall, *Medieval and Renaissance Manuscripts in the Walters Art Gallery*.
11 Clark, "Beyond Saints," 213.
12 Fulton, "Praying with Anselm," 732.
13 One such survey that attends to devotional texts in addition to visual representations in books of hours is Wieck, *Painted Prayers*.
14 de Pizan, *The Treasure of the City of Ladies or the Book of the Three Virtues*, 68.
15 Hindman, "Books of Hours," 5.
16 Meurier, *Traicté de l'institution*, fol. 43r.
17 Wieck, *Time Sanctified*, 40; Reinburg, *French Books of Hours*, 6–8.
18 Penketh, "Women and Books of Hours"; Reinburg, "'For the Use of Women.'" See also Bell, "Medieval Women Book Owners"; Driver, "Mirrors of a Collective Past"; and Bennett, "A Thirteenth-Century French Book of Hours for Marie."
19 Duffy, *Marking the Hours*, VIII.
20 The rationale can be found in *ibid.*, 4. Duffy's focus on devotional texts and special charms and prayers in English books of hours (*primers*), however, are profitably detailed in *The Stripping of the Altars*, 233–298.
21 Sheingorn, "Performing the Illustrated Manuscript," 57.
22 See, for example, the essays in Fulton and Holsinger, *History in the Comic Mode*.
23 Reinburg, "Oral Rites," 376–79; Reinburg, *French Books of Hours*, 4, 140.
24 See four articles by Bowles, "A Checklist of Musical Instruments . . .," each surveying a major library or museum (British Museum, Pierpont Morgan Library, Walters Art Gallery, and the Bibliothèque nationale de France).
25 Owens, "Musical Subjects."
26 Neither type of prayer book, however, has fielded much musicological attention, though other early pre-modern sources without notation have drawn rightful attention. See, for example, Watt, *Cheap Print and Popular Piety*, and McIlvenna, "The Power of Music." English books of hours that contain notation for the Office of the Dead are explored in Schell, "The Office of the Dead in England."
27 Brown, "The Mirror of Man's Salvation."
28 Blackburn, "Te Matrem Dei Laudamus," 58; Blackburn, "The Virgin in the Sun"; Blackburn, "Messages in Miniature," 161–62; Rothenberg, *The Flower of Paradise*; Rothenberg, "The Most Prudent Virgin," 40–46; Cumming, "Petrucci's Publics"; Bazinet, "Singing the King's Music"; Macey, "Josquin, Good King René"; Constant, "A Book of Hours for Pope Leo X," 330–332; Crook, "The Exegetical Motet."
29 Van Orden, "Children's Voices."
30 Saenger, "Books of Hours and Reading Habits."
31 Williamson, "Sensory Experience in Medieval Devotion."
32 Shephard et al., "Music, Silence, and the Senses."
33 Augustine, *Confessions*, 97–98 (Bk. VI, iii).
34 Isidore of Seville, *The Etymologies*, 95.
35 The earliest notated sources (for example, BnF, lat. 1154 and lat. 1240) are generally dated around the end of the ninth century.
36 For a discussion of Notker's *Liber ymnorum*, see Bower, *The Liber ymnorum of Notker Balbulus*, 1: 1–55.
37 Lord (*The Singer of Tales*) and Parry (*The Making of Homeric Verse*) tended to view orality and literacy as opposites. The complex interaction of the two was recognized in later scholarship. See,

for example, Ong, *Orality and Literacy*; Goody, *The Interface Between the Written and the Oral*; Stock, *The Implications of Literacy*. Among the major musicological studies, particularly involving memory and notation, see Busse Berger, *Medieval Music and the Art of Memory*; Boynton, "Orality, Literacy, and the Early Notation of the Office Hymns."
38 Williamson, "Sensory Experience in Medieval Devotion," 42–43.
39 Dillon, *The Sense of Sound*, 174, 188.
40 Edwards ("Dynamic Qualities," 52) has alluded to the different kinds of sonic contrasts in the liturgy.
41 Zieman, *Singing the New Song*, 36–37.
42 Sheingorn, "Performing the Illustrated Manuscript," 64–67.
43 Unsurprisingly, these extensive prayers have no links to the world of plainchant or polyphony. Johannes Ockeghem's *Intemerata dei mater* (*Collected Works*, 3: 8–12) shows no resemblance to the text from books of hours after its first address of the Virgin Mary. And while the Josquin-attributed motet *Obsecro te domina* (*New Josquin Edition* 24.8, incl. Critical Commentary volume) does paraphrase the conventional opening text of the "Obsecro te" from books of hours, the connection stops after the first 11 words and adds just a few additional phrases.
44 Le Grand, *Statuts*, 37–38.
45 Morgan, "English Books of Hours," 75; Boynton, "Prayer as Liturgical Performance," 897.
46 Reinburg, *French Books of Hours*, 6.
47 Zieman, *Singing the New Song*, 83.
48 Cohen and Twomey, *Spoken Word and Social Practice*, 9–10.
49 On the efficacy of the murmur to avoid distraction in a meditative state, see Quintilian, *The Institutio oratoria*, XI, ii, 33–34.
50 Baroffio, "Testo e musica."
51 For examples highlighting John, Duke of Berry, see Avril et al., *Les petites heures de Jean, duc de Berry*; Limbourg and Colombe, *The Très riches heures of Jean, Duke of Berry*; Meiss et al., *French Painting in the Time of Jean de Berry*. Ghent, Bruges, Flanders, and Utrecht, were also major centers of production for books of hours.
52 Labarre, *Le livre dans la vie amiénoise*, 166.
53 Plummer, "'Use' and 'Beyond Use'"; Clark, "Beyond Saints," 224. Variant usages could number in the hundreds.
54 See, for example, Smith, *Art, Identity and Devotion*, which investigates three books of hours separately in a single volume.
55 Leroquais, *Les livres d'heures manuscrits*, 1: xv–xvi.
56 On the Marian and Christological connections between the antiphons and the Psalms as a reflection of the ancient Temple worship tradition, see Fulton, *Mary and the Art of Prayer*, 107.

Part I
Music of the Offices

1 Psalms

*

> "All things being equal . . . it is better to draw affects of devotion from the Psalms than to go looking for any other object."[1]
>
> —Johannes Mauburnus

> "In fact, what can be more musical than the Psalter?"[2]
>
> —St. Jerome

The Psalms of the Old Testament infused all parts of medieval Christian life. For youth, they formed part of the backbone of elementary education. While central prayers such as the Pater noster and Ave Maria were memorized at a young age, one learned to read with the help of a psalter.[3] As readers advanced with the Psalms, the poetry prompted understanding of Christian doctrine. For both clerics and laypersons, psalm texts also served as the substance of personal devotion. The great utility of the Psalms is more than enough to explain their pervasiveness in medieval liturgies. Lying at the heart of the observances of the Divine Office, the Psalms constitute the core of a book of hours. Extant manuscript copies of psalters—to say nothing of commentaries on the Psalms—survive in greater numbers than any other book of the Bible; yet, scholarship has not nearly matched the widespread appetite for these omnipresent praises from the Old Testament.

In a book of hours, one encounters the Psalms in three key places—the Office of the Virgin, the Seven Penitential Psalms, and the Office of the Dead. Though they occupy most of the folios of these precious devotional books, the Psalms have generally been overlooked in studies of books of hours, presumably for being standardized texts. Such neglect in part reflects assumptions of rampant illiteracy among lay Christians. As Kate van Orden has shown in her investigation of connections between literacy and liturgy in sixteenth-century France, Latin psalters were often used to teach children how to render letters and phonemes.[4] That the script size used for psalms is typically the largest one would find in hand-copied books of hours suggests its clarity was paramount in discerning, even performing, the psalm.[5] Aiding the presentation of these imposing texts was the length of the individual psalm verses, calibrated relatively consistently across the pages of a psalter or book of hours. Most verses range between 10 and 15 words, putting the lines within the reach of a "mental glance," to invoke the parlance of memory studies of the Middle Ages.[6]

DOI: 10.4324/9781003140511-3

18   *Music of the Offices*

As Katherine Zieman reminds us, "the ritualized, performative context of elementary reading becomes increasingly marked by pairing it with 'singing.'"[7] Indeed, we need not look far to discover a musical connection to the Psalms: the verb *psallere* and its derivatives often served as synonyms for singing (*cantare*) and music-making. Further, references to singing, hymns, and instrumental accompaniment are abundant in the Book of Psalms; Psalm 150 alone invokes the trumpet, psaltery, harp, choir, timbrel, strings, pipe, and cymbals as instruments of praise. King David, the presumed author of the Psalms, may also be viewed as a progenitor of liturgical music and singing in the Temple.[8] Users of illustrated books of hours witness David's musical talent in the Seven Penitential Psalms, as we will see in Chapter 6. In medieval monastic practice, psalms flooded the liturgies, and religious communities sang them on "psalm tones." As communal recitation of familiar texts, psalmody would have resounded outside of formal institutions, particularly among nobles and elites who sometimes retained a chapel of singers on their behalf to sing this music. Poetic paraphrases of the Psalms and other versified translations in the vernacular ensured the wide circulation and high level of memorization of these central texts.[9]

While we cannot assume that private engagement with the Psalms necessarily featured singing as we perceive it now, we must still recognize that those texts sung daily throughout Europe do not mysteriously lose their status as songs once extracted and presented in books of hours.[10] At minimum, these vital texts represent voices, as the twelfth-century philosopher John of Salisbury suggested in the *Metalogicon*: "Fundamentally letters are shapes indicating voices. Hence, they represent things which they bring to mind through the windows of the eyes. Frequently they speak voicelessly the utterances of the absent."[11] The Psalms are not muzzled when the texts meet the eye in a psalter or prayer book: they encourage recollection through the sound medium.[12] If we regard psalm texts in books of hours as a shadow of the ancient psalmodic strains, we unleash a rich network of associations—lexical, poetic, historical, theological, and musical—some of which point productively to the sonic potentiality of a devotional practice and away from the silence typically attributed to the act of reading. Some evidence from fifteenth-century devotional literature suggests that the Psalms were at minimum read aloud. In the *Lives of St. Colette*, the saint's companion, Sister Perrine de la Roche, reported that Colette's favorite prayers to perform with the voice were the Psalter, the Seven Penitential Psalms, and the Litany—all of which are found in books of hours.[13] The poetic versification, extraordinary allusions, and inward-looking expressivity of the Psalms, especially if known from a young age, can be imagined not only as pronounced aloud but also "envoiced" musically.

Unfolding the psalms across the hours

Psalms dominate the liturgical offices in books of hours. For centuries in monasteries, novices learned them by heart in the order they occurred in the offices.[14] Lay users of books of hours were unwittingly partaking in this practice in their experience with the psalms of the prescribed liturgies therein. The Office of the Virgin and the Office of the Dead contain numerous psalms, but by no means encompass the full Psalter. Still, they present some of the most poignant and memorable of the 150 psalms for devotees. The highly condensed auxiliary offices of the Hours of the Cross and the Hours of the Holy Spirit, which contain only seven canonical hours each (omitting Lauds), do not offer psalms.

If hebdomadal prescriptions were made in the service of Matins, then 37 psalms would be slated for the eight services that make up the Office of the Virgin in a given week. Table 1.1 shows the common progression of psalms in this office across the canonical hours. Matins

Table 1.1 Psalms in the Office of the Virgin

Matins	94 / i: 8, 18, 23 / ii: 44, 45, 86 / iii: 95, 96, 97
Lauds	92, 99, 62, 66, [Canticle of the Three Children], 148, 149, 150 [Canticle of Zechariah]
Prime	Variable [common: 53, 84, 116]
Terce	119, 120, 121
Sext	122, 123, 124
None	125, 126, 127
Vespers	109, 112, 121, 126, 147, [Canticle of Mary]
Compline	128, 129, 130 [Canticle of Simeon]

provides the most psalms—ten in total at its maximum. Apart from the staple of Psalm 94 ("Venite exultemus"), groups of three psalms are specified for different days of the week. The first group (Psalms 8, 18, 23) are sung on Sundays, Mondays, and Thursdays; Psalms 44, 45, and 86 fall on Tuesday and Friday; and Psalms 95–97 on Wednesday and Saturday. The following service of Lauds bears seven psalms; psalms 62 and 66 appear consecutively, as do the three "Praise Psalms" (Psalms 148–150).[15] Vespers carries five psalms, while the remaining "little" hours and Compline offer three each.

The three psalms for the service of Prime are variable in the Roman usage, but Psalms 53, 84, and 116 are a common prescription. The progression through 12 of the 15 Gradual Psalms 119 to 130 may be seen from the service of Terce through the concluding office of Compline. The series is interrupted by the psalms of Vespers, which introduces a handful of nonconsecutive psalms beginning with Psalm 109. Psalm 121 finds itself in the liturgies of both Terce and Vespers; Psalm 126 similarly appears in the adjacent offices of None and Vespers. Although one might expect the repetition of a text to be abbreviated or cross-referenced in a manuscript, most books of hours will almost always write out Psalms 121 and 126 when they are encountered for the second time in the Vespers service. This practice suggests that the complete recitation and flow of psalm texts in their designated position in Vespers was valued in the performing experience. Instructions to locate a psalm earlier in a book of hours manuscript—a practice in some liturgical books to save space—was evidently seen as a disruption in praying the hours. In taking the extra effort and space to recopy psalms already within the manuscript, scribes and compilers often defied traditional economizing tactics in book production.

Aside from the Seven Penitential Psalms (the subject of Chapter 6), the Office of the Dead presents the next big well of psalms in books of hours. The services make up one of the longest sections of the book of hours, despite only featuring three of the eight possible canonical hours (Vespers, Matins, and Lauds), bearing a resemblance to the ancient vigils. The standard nine lections across three nocturns of Matins account for the office's length, compared to the three customary readings assigned to the Office of the Virgin. In general, one expects to see 22 psalms in the Office of the Dead. Table 1.2 reveals the typical sequence of psalms in the three commemorative services for the deceased.

Table 1.2 Psalms in the Office of the Dead

Vespers	114, 119, 120, 129, 137, [Canticle of Mary], 145
Matins	I: 5, 6, 7 / II: 22, 24, 26 / III: 39, 40, 41
Lauds	50, 64, 62, [Canticle of Ezechias], 148, 149, 150, [Canticle of Zechariah], 129

Similar to the Office of the Virgin, duplicate psalms continue to be in evidence with the Office of the Dead. Convention again dictates that these psalms be written out in the *horae*; scarcely are they cross-referenced to an earlier office in the book. Psalms 62, 119, 120, and 129 typically occur in both offices. The "Praise Psalms" likewise can be found consecutively in the service of Lauds in the two offices. Psalm 129 (*De profundis clamavi*, "Out of the depths have I cried") remains a central Christian prayer for the defunct, found twice in the Office of the Dead, once in the Seven Penitential Psalms, and even once in the Office of the Virgin (Compline).

Psalms in more luxurious books—no small amount among extant fifteenth-century sources—are often presented with decorative enhancements as part of the *mise-en-page*. These features not only direct the eye but can stimulate the ear for the user to be reminded of the sounds of the parallel verses. Certain recurring cues on a folio can point the owner toward a way of performing aloud, audiating internally, or even singing the texts before them. Large capital letters, for example, can occupy substantial space at the beginning of each verse, sometimes spanning multiple lines. Like an *aide-mémoire*, the capitals offer a fresh start to the poetic "sense unit" of the psalm verse.[16] Rich use of opposing ink colors (red and blue, or blue and gold), typically used with alternating psalm verses, further alert the supplicant to the structure of the verses. As each psalm verse comprises two half verses, some books of hours signaled the partition with a colon, which prompted silence instead of sound. The concluding line-fills (German: *Zeilenfüller*)—the notorious habit of illustrators at pains to consume bits of empty space in manuscripts—further emphasize that the user should take or imagine rest within and between verses, collecting breath and recentering energy for the succeeding verse. Verses rarely run on top of each other; most characteristically start anew flush left, organizing the recitational experience. A typical example comes from the workshop of the Master of the Burgundian Prelates in a book of hours prepared for the noble Bochard family of Vézelay (Figure 1.1). In this manuscript from the last quarter of the fifteenth century, the artist provides a floral scene with the capital "C" at the beginning of Psalm 18 (*Celi enarrant*, "The heavens shew forth") consuming two line spaces. Conventional alternation of ink for capitals and contrasting line-fills are also in evidence on this single folio.

At the end of a chanted psalm recitation or following a group of psalms, the convention is to conclude with the Lesser Doxology, or *Gloria patri*. When the verses of the psalm have been exhausted, the valedictory verses of the doxology acknowledge that the glory of God remains forever and is worthy of praise. In its reverence of the Trinity, the *Gloria patri* provided a Christian overlay to the preceding Old Testament texts. The doxology consists of two full chanted verses divided into four parts: "Gloria patri, et filio / et spiritui sancto // Sicut erat in principio, et nunc, et semper / et in saecula saeculorum. Amen." In the Office of the Dead, the *Gloria patri* is customarily replaced by a single verse of two clauses: "Requiem aeternam dona eis Domine/et lux perpetua luceat eis." These concluding formulas, prescribed with far more regularity than the individual psalms themselves, are almost always given as incipits ("Gloria patri" and "Requiem aeternam"). Prompts of this nature are enough to call to mind texts that were no doubt learned by rote from a very early age. They are testimony that what we see on the page and what we hear, utter, sing, or experience may be vastly different.

Choral alternation

In the office liturgies, psalm-singing would not be mistaken for any other type of vocal texture. It is functional music designed to deliver the verses efficiently but with syntactical divisions to ensure the sense and meaning of the text. As musical poetry associated with King

Figure 1.1 Psalm 18. Paris, BnF Ars. Ms-645 réserve, fol. 33r.

David, the psalms in books of hours gesture toward voices in presentation. Roger Wieck believes that owners did not simply practice the hours in their minds, but recognized the types of inherent voices suggested in the alternating sound from psalm to antiphon, reflective of a monastic performance of the Divine Office.[17] The antiphon indeed represents a different musical profile from the psalm, as we will see in Chapter 2, but for the moment, we can focus on the more obvious aspect of alternation within psalm recitation itself in books of hours.

Alternation of choral groups in the execution of psalmody is in fact one of the principal features of its recitation from the central Middle Ages onward. Although communal performance of the psalms emerged in the ninth century after solo performance diminished, the recitation by choirs appears to be no Christian invention, but rather traceable to Jewish practice described in the Talmud. Christians took up this practice of chanting antiphonally, or back and forth, with two groups of singers; sometimes a soloist declaimed the initial half verse to establish the psalm tone that would be used. In cathedral settings, the two groups that take up the musical delivery of psalms have names—*decani* and *cantoris*—echoing the opposite positioning of the stalls of the high-ranking dean and the cantor (or precentor).[18] The division at a psalm's half verse did not necessarily map to a choral assignment, however. Andrew Hughes has written that choral alternation in psalmody was so commonplace that, ironically, it is impossible to know how the alternation was generally applied: alternation at the verse or at the half verse?[19] While practices in the synagogue included the alternation of half verses by the cantor and the congregation, evidence in Christian psalm-singing leans toward alternation of entire verses.[20] The colon at the half verse provided in many books of hours may thus be taken to act as a point of rest for a select group of voices.

Performative alternation of choirs may be suggested visually. Scribes have long used large capitals to articulate the structure of medieval texts for users, and the rotation of color in these initials was likewise a tradition seen in psalters, liturgical books, books of hours, and other genres. Alternation of blue and red capitals was common as these inks were widely available. (In the Middle Ages, illustrators preferred red for headings, bequeathing the term "rubric.") The specific alternation of color in the psalms of books of hours could take on more intricate forms, such as gold capitals with red and blue penwork alternating in the background of the letters. A typical scheme can be found in a book of hours prepared for a member of the French royal family (either Anne of Beaujeu or Jeanne of France) in the last third of the fifteenth century (Figure 1.2), which reveals the opening verses of Psalm 8 ("Domine Dominus noster"). Red and blue ink are used together in the presentation of capitals, but at two different levels. While gold traces the letter itself, one color consumes the interior of the letter and can be seen to alternate with the opposing color down the folio. The contrasting ink also plays a different role, thinly filling in the background of a letter dominated by the other color. As is common in illustrated manuscripts, the line-fills at the end of each psalm verse further participate in the alternation, being split into two or three parts of red and blue separated by a gold bead.

While it is unclear why the alternation of colors became a standard in medieval texts of all sorts, the result in the context of books of hours has the potential to signal the change of vocal grouping that would have taken place in the walls of a cathedral or monastery. Whatever the alternating scheme that was chosen for a manuscript, the practice finds an analog in the alternating choirs in psalmody, the unceasing practice of monastic institutions. In execution, the voices of the choirs volley the sound back and forth, creating sonic symmetry in the space where they are gathered. As each semi-chorus reaches the end of a verse, they exchange responsibilities with the other group and rest. Collecting breath, they prepare to sing again, usually within 10 or 20 seconds. As they stay silent, they also experience the

Figure 1.2 Psalm 8. Paris, BnF, Ars. Ms-644 réserve, fol. 30r.

psalm aurally. The handover of the vocal duty after each verse may be subtle to witness without hearing it live. The larger the community envoicing the psalm, the more homogenous the choral sound. A small coterie of singers, however, may produce an outstanding singer or two in each semi-choir, despite the goal of seamlessness between groups. The symmetry of the alternating colors found throughout manuscript books of hours may be recalling the bifurcated choral arrangement.

We may add further that the use of color may offer an *aide-memoire* for users of books of hours, whether young or old. On the process of memorizing the Psalter, the twelfth-century philosopher and theologian Hugh of St. Victor wrote that memory devices not only come from the "number and order of verses or ideas, but at the same time the color, shape, position, and placement of the letters, where we have seen this or that written, in what part, in what location (at the top, the middle, or the bottom) we saw it positioned, in what color we observed the trace of the letter or the ornamented surface of the parchment."[21] At minimum, the alternating use of color in books of hours allows for a rudimentary type of separation among verses in the mind. More likely for users, the visual display prompted sounds and perhaps even performances of the texts. What we see in the book of hours reflects how we internalize, hear, perform, and store texts.

Silence and the medial distinction

Performative cues lie not just between the verses of a psalm but also within them. The consistent two-part construction of individual psalm verses generates a powerful and persuasive meaning in the act of recitation. James Kugel has most lucidly explained the bipartite construction (A/B) of psalm verses.[22] What he calls the "short sentence-form that consists of two brief clauses" is crucial in understanding the psalms as sounding phenomena in books of hours. In psalmodic practice, the two parts are intoned with special formulas that each have the capacity to accommodate the poetry of the Psalter. The caesura after A is likewise of poetic significance, as Kugel has described: it paves the way for B to engage in a "particularizing, defining, or expanding" function relative to A. The pause (or "comma") between A and B is called the *media distinctio* ("medial distinction"). At that juncture, the sense is complete, but more of the *sententia*, the full substance of the thought, remains to be heard.[23]

Pauses in the delivery of texts and other acts of observing punctuation to make sense of phrase units were articulated in antiquity, embraced by Quintilian and others.[24] The Roman grammarian Donatus even went so far as to assign different time values to the assorted pauses one could produce when reading.[25] Being as frequently "performed" and "heard" as much as psalm verses themselves, the silence produced at the *media distinctio* has not gone unnoticed. The mid-way rest had different functions in the monastic ritual of chanting the psalms. On one hand, it was a necessary caesura to articulate the poetry of the first clause A and to let its premise settle in the mind. The break also allowed for a meditative or devotional moment in the musical delivery of verses. Whether assigned to the semi-chorus singing or to the group listening, the monk, nun, or cleric could contemplate the meaning and teaching suggested in the preparatory A clause and anticipate its B rejoinder.

On a physical level, the medial distinction was also a short-lived instance of vocal rest for the members of the communities. For those present, the gap of rest between a psalm's half verses allowed the cadence of the initial clause A to bloom and resound in the sacred space. Comparing the silence to Boethius's unhearable *musica mundana*, Beth Williamson has written about the medial distinction in psalm-singing: "The music may not be sounding, but it has not stopped. The singers are aware, within their own interiority, of its continuation, and though they do not hear it in their physical ears, they hear it still inwardly. In this moment of silence, the music does not disappear, but functions temporarily—and temporally—on a different level."[26]

The pause not only signaled a moment of repose but also offered the opportunity for the appointed group to inhale as part of their intonation of the verse. The circular act of breathing in declaiming the half verses of the psalm was invested with great significance in the Middle Ages. Christians have long associated breath with the Holy Spirit. The word "spirit" in both Hebrew (חור) and Greek (πνεῦμα) translates to "breath" or "wind." Acts 2:2 describes the presence of the Holy Spirit on Pentecost as a violent "wind" that filled the whole house where Jesus's disciples were gathered. The suspension of a psalm verse for breath at the medial distinction was thus a moment for the Holy Spirit to enter into the souls of the faithful in their devotional act of singing the psalms.[27] Emma Hornby has noted the complexity of the medial distinction in psalmody, bearing witness to its ability to bring together a community assembled in ceremonial song.[28] The spiritual unanimity achieved through performance of the psalms and their requisite silences were conceivably transferred into a user's experience with the book of hours.

Many scribes suggest the medial distinction in books of hours, indicating their own performance memory of the pause or their desire to parse the verse for the owner. Some will place a colon or other mark at the half verse to recognize the performative caesura. A full opening from a northern French book of hours produced in the last decade of the fifteenth century may serve as an example (Figure 1.3). In the middle of Psalm 24 from the second nocturn of Matins in the Office of the Dead, the text scribe consistently places a colon at the medial distinction of every verse. The consistent punctuation divides the verse evenly for the user, allowing the sense units to form for execution of the psalm.

A more exceptional example of rendering the pause comes from a manuscript *horae* prepared in Rouen and illustrated by the anonymous Master of the Bishops of Rouen in the second half of the fifteenth century (BnF, Ars. 562). In this book of hours, the illuminator has provided large colored initials at the start of each psalm verse; these initials alternate blue and gold against red and gray fields, respectively. As it concerns the medial distinction, the scribe of this book of hours regularly provides punctuation at the half verse of the psalm to indicate the pause for the user. Figure 1.4 demonstrates the effect in the context of the middle of Psalm 18 in the first nocturn of Matins in the Office of the Virgin.[29] Throughout this manuscript, the owner of this book was treated to two different kinds of partitions at the medial distinction—a colon and dot of division. The dot of division nearly resembles a period, and all verses shown reveal a period at the end of each verse. Whatever punctuation mark the scribe chooses at the medial distinction (it appears arbitrary), the user sees ample space around these caesurae, separating the clauses.

In other books, the colon may be inconsistent verse to verse, or absent entirely from the psalms. If a user had already memorized the Psalter to some extent and recalled some or all of the poems by heart, explicit cues for the performative caesurae would mean less than they do for the modern observer. Some devotees might have needed a reminder only at the beginning of each psalm verse to prompt the full verse. Others might have rehearsed everything in the mind, minimally attentive to the page at all. Imitating the practice of the monastery, the supplicant cannot have consistently relied on written indications for corporate breath, but neither was she prevented from inhaling the vapor of the Holy Spirit at each half verse and between full verses.

Psalm intonation

With a sense of liturgical assignment and parsing of the biblical poetry, we are in a position to examine the practice of psalmody. There are, of course, real musical sounds associated with

Figure 1.3 Psalm 24. Philadelphia, Philadelphia Art Museum, Department of Prints, Drawings, and Photographs, MS 1945-65-13, 290–291. Image: Bibliotheca Philadelphiensis.

Figure 1.3 (Continued)

Figure 1.4 Psalm 18. Paris, BnF, Ars. Ms-562 réserve, fol. 24v.

the Psalms derived from the venerable "psalm tones." While it is possible that some or even many owners of books of hours did not envoice the psalm texts musically, it would nonetheless be close-minded to think that all users separated the psalms in books of hours from those that would have been sung and heard from lived experience, for example at funerals or in community procession. Since we are in no position to draw a line between these types of users, it is thus worthwhile to be reminded of the sounding potentiality of the psalms in these cherished personal books.

Psalmody was among the most versatile types of music-making one finds in the practice of the liturgy and, by association, in the book of hours. The melodic formulas of the psalm tones, varying in their level of decoration, ensure delivery of the text not just completely but persuasively. It is impossible to know how ancient the psalm tones are, particularly since soloists tightly guarded the practice until around the ninth century. The musical tradition of applying melodic formulas to sacred texts seems to echo Jewish psalmodic recitation practice.[30] A psalm tone contains several parts: an incipit (or introductory gesture); a recitation tone; a cadential figure before the medial distinction; a continued recitation; and a termination formula. As David Hiley has written, the psalm tone is a "sort of chant in itself."[31] The melodic incipit (*intonatio*) may be applied to the first verse only or all the verses. The prescribed recitation tone is a pitch that governs the delivery of the psalm text. This tone is interrupted by the medial cadential figure, which is typically based on text accent at the end of the first clause. The termination formula or *differentia* was sometimes pegged to the text accent (a "tonic" cadence, rhetorically inspired); other times, the text was subject to a "cursive" cadence, requiring the singer to count "back" the appropriate number of syllables in applying the concluding formula. The latter was the more artificial and more rigorous practice of psalmody in monastic life—and the more unforgiving. Both performance possibilities, however, allow the recitation tone to expand flexibly to accommodate the end of each verse. A liturgical book such as a breviary does not provide all elements of the psalm tone. Usually, the copyist reveals only the notes of the *differentia* to unlock the psalm tone. This group of pitches maps to the final two words "seculorum Amen" of the concluding *Gloria patri*.

The recitation tone—a single musical note—dominated the presentation of both clauses of the psalm text, decorated by the introductory inflection, medial articulation, and termination formula. The note on which psalm tone recitation occurred was a clue to a musical "mode," an abstract kind of "tonality" for a chant, the full extent of which was evinced in the antiphon paired with the psalm (see Chapter 2). There were eight modes in the realm of Latin ecclesiastical plainchant in circulation since the ninth century, likely derived from Byzantine practice. The possible musical notes for the reciting tone were f (mode 2), a (mode 1, 4, and 6), c (mode 3, 5, and 8), and d (mode 7). The context surrounding these reciting pitches confirms the modal assignment. Each mode could have several options for terminating formulas. As it concerns the musically engaged user of psalms in the book of hours, the letter names of the pitches mean very little. In truth, a recitational pitch may be any sounding note; what creates the appropriate melodic shape of the psalm tone delivery and confirms the mode are the musical intervals surrounding the sung or imagined reciting pitch.

The practice of psalmody is flexible enough with its accommodation of syllables and options for the *differentia*. The exercise becomes even more elastic when one considers that the psalm texts were not assigned to particular modes. This did not mean, however, that a supplicant was free to murmur or conjure the psalm in whatever mode came to mind. The user who sang or recalled the psalm tone was theoretically constrained by the tonality of the antiphon with which it is paired. The antiphon in fact determines the psalm tone. More will be said on the sonic phenomenology of executing the antiphon and psalm in Chapter 2.

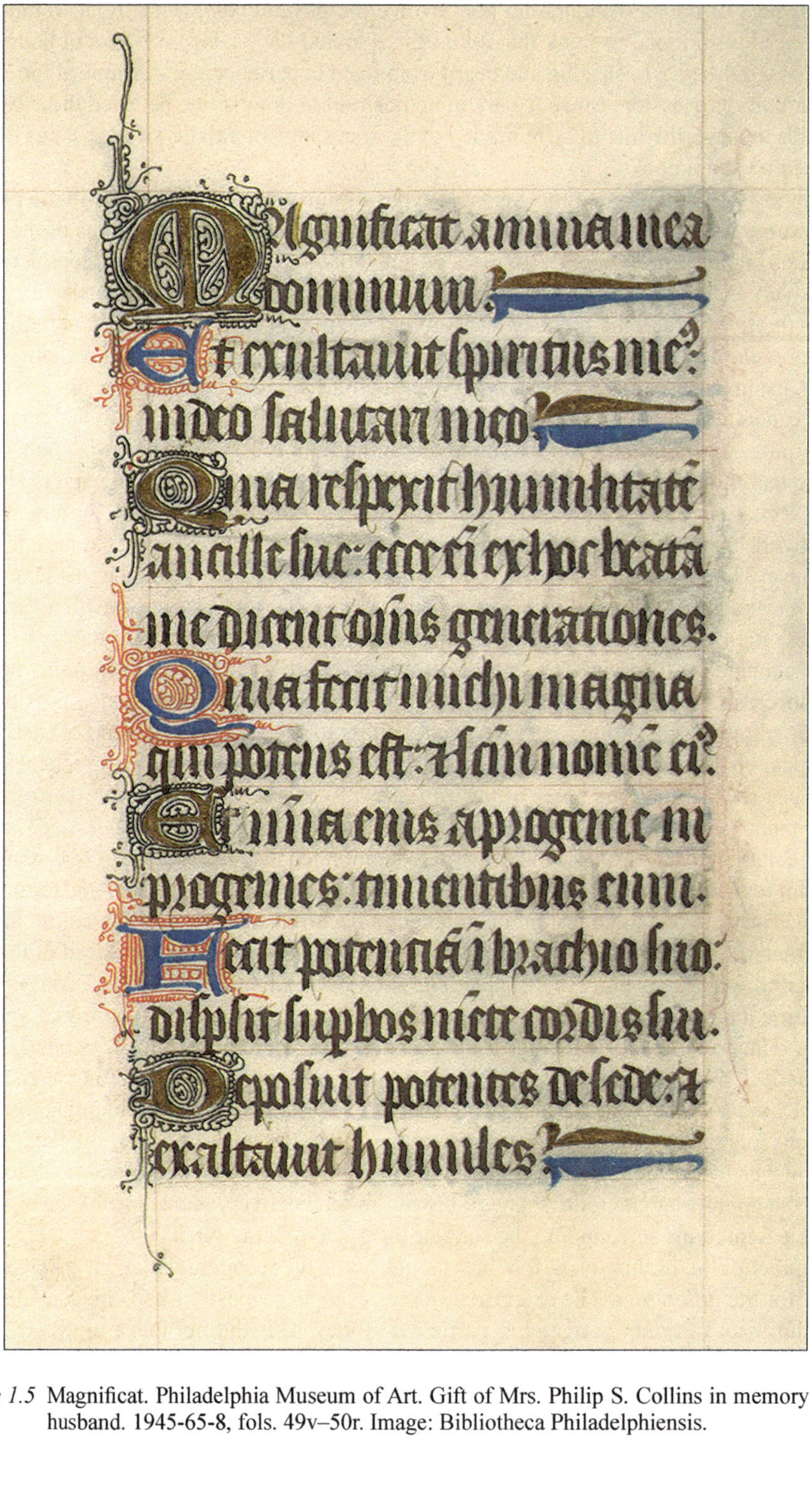

Figure 1.5 Magnificat. Philadelphia Museum of Art. Gift of Mrs. Philip S. Collins in memory of her husband. 1945-65-8, fols. 49v–50r. Image: Bibliotheca Philadelphiensis.

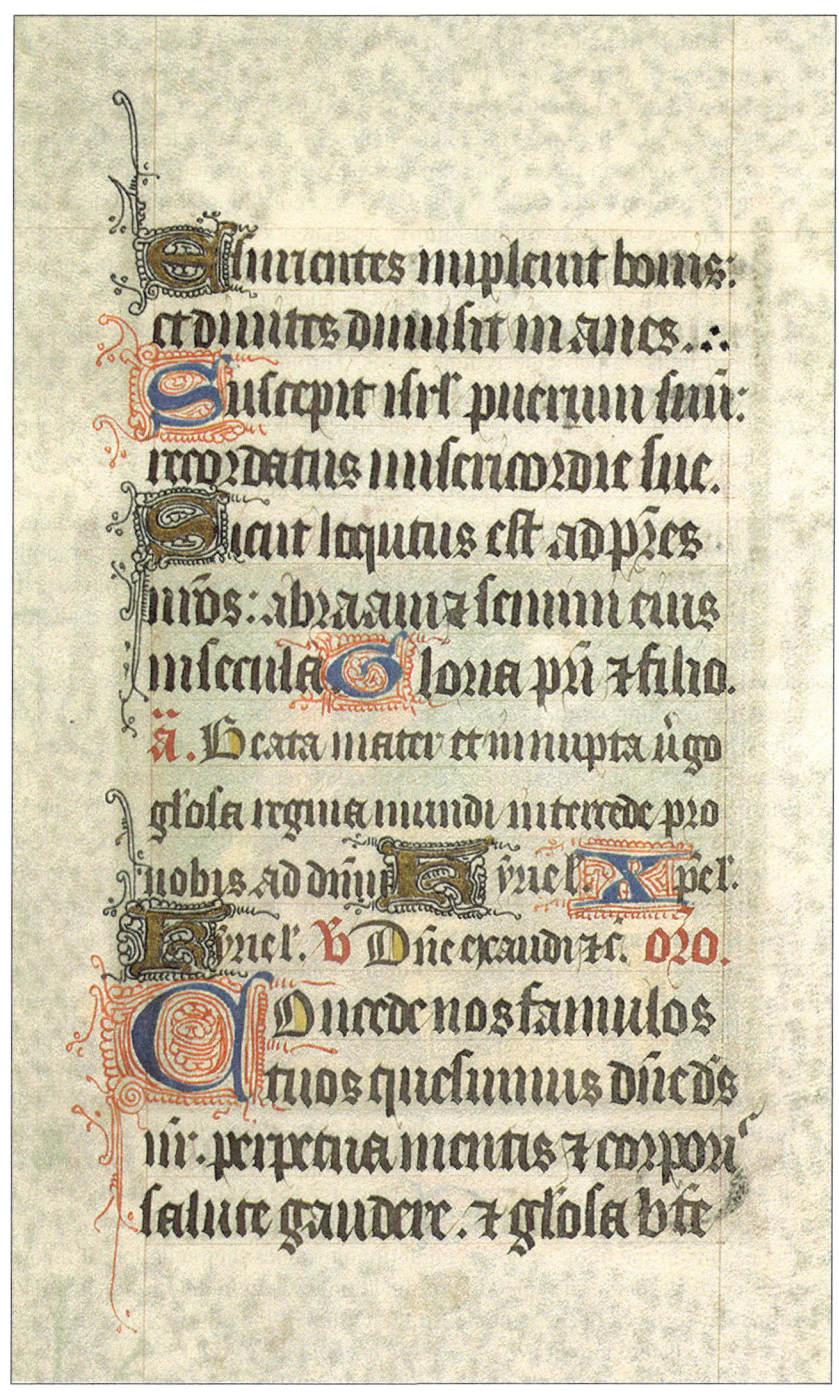

Figure 1.5 (Continued)

The Magnificat and other canticles

The Magnificat, or Canticle of Mary, was held up consistently through the centuries as a text central to the Incarnation of Jesus. Set in the first person in its opening verses (Luke 1:46–49), Mary's song allowed the faithful to experience the text in an intimate way. Its presence is thus fitting in the personal experiences offered by the *horae*. The canticle usually appeared twice in a book of hours, once in the evening services of Vespers in the Office of the Virgin and again in the same position in the Office of the Dead. Its enduring placement near the end of the eventide service was a climax of that liturgy, stipulated as early as the sixth-century Rule of St. Benedict.[32] The Magnificat followed the recitation of five psalms with antiphons, a chapter reading, the hymn *Ave maris stella*, a versicle, and short response. Stationed at a high liturgical moment, the canticle was often amplified ceremonially by a censing of the altar or the ringing of bells on particularly high feasts. Through the sixteenth century, this song of Mary was most widely and uniformly experienced in the form of musical recitation.

From a performance standpoint, the Magnificat was treated like a psalm tone on account of its unfolding of bipartite verses and the inclusion of the *Gloria patri* at its conclusion. Unsurprisingly, then, Mary's song is copied in the style of a psalm in books of hours. The verses often begin with elaborately drawn and colored capital letters; scribes may also denote the medial distinction to separate the half verses. We may witness these features in an example of the Magnificat from a mid-fifteenth-century manuscript from the Provençal city of Carpentras (Figure 1.5). The initial gold "M" of Magnificat on the verso spans two lines and alternates with blue capitals for the beginning of each verse of Mary's song. In all of the verses except the first, colons signal the performative pause at the medial distinction, much like a psalm. In liturgical practice, the opening word, "Magnificat," might have been declaimed by a soloist to cue the choir. While a book of hours user is rarely treated to an indication of a pause after that intonation, a textural change from solo to choir could be reasonably imagined.

In the concluding doxology on the recto, the scribe provided more than the usual two-word prompt "Gloria patri," supplementing with the succeeding words "et filio," evidently to fill out the line space. Still the reduction of the *Gloria patri* from two full verses to a few words must be taken as a sign that the formulation was easily recalled, especially being the concluding verses to most psalms in books of hours.[33] Although the doxology is not formally connected to the Magnificat, the psalm-like treatment of the canticle facilitates not only a visual link in the versified structure but also an aural-performative link. To wit, the formula applied to the *Gloria patri* is that of the tone assigned to the Magnificat. No matter how users engaged with their books of hours, the musical shape of the doxology was the same as that heard in the recitation of the Magnificat. There is a shift in the vocal intensity of sound here, though, as in all psalmody. In monastic practice, the split-choir arrangement for psalm recitation would cease at the doxology, and the full community would join at the *Gloria patri*. The return to a full sound prepares the performer or listener for the communal texture required for the repeat of the antiphon that follows the Magnificat recitation.

As with most psalms in the book of hours, an antiphon frames the recitation of the Magnificat in the service of Vespers. The selection of the antiphon would determine the melodic mode and termination formula of the canticle. In the Office of the Virgin, Roman liturgical usage dictated the use of the antiphon *Beata mater et innupta* (CAO 1570) to bracket the Magnificat. This antiphon was also assigned to different positions in various Marian liturgies, mainly for the feasts of the Assumption and Purification.[34] Cast in second mode, *Beata mater et innupta* required a psalm tone to pair with that mode for the recitation of Mary's song. The tone for the canticle is rarely found in medieval sources, a potential indicator of

Example 1.1 Magnificat, Mode 2 tone

its popularity rather than its obscurity. Example 1.1 shows a possible mode 2 formula for the Magnificat from modern chant books. From what can be gathered from medieval sources, there seems to be some contrast between recitation of the Magnificat and that of a conventional psalm: the Canticle of Mary appears to be chanted with a slightly more elaborate tone than one would sing for a regular psalm.[35] One subtle distinction may be found in the intonation (or "run-up") to the recitation tone, as well as in other two-note groupings before the medial cadence. The intonation often follows a "cursive" style in which syllables are fitted to the "course" of the initial formula.

Finally, it should be noted the Magnificat was treated as a kind of psalm not only from a performative standpoint but also from a conceptual one in books of hours. One sees proof of this in the rubrication of the Magnificat in the Carpentras *horae*. On the preceding folio (not shown here), the genre accorded to the Magnificat is "ps. david." This manuscript is not alone; scribes of other books of hours provide the rubric "psalmus," "ps.," or "psalmus david" preceding Mary's canticle.[36] The psalm designation is plainly incorrect: the Magnificat is no Old Testament text from the Book of Psalms. But neither was it an isolated mistake; the genre designation was not uncommon in books of hours. The labeling of the Magnificat as a "psalmus" was not unique to books of hours; even scribes of liturgical books were known to rubricate the Magnificat in this same way.[37] We will see other unexpected genre names appear in the course of this book.

There are other canticles besides the Magnificat that were used liturgically and reflected in the offices of books of hours. Though none are properly psalms, all of them are treated as psalm-like in their appearance and execution. The most recognizable is the Canticle of Zechariah sung at Lauds. Known as the Benedictus, it occupies a similar position to the Magnificat in Vespers, following a group of psalms. Also like the Magnificat, the Benedictus draws its text from the Gospel of Luke (1:68–79) and can be found in both the Office of the Virgin and the Office of the Dead. Its bipartite verse structure again mirrors that of psalms, and the canticle too is sometimes rubricated as "psalmus" in manuscript books of hours.[38] The brief *Nunc dimittis*, or Canticle of Simeon, is the third and final Gospel canticle from Luke (2:29–32). Divided into two-part verses, the *Nunc dimittis* is likewise ripe for psalmodic treatment and occasionally denoted as a "psalmus."[39] The canticles of Zechariah and of Simeon both conclude with the doxology, confirming a liturgical and performative connection to the exercise of the psalms. The three New Testament (or "evangelical") canticles were patterned after seven Old Testament canticles, one of which appears in books of hours.[40] The Canticle of the Three Children (Daniel 3:57–88, 56)—"Benedicite omnia opera" ("Bless the Lord, all you works of the Lord")—is notable for its length and striking appearance in books of hours, each verse beginning with the command "Benedicite" ("bless").[41] Assigned as the Old Testament canticle for Lauds on Sundays and feast days, this canticle was customarily positioned within the psalms of Lauds in the Office of the Virgin Mary.

*

It cannot be emphasized enough that psalms and psalm-like canticles account for much of the music-making in the liturgical day and correspondingly in the experience in the book of hours. Being recitational in character with maximum flexibility to accommodate poetic texts, the psalms bear a musical style that is necessarily conservative. As has been suggested, antiphons routinely attach to either side of the psalms of the offices, on one hand orienting the texts more intensely toward their devotional objective while on the other presenting a richer and more specialized musical experience for those who recalled or uttered the inherent sounds of the Divine Office. In some ways, we journey into the crevices of the book of hours as we explore the antiphons associated with the psalms. From another perspective, we open up a sonorous world that psalms could never approach.

Notes

1. Mauburnus, *Rosetum exercitatorium spiritualium*, 163.
2. Fremantle and Martley, *Jerome: Letters and Select Works*, 6: 484.
3. Brown, "The Psalms as the Foundation"; Zieman, *Singing the New Song*, 36.
4. Van Orden, "Children's Voices," 215.
5. Script sizes differ in liturgical books such as missals, demarcating changes of genre or prominence for the user. See, for example, BnF, lat. 17315.
6. Carruthers, *The Book of Memory*, 102.
7. Zieman, *Singing the New Song*, 36.
8. See, for example, 1 Chronicles 23:5.
9. The Old English *Metrical Psalms* from the late ninth or early tenth century represents one such text to engage the wider public. See Leneghan, "Making the Psalter Sing."
10. Dillon, "Unwriting Medieval Song," 602.
11. John of Salisbury, *Metalogicon* (Bk 1, Ch. 13), 32. Translation from Clanchy, *From Memory to Written Record*, 253.
12. For a case study on the sounds suggested in the fourteenth-century Luttrell Psalter, see Buckland, "Sounds of the Psalter."
13. Saenger, "Books of Hours and Reading Habits," 147.
14. Carruthers, *The Book of Memory*, 102–103.
15. The three Praise Psalms form the etymology of the service of "Lauds" in the Divine Office and further match the psalms that are recited daily for Jewish morning services. See Yuval, "The Other in Us," 370.
16. This layout is akin to the *per cola et commata* style of division with major clauses or phrases placed at the beginning of a line. For discussion of the layout and punctuation of verse in antiquity and the Middle Ages, see Parkes, *Pause and Effect*, 97–106.
17. Wieck, *Time Sanctified*, 41.
18. Dyer, "The Psalms in Monastic Prayer," 76; Nicholas Temperley, "Decani and Cantoris," *NG* 7: 119.
19. Hughes, *Medieval Manuscripts*, 30–31.
20. Taft, "Christian Liturgical Psalmody," 19–21.
21. Hugh of St. Victor, *De tribus maximis circumstantiis gestorum*, trans. in Carruthers, *The Book of Memory*, 342.
22. Kugel, *The Idea of Biblical Poetry*, 1–2, 8.
23. Parkes, *Pause and Effect*, 67.
24. *Ibid.*, 65–70.
25. *Ibid.*, 13. The various pauses (*distinctiones*) are not absolute time designations but rather relative to one another. The minor medial pause is the shortest, followed by the major medial pause and the final pause at the end of a sentence.
26. Williamson, "Sensory Experience in Medieval Devotion," 31–32.
27. Van Dijk, "Medieval Terminology," 12.
28. Hornby, "Preliminary Thoughts," 143.
29. Psalters and books of hours will divide the verses differently in Psalm 18. In many renderings, the first half of 18:7 falls at the end of 18:6.
30. John Arthur Smith, "Psalm I, 3: Ancient Judaism," *NG* 20: 450.

31 Hiley, *Western Plainchant*, 61.
32 The monastic rule of Aurelian of Arles (d. 551) assigned Mary's canticle to morning recitation. See Anderson, "Magnificat."
33 When the *Gloria patri* is replaced in the Office of the Dead, the verse "Requiem aeternam" is likewise cued only with a one- or two-word incipit.
34 For example, *Beata mater et innupta* was commonly situated as the sixth antiphon of Matins on the feast of the Purification.
35 Peter Wagner published two versions of the Magnificat tone (*Einführung in die gregorianischen Melodien*, 3: 98–99, 102–103).
36 BnF, Ars. 562, for instance, calls the Magnificat both a *canticum* (fol. 59r) and a *psalmus* (fol. 107r).
37 Edwards, *Matins, Lauds, and Vespers for St. David's Day*, 110.
38 The Benedictus is called a *psalmus david* in BnF, lat. 1184, fol. 38v.
39 See, for example, BnF, Ars. 434, fol. 131v.
40 The canticles, sometimes misleadingly referred to as hymns, were assigned liturgically to the service of Lauds in the Office of the Virgin, one for each day of the week. See Velimirović et al., "Canticle," *NG* 5: 49–51.
41 See the psalm, for example, in BnF, lat. 1369, 97–98, one of four books of hours associated with Isabella Stewart. For discussion of this book, see Deuffic and Booton, *Le livre d'heures enluminé en Bretagne*, 93–97.

2 Antiphons

*

In books of hours, as in the liturgy, psalm recitation is usually incomplete without the enclosure of an antiphon. A breviary containing the Divine Office for the year (or part of a year) may easily contain a thousand antiphons to pair with psalms, the bulk reserved for feast days requiring proper liturgical chants. Those prescribed in books of hours are much fewer because there are only two core offices. One might expect around 50 antiphons across the offices in a given book of hours. Antiphons may further be found in the suffrages of a book of hours, about which more will be said in Chapter 8.

Antiphons are short liturgical chants with a prose text. The name of the genre is regrettable, as nothing in the performance of the antiphon proper requires alternation, or "antiphony," as we find in the practice of psalmody. A psalm and its assigned antiphon have a connection, though, one to which Rachel Fulton has called attention in her illuminating study of the Office of the Virgin Mary. There is a "dialogue" between psalms and the antiphons that frame them, an interchange infused with Marian meaning, not obvious on the face of it, but recognized by medieval exegetes.[1] Scribes too read antiphons as Marian that were not plainly so. A rubric for the antiphon *Pulchra es decora* in one book of hours indicates that the Old Testament text (Song of Songs 6:3) is an antiphon for Our Lady (*antienne de n[ost]re da[m]e*).[2] But a different dialogue is also at play between psalm and antiphon in the offices—namely, a musical one.

Structurally, the antiphon wraps around the psalm, setting it up tonally and then securing the proper chant at the psalm's conclusion. The return of the antiphon strengthens the conversation between the poetry of the psalm and the antiphon's brief statement. A governing tonality binds the dialogue. In Chapter 1, it was mentioned that an antiphon's tonal classification, known as the melodic mode, in fact determines the recitational pitch of the psalm tone. The tonal linkage between the psalm and assigned antiphon further creates a cohesive musical experience that separates them from other parts of a liturgical service. Antiphons were cast in one of the eight modes. Once that mode is ascertained, the recitation tone can be determined, drawn from a number of *differentiae*. In the ear or voice of the user, the execution of the antiphon and psalm holds both limiting and liberating aspects. The antiphon's mode fixes relationships among pitches, but the sounding pitch frequency on which the melody is placed may vary widely, though usually in an unstrained vocal range. As the mode is affirmed through the singing of the antiphon, the structure of the psalm tone is foreshadowed, even though a concluding formula has not been articulated. The shared mode draws the two parts together in an exchange.

DOI: 10.4324/9781003140511-4

The dialogue between antiphon and psalm continues yet further in the area of musical style. Antiphons are modest in their melodic shape, but contrast noticeably with the conservative, static style of a psalm tone.[3] The mode of the antiphon often had a powerful influence on its melodic contour, as stock gestures within a mode began to act as recurring possibilities for navigating tonal space.[4] Important for study of the book of hours, more narrowly defined options for melodies were likely a boost to memory, especially for those who had knowledge of the antiphons and were familiar with their basic melodic profile.

This chapter does not set out to examine all of the antiphons one would witness in a book of hours; rather, it provides an overview of the topic and explores select issues that emerge in the study of the genre in these precious xbooks. After a survey of antiphons commonly found in the offices of the *horae*, the investigation turns to the realm of performance by examining the use of incipits in the execution of antiphons. It then focuses on a peculiar treatment of the first antiphon found in the Office of the Virgin—the invitatory *Ave Maria gratia plena*. The chapter concludes with observations of select antiphons, including the famous Marian antiphons and the prevalent antiphon *Veni sancte spiritus*.

Antiphons for the core offices

Some global observations can be made about the antiphons that lie within the Office of the Virgin and the Office of the Dead. First, scribes regularly provided rubrics for them, usually with *a.*, *an.*—also *antiphona* or *antienne* when spelled out. They also tended to record the antiphon in a script size noticeably smaller than one finds with the psalms (and hymns too, as we will see in Chapter 3). It is tempting to view the reduced script size as signaling something unimportant or possibly unperformable by the user. Katherine Zieman has remarked that the smaller script in books of hours was reserved for texts that were "sung," but she saw no reason to posit a special kind of performance.[5] If we cannot penetrate the level of engagement of books with such a broad usage, we might still make some observations about how to understand the genre. Given the close adherence to the liturgy in books of hours, it is unlikely that the user disengaged at the sight of the antiphon. Instead, we could reasonably suggest that a demonstrable change of vocal texture took place between antiphon and psalm, whether understood aurally or enacted physically. The intentional and pervasive changes in script size may awaken what Emma Dillon calls the "visual map of the musical memory."[6] From a sonic point of view, the diminished script may thus be understood as an exchange of vocal textures from a contoured antiphon to a recitation-dominated form of speech-song. Or vice versa: antiphons resounded on either side of the psalm.

But not always. While antiphons generally frame psalms in liturgical practice, they do not always frame them individually in books of hours. Occasionally, psalms may appear in groups of two or three, and the full set is wrapped by a single antiphon. Groups of three are common in the more modest minor hours in the Office of the Virgin (Prime, Terce, Sext, and None). Table 2.1 shows common antiphons found in the Roman rite for the Office of the Virgin, building on Table 1.1 from earlier. Being from some of the earliest layers of ecclesiastical plainchant, the antiphons include the CAO number from Hesbert's seminal *Corpus antiphonalium officii*. Compilers imported the antiphons from two main reservoirs, the Common of Virgins and Marian feasts (Assumption, Purification, and Nativity especially). The indicated mode is the prevailing classification asserted by those who have cataloged the extant sources, with privilege given to French liturgical books. The table italicizes the antiphons of the minor hours, since these melodies are recycled from the service of Lauds. From a textual perspective, it may be noted that *Benedicta tu in mulieribus* (MA1) builds on the preceding invitatory antiphon *Ave Maria gratia plena*. Even though the items are discrete in practice, they pair well in devotion, together constituting what was the most widely uttered prayer in Christian devotional life—the "Ave Maria."[7]

The melodic modes of the antiphons for the Virgin Mary are crucial for narrowing the sound world of this office in books of hours. By securing the most likely mode of these framing antiphons, the user is constrained in the possibilities for how the psalm will sound, though each mode still had several options for a termination formula. The musical choices for the psalm tone are further limited when we consider the repetition of the modes in the Office of the Virgin. Users might well apply a single tone in their experience, avoiding formulas with slight variants. There is in fact evidence supporting the idea that the design of the Office of the Virgin relied on melodic exemplars that likely eased recollection and execution.

Owners of books of hours could not only apply a consistent formula in the practice of psalmody but also streamline sounds of several antiphons as well. In the late Middle Ages, newly developed liturgical offices often followed a strict pattern of modal ordering through the offices, antiphons cycling through the eight modes systematically in Matins (MA1=mode 1; MA2=mode 2, etc.).[8] Table 2.1 shows no such evidence of this practice in the antiphons of the Office of the Virgin. A pattern of modal organization of a different sort does emerge in

Table 2.1 Antiphons for the Office of the Virgin

Service	Position	Antiphon	CAO no.	Mode	Psalm/Canticle
Matins	MI	Ave Maria gratia plena	1041	7	94
	MA1	Benedicta tu in mulieribus	1709	4	8
	MA2	Sicut myrra electa	4942	4	18
	MA3	Ante thorum huius virginis	1438	4	23
	MA4	Specie tua et pulchritudine	4987	7	44
	MA5	Adiuvabit eam Deus	1282	7	45
	MA6	Sicut letantium omnium nostrum	4936	7	86
	MA7	Gaude Maria virgo	2924	4	95
	MA8	Dignare me laudare te	2217	4	96
	MA9	Post partum virgo	4332	4	97
Lauds	LA1	Assumpta est Maria	1503	7	92
	LA2	Maria virgo assumpta est	3707	8	99
	LA3	In odorem unguentorum	3261	4	62, 66
	LA4	Benedicta filia tu	1705	7	Canticle of the Three Children
	LA5	Pulchra es decora	4418	1	148, 149, 150
	LAB	Beata dei genetrix	1563	8	Canticle of Zechariah
Prime		*Assumpta est Maria*	*1503*	7	53, 84, 116
Terce		*Maria virgo assumpta est*	*3707*	8	119, 120, 121
Sext		*In odorem unguentorum*	*3261*	4	122, 123, 124
None		*Pulchra es decora*	*4418*	1	125, 126, 127
Vespers	VA1	Dum esset rex	2450	3	109
	VA2	Leva eius sub capite	3574	4	112
	VA3	Nigra sum sed formosa	3878	3	121
	VA4	Iam hiems	3470	4	126
	VA5	Speciosa facta es	4988	4	147
	VAM	Beata mater et innupta	1570	2	Canticle of Mary
Compline	CA	Sub tuum presidium	5041	7	Canticle of Simeon

the service of Matins: the three antiphons assigned to each of the three nocturns of Matins bear the same mode. MA1 through MA3 and MA7 through MA9 present mode 4 antiphons, while the intervening second nocturn (MA4 through MA6) carries three mode 7 antiphons. Modes 4 and 7 in fact account for more than two-thirds of the antiphons in the Office of the Virgin. Modal conformity alone does not necessarily simplify musical material as individual gestures can vary in theory. The musical constraints extend further than this, effectively narrowing the set of melodies users committed to memory.

The mode 4 antiphons adhere to a model that accommodated the brief texts assigned to them. Example 2.1 reveals the remarkable melodic uniformity of these antiphons, as seen in early fourteenth-century breviaries from the Cathedral of Notre Dame of Paris (BnF, lat. 15181 and 15182), sources that will be valuable for melodic reference throughout this study due to their geography, chronology, and notational clarity. As Rebecca Baltzer has shown, the cathedral was one of the early cultivators of the "Little Office" of the Virgin.[9] Each of the mode 4 antiphons are transposed up a fourth, finishing on *a* with secondary emphasis on *d*. The antiphons of the first nocturn (MA1–MA3) consistently open with the notes *g-a-c-d*, two of them establishing a narrow compass around *c-e* toward the midpoint of the antiphon. The second half of these three antiphons descends to the *f* below the final, rising up past it precisely to *c* before descending by skip or step to the final *a*.

The three antiphons from the third nocturn (MA7–MA9) all begin with similar gestures (*c-g-a-c-d*), nearly identical to the first set of mode 4 antiphons except for the initial descent of a fourth. These three antiphons also share with MA1 and MA2 the skip down of a minor

Example 2.1 Antiphons from the Office of the Virgin, transcribed from BnF, lat. 15181, fols. 445v–446r (MA1, MA2), 448v–449r (MA7, MA9), 530r (MA3) and BnF, lat. 15182, fol. 309r (MA8).

Example 2.2 Mode 7 Antiphons MA4–MA6 from the Office of the Virgin, transcribed from BnF, lat. 15181, fol. 447r (MA4, MA5) and BnF, lat. 15182, fol. 307v (MA6).

second (*d-b*). This skip breaks the recitational emphasis around *d* in each chant and unleashes the concluding gesture toward its final. Since the common musical gestures were limited among these six Matins antiphons, one presumes that by seeing the text, a user could easily unlock the short, near-formulaic mode 4 melody. The melody of the antiphon *Ante thorum huius virginis* (MA3), however, reminds us of the thorny issues around *b*-flat. This pitch would normally be assumed in a transposed mode 4, but it is ambiguous in the sources. In the experience of a book of hours, owners bypass the problem of notation and modal theory, relying on memory to recreate the sound of the antiphons from the written words alone.

There are four additional mode 4 melodies deployed in the Office of the Virgin (LA3, VA2, VA4, VA5). *In odorem unguentorum* appears in both Lauds and the service of Sext and takes the same melodic shape as the antiphons from Matins. VA, VA3, and VA5 follow suit, most resembling the first three Matins antiphons in their initial pitches (*g-a-c-d*). The homogeneity of the mode 4 antiphons in the Office of the Virgin greatly reduced the sounds a book of hours user needed to remember in the execution of this office.

Mode 7 antiphons are also overrepresented in the Office of the Virgin. Here too we see unusual consistency among some of them that would have likely strengthened aural recall of the melodies in the absence of notation in books of hours (Example 2.2). The three consecutive mode 7 antiphons of Matins (MA4 to MA6) each unfold in two brief musical phrases ending on the final *g*. They all begin with same five pitches above the final (*d-b-d-e-d*). Emphasizing the mode's recitation tone on *d*, these chants traverse the pentachord down to the *g* at the conclusion of the first phrase. The second phrase takes up a recitation of between three and six notes on *c*; it then dips down to *a* and returns to *c*. The phrase winds down by filling in the tetrachord down to the final again before a short, arched concluding formula (*g-a-b-a-g*). The model is simple but distinct, each phrase beginning above the final almost recitationally and working its way down to *g*.

Comprising only three services of Vespers, Matins, and Lauds, the Office of the Dead in books of hours offers 22 antiphons, five fewer than the number found in the Office of the Virgin. Compared to the Marian office, the antiphons for the defunct are even shorter in length, many just a single musical phrase.[10] The Office of the Dead is sometimes referred to simply by its opening Vespers antiphon, *Placebo*, an incipit that may either precede or lie beneath a miniature depicting the funeral service. Table 2.2 reveals the progression of antiphons encountered in the Roman rite along with their presumed modes.

Table 2.2 Antiphons for the Office of the Dead

Service	Position	Antiphon	CAO no.	Mode	Psalm/Canticle
Vespers	VA1	Placebo Domino	4293	3	114
	VA2	Heu mihi	3038	2	119
	VA3	Dominus custodit	2402	8	120
	VA4	Si iniquitates observaveris	4899	8	129
	VA5	Opera manuum	4159	2	137
	VAM	Omne quod dat	4115	7	Canticle of Mary
Matins	MI	Regem cui omnia vivunt	1131	6	94
	MA1	Dirige Domine	2244	7	5
	MA2	Convertere Domine	1921	8	6
	MA3	Nequando rapiat	3875	8	7
	MA4	In loco pascue	3250	8	22
	MA5	Delicta iuventutis	2146	8	24
	MA6	Credo videre bona	1948	4	26
	MA7	Complaceat tibi	1861	2	39
	MA8	Sana Domine	4696	2	40
	MA9	Sitivit anima	4972	2/8	41
Lauds	LA1	Exultabunt Domino	2810	1	50
	LA2	Exaudi Domine	2767	8	64
	LA3	Me suscepit dextera	3725	7	62
	LA4	A porta inferi	1191	2	Canticle of Ezechias
	LA5	Omnis spiritus	4154	7	148, 149, 150
	LAB	Ego sum resurrectio	2601	2	Canticle of Zechariah

Unlike the Office of the Virgin, no antiphon is slated to repeat across the services. Nearly all are drawn directly from the psalms with which they are paired, reinforcing the texts with different vocal expressions.[11] Across the services, mode 8 dominates the collection of antiphons, with G-mode chants (modes 7 and 8) accounting for at least half of the modes in the Office of the Dead.[12] The low-ranging Mode 2 also plays a noticeable role in the melodies of this office. The four consecutive mode 8 antiphons in Matins do not assume a consistent formula beyond adhering to basic modal behavior. One could not fall back on a prescribed melodic shape for recalling the antiphons in this office. Yet, it will be recalled that they were heard in public with regularity. Any variations in melodic shape are tempered by the antiphons' general conciseness.

Incipits

For all of the built-in brevity of the office antiphons, there is another level of succinctness that accompanies their presentation in the *horae*. A careful eye will notice in the unfolding of antiphons that only the incipit is given at its initial appearance before the psalm. One must wait until the end of the psalm or group of psalms for the full text of the antiphon to be revealed. This customary asymmetrical feature has not been addressed in scholarship on books of hours nor in the musicological literature. The phenomenon can be witnessed in two contrasting examples, one from each of the core offices in books of hours.

We may first examine the incipit of a brief chant, characteristic of the antiphons in the core offices. *In loco pascue* (CAO 3250) is the fourth antiphon of Matins in the Office of the Dead. Figure 2.1a places us in the transition from the first to the second nocturn in the service. In the middle of the folio, the three-word incipit *In loco pascue* follows the truncated rubrication of that antiphon (*antipho[na]*). This incipit, written in a slightly smaller script, leads directly to the recitation of Psalm 22 ("Dominus regit me"), rubricated *psalmus* and

Figure 2.1 a/b Antiphon, *In loco pascue* with Psalm 22 (beginning and end). Paris, BnF, Ars. Ms-637 réserve, fols. 122r, 123r.

Figure 2.1 (Continued)

Example 2.3 Antiphon, *In loco pascue*. Transcribed from BnF, lat. 15182, fol. 423v.

drawn with larger script as was conventional. The antiphon text is extracted from the end of the first verse of Psalm 22: "He has set me in a place of pasture." The psalm's opening letter "D" of *Dominus* spans two lines and features a large gold capital filled with a red interior and a surrounding blue field, a pattern that will alternate in the succeeding psalm verses.

The third and fourth lines of Figure 2.1b in turn divulge the complete text of *In loco pascue*, a scant six words capping the nine verses of the psalm (five not shown) plus the doxology-like "Requiem." The incipit and the full antiphon differ only by the concluding clause of just three words ("ibi me collocavit") usually cast syllabically to the letter notes *b-c-a-b-a-g-g* in the eighth melodic mode, as shown in Example 2.3. The six-syllable intonation "In loco pascue" (*g-f-a-c-c-bg*) sets up the seven-syllable conclusion, but only after the recitation of the psalm. Limited to a perfect fifth in its range, the mode 8 *In loco pascue* is built for any voice to murmur or sing out in performing the psalm. Like other short antiphons in the offices, the intonation of *In loco pascue* is about half the length of the antiphon itself, highly memorable on its own and helped by its syllabic melodic profile.

A second example shows a lengthy antiphon, *Beata dei genetrix* (CAO 1563), which frames the Benedictus at Lauds in the Office of the Virgin. Figure 2.2a indicates the incipit, again kept to just three words. The return of the antiphon at the end of the Canticle of Zechariah (Figure 2.2b) is extensive and far more ornate than *In loco pascue*. While the incipit of *Beata dei genetrix* consumes about half a line, the complete mode 8 antiphon occupies more than a third of the page's text block, even with a script noticeably smaller than the preceding verses of the canticle. Still, a musical response could reasonably be enacted. *Beata dei genetrix* retains a relatively syllabic profile with occasional two-note groupings, but full of familiar mode 8 gestures.[13]

The incipits themselves are an especially curious feature in the presentation of antiphons in books of hours. Were they supposed to signal a full recitation of the antiphon? At the end of a psalm, for example, the *Gloria patri* was to be said in full, but usually only those two words are provided. Do the first two or three words of the antiphon function similarly? If the full antiphon was to be sung at the beginning, why was it invariably written out after the psalm or group of psalms were completed? Our modern "textbook" understanding of antiphons is that they were to be declaimed in full both before and after the psalm recitation. And while a cantor may intone the incipit of the antiphon, the choir seems to have performed the antiphon in full before proceeding to the psalm.[14] This uncontested principle of practice does not concord with the prescriptions given in books of hours. What was the convention?

A clue can be found in the rare instances in which the psalm is abbreviated because it is found earlier in a book of hours. On these occasions, it would seem like some condensing of the antiphon might be in order. An example from BnF, n.a.l. 3258 (illustrated by the Master of the Hours of Louis of Savoy) is representative of the scribal inclination to delineate liturgical practice even in the face of a compressed liturgical item.[15] Though the psalm is found elsewhere in the book of hours (and could well have been memorized by the user), the incipit and full antiphon still surround the cue for the psalm in the customary fashion.[16] The third line of Figure 2.3 indicates the antiphon *Nigra sum sed formosa* (VA3 in the Office of the Virgin), leading to its usual psalm "Letatus sum" (Psalm 121) in large script. A rubric alerts the owner to seek (*require*) the full psalm earlier in the Office of the Virgin in the minor hour

Figure 2.2 a/b Antiphon for the Benedictus at Lauds, *Beata dei genetrix* (beginning and end). Paris, BnF, lat. 1160, fol. 59v, 60v.

Figure 2.2 (Continued)

Figure 2.3 Vespers Antiphons in the Office of the Virgin. Paris, BnF, n.a.l. 3258, fol. 67v.

of Terce.[17] The complete *Nigra sum* follows, consuming three lines. The pattern continues on this folio with the fourth antiphon of Vespers (*Iam hiems*). The incipit gives way to Psalm 126 "Nisi Dominus" and an instruction to turn back earlier to the service of None for the psalm's remainder; the item then resolves with the full provision of *Iam hiems*.

The incipit specified before the psalm was both necessary and sufficient in its prescription. With more space presumably available from the abbreviated psalm, the framing antiphon retains its two forms. No full declamation of the antiphon was required before the psalm recitation in the Office of the Virgin or the Office of the Dead. This arrangement was rigorously reflected in liturgical practice. For celebrations that were not major, which included these office liturgies, a cantor intoned only the incipit before the choir chanted the psalmody, after which the choir sang the whole antiphon for the first time. Early evidence for this practice can be found in the *Liber quare*, an eleventh-century treatise about the liturgy, set in the form of a catechism.[18] Subsequent testimony of this custom of singing of antiphons and psalms comes from the anonymous *Speculum de mysteriis ecclesiae* and Iohannes Beleth's *Summa de ecclesiasticis officiis*.[19] The influential thirteenth-century bishop and liturgical writer Guillaume Durand further bore witness to the tradition in detail in the famous *Rationale divinorum officiorum*.[20]

Only on the church's major feast days (Easter, Christmas, Epiphany, Ascension, etc.) could one witness the "textbook" practice of singing the antiphon in full before and after the psalm. This "double" performance of the antiphon in fact explains the notion of a *duplex* feast, a classification of high rank and solemnity.[21] Capturing the full extent of the calendar feasts, medieval breviaries and psalters regularly show what we find in books of hours—the intonation only before a psalm or canticle. Corroborating this practice from a different point of view, extant books prescribing liturgical rituals and movements called ordinals refer to special cases of the "doubling" practice with the instruction *antiphona duplicatur*. Therefore, we can similarly deduce that the conventional practice must have been to deliver only the incipit before the antiphon. The book of hours thus represents a norm of the liturgical rite, not an exception, in its precise deployment of incipits in the office antiphons.[22]

The length of the incipit for a given antiphon was not uniform across books of hours, raising questions about the envoicing or audiation of the sounding fragment. The inconsistency was no doubt a function of space more than a reflection of practice. Depending on the available line space at the beginning of the antiphon *In loco pascue* (MA4, Office of the Dead), for example, the scribe may opt for either "In loco" or "In loco pascue" as the incipit, leaving the musical gesture at differing points if strictly adherent to the written words (Example 2.3). In practice, a cantor would have been unlikely to halt the incipit after "loco" in the midst of the mode 8 antiphon's characteristic rising gesture *f-a-c*. Extreme truncation of incipits to a single word (or even an initial syllable) occasionally occurred, again producing an unreasonable-sounding melodic fragment to establish a stable tonality if taken literally on the page.[23]

Invitatory intercalations

If the intonation of the antiphon before the psalm was a conventional practice, there was one antiphon in the Office of the Virgin that did not follow this routine and instead called for extraordinary execution in books of hours. While we have seen the antiphon abbreviated in the case of the incipit, we now see this antiphon multiplied, encroaching on the territory reserved for the psalm in the *mise-en-page*. This invitatory antiphon of Matins, *Ave Maria gratia plena*, frames the singing of Psalm 94 ("Venite exultemus")—and then some. Opening the Night Office, the psalm's inaugural command "Venite" ("Come") summoned the monastic community out of its sleep to worship. The owner of the book of hours could imagine or act out the experience of Matins similarly.

Antiphons 49

There are two invitatory melodies with the title "Ave Maria"—CAO 1041 and 1042. Neither will be familiar to modern ears. The well-known antiphon of the same title (CAO 1539) is a syllabic setting in mode 1 known for its rising fifth and neighbor tone *b*-flat. This antiphon was found in numerous positions for the feasts of the Virgin Mary, but never accompanying the invitatory psalm. Between the two *Ave Maria* invitatories, CAO 1041 was clearly the one called for in books of hours. Not only is it the more widespread of the two, but CAO 1042 includes text that exceeds the prescription at the beginning of Matins.[24] Namely, it extends beyond the six words of the angel Gabriel ("Ave Maria gratia plena Dominus tecum"), appending Elizabeth's words from Luke 1:42 ("benedicta tu in mulieribus"). Example 2.4 juxtaposes the ornate invitatory CAO 1041 with the popular and more modest *Ave Maria* antiphon (CAO 1539), which also attaches Elizabeth's declaration at the scene of the Visitation. With the invitatory CAO 1041 in mind, we can examine its peculiar unfolding at the beginning of Matins for the Virgin Mary.

The invitatory antiphon *Ave Maria* not only appears in its entirety before Psalm 94, but it is remarkably interlaced in the course of the psalm's recitation. The practice was not novel for books of hours but rather a centuries-old practice, if little acknowledged. Joseph Dyer found evidence in early Christian psalmody of antiphon repetitions between verses of the psalm. The number of times the antiphon was intercalated into the psalm verses "varied according to circumstances which may never be understood." As the Christian monk and theologian John Cassian observed in the fifth century, this practice greatly prolonged the performance of the psalms. Dyer noted that there were certainly cases in which the antiphon was repeated by the choir after every psalm verse.[25] The great Carolingian chronicler Amalarius of Metz appears to suggest this type of execution in his description of the organization of the Night Office.[26] A modified version of this practice was maintained into the later Middle Ages in only a single liturgical genre—the invitatory.

The practice of interpolating the antiphon in the recitation of Psalm 94 was consistent in books of hours but not straightforward. In the course of the psalm intonation, the antiphon resurfaced in two different ways. At the end of odd-numbered verses, the antiphon was sung in its entirety. After even-numbered verses and after the doxology, the choir declaimed only the final words of the invitatory antiphon, "Dominus tecum."[27] As would happen with any antiphon and psalm in the office, the invitatory antiphon is repeated in full to conclude. In the Office of the Virgin in books of hours, the *mise-en-page* reflects the liturgical practice at every turn, mirroring the proper repetitions so that the eyes and ears can experience the extraordinary and refreshing appearance of the antiphon throughout Psalm 94.

Figure 2.4 demonstrates the characteristic unfolding of *Ave Maria gratia plena* in Psalm 94, as shown in a book of hours from the city of Rennes in France's Brittany region ca. 1420 (BnF, Ars. 616).[28] As was the convention, the invitatory antiphon on the verso follows the

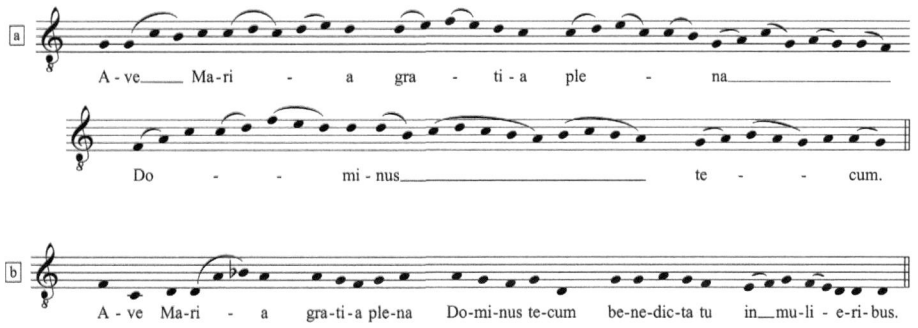

Example 2.4 (a) Invitatory, *Ave Maria gratia plena*, CAO 1041; and (b) Antiphon, *Ave Maria gratia plena*, CAO 1539. Transcribed from BnF, lat. 15181, fols. 467v, 471r.

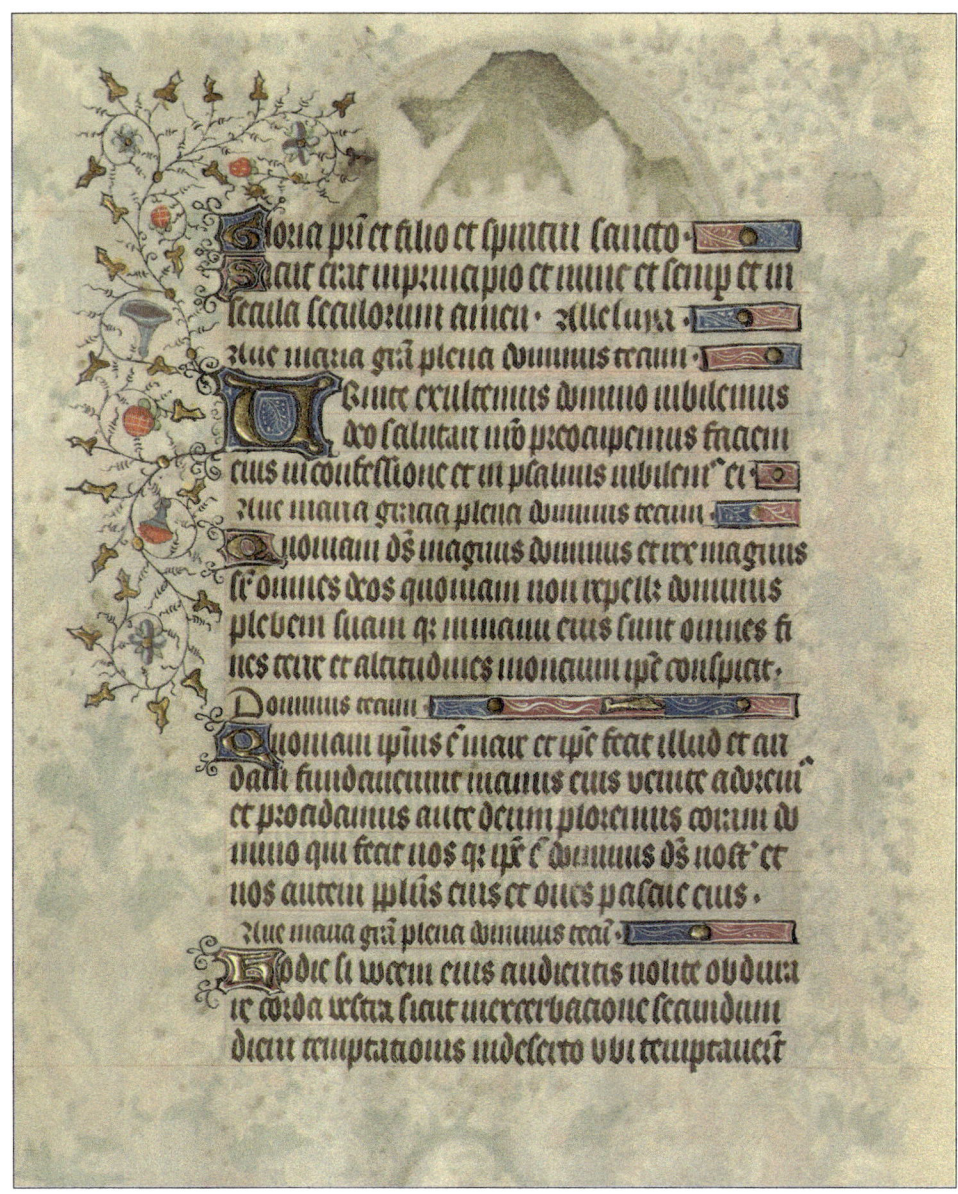

Figure 2.4 Invitatory antiphon, *Ave Maria gratia plena* with Psalm 94. Paris, BnF, Ars. Ms-616 réserve, fols. 13v–14r.

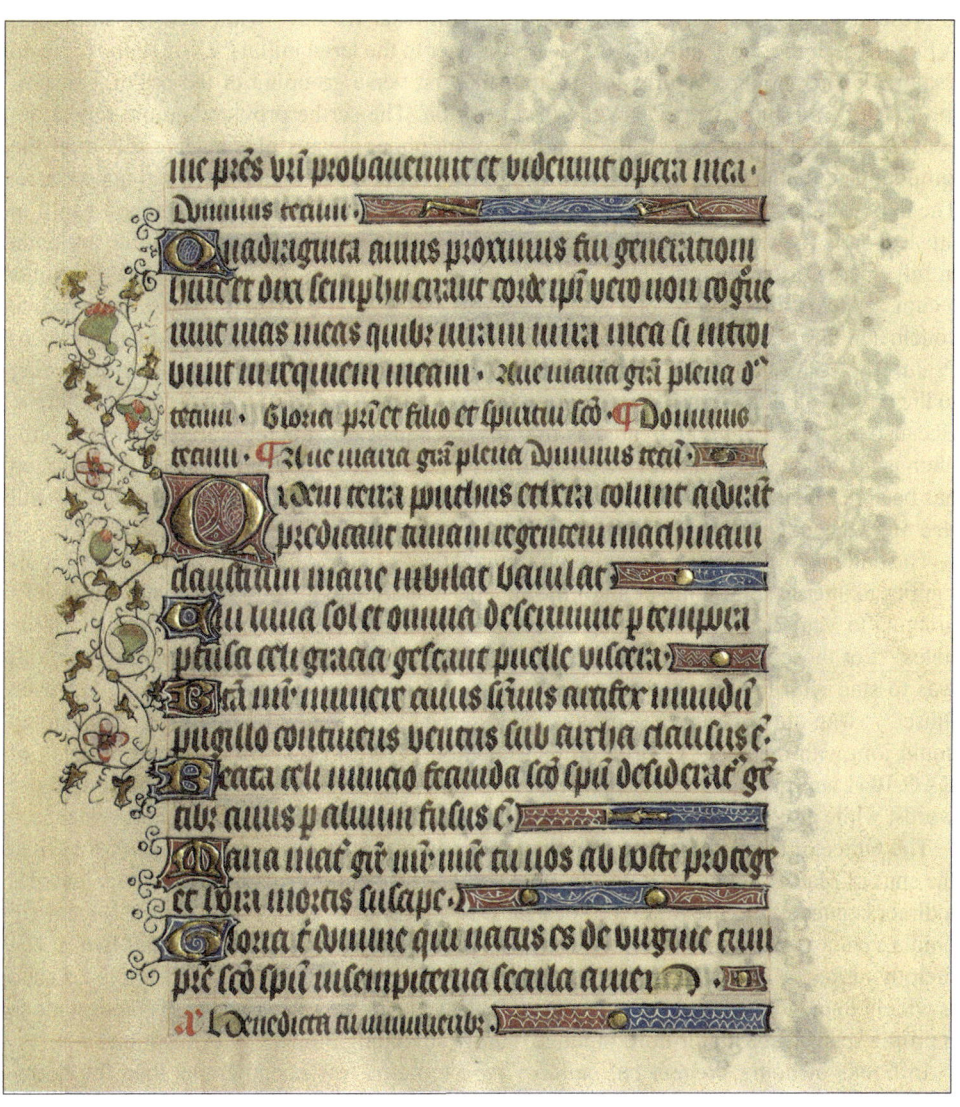

Figure 2.4 (Continued)

52 *Music of the Offices*

doxology of the opening versicle and response of Matins in the Office of the Virgin. Its genre of antiphon unrubricated, *Ave Maria gratia plena* appears on the fourth line of the verso; it is presented in a small script size, consistent with what we have witnessed for antiphons. A line-fill after the short antiphon text leads the user to the large initial "V" of *Venite* to begin Psalm 94. The antiphon returns in full after the first verse grouping of the psalm, consuming much of the line as it did for the first iteration. The scribe provided ample separation between the psalm verses and the interleaved antiphon, always placing line-fills after the antiphon and maintaining the antiphon's reduced script size to match its initial appearance. The delineations do not signal a change of forces—both were choral—but perhaps a shift in musical style (from recitational to more contoured). As expected, the return of the antiphon in full emerges after the first, third, and fifth verse combinations, while the partial "Dominus tecum" appears after the second and fourth pairings.[29] As the invitatory comes toward its conclusion on the recto, the words of the angel Gabriel intensify. After the final verses of Psalm 94 (10–11, beginning "Quadraginta annis"), the complete antiphon is heard according to the pattern of alternation. The doxology follows, curiously in small script in this example. Because the *Gloria patri* is treated as psalm verse musically, another reference to the antiphon is in order with the abbreviated "Dominus tecum." Even though the end of the antiphon has been reached at that point, it was only partially accomplished, which means that the full *Ave Maria* would be heard again in its entirety.

The braiding of the *Ave Maria* through Psalm 94 gave books of hours users multiple opportunities to utter in song some or all of the angelic salutation at the outset of Matins. Gabriel's greeting to Mary had overwhelming significance in late medieval Europe. As Rachel Fulton notes, "For those who were able, the most perfect service [of Mary in order to serve God] was to sing with the angels the psalms that they sang before the throne of God, but even those . . . who did not know the psalms could serve her with their bodies and hearts, and all could join with the angel Gabriel in his salutation."[30] With each full or partial iteration of CAO 1041 amid Psalm 94, the supplicant steps into the role of the angel by repeating those words, while also savoring the mystery of the incarnation contained in that short sentence.

The Office of the Dead featured a parallel invitatory antiphon *Regem cui omnia vivunt* at the start of Matins. Its full text, also a mere six words like the *Ave Maria* invitatory, evinces a direct connection to the first word of Psalm 94 that should not go unnoticed ("Regem cui omnia vivunt venite adoremus" or "Come, let us adore the King, unto whom all live"). The melody of *Regem cui omnia vivunt* can be securely mapped to CAO 1131 (Example 2.5) and is widely found in liturgical books assigned to the same office *pro defunctis*. Its modest mode 6 profile spans just a major third in range, hardly stretching the voice in execution.

In books of hours, *Regem cui omnia vivunt* remains less conspicuous than the corresponding invitatory in the Office of the Virgin, not only because the office falls much later in the book, but also because Vespers, not Matins, is the opening service of the Office of the Dead. It is not uncommon to see only the incipit for Psalm 94 provided to avoid duplication with the earlier Matins invitatory psalm. When *Regem cui omnia vivunt* does

Example 2.5 Invitatory antiphon, *Regem cui omnia vivunt*. Transcribed from BnF, n.a.l. 1535, fol. 129r.

appear with the full Psalm 94, it is typically threaded into the psalm like its counterpart in Office of the Virgin. The antiphon unfolds in two musical phrases, with a brief medial cadence before the "venite." Grammatical and musical intuition alone could make us confident of the moment of division between these phrases, but we are assured of the partition by following cues for partial repetition of the antiphon interpolated into Psalm 94 in the Office of the Dead. An exquisite book of hours thought to be in the possession of Charles of Orléans, Count of Angoulême (1459–1496) and Louise of Savoy (1476–1531) reveals the expected interweaving of *Regem cui omnia vivunt* with the invitatory psalm (Figure 2.5).

Encased by the stunning marginal images of both nature and the specter of death, the opening of Matins highlights the varied textures of the invitatory, toggling between the melodious antiphon, delineated in smaller script, and the more imposing verses of Psalm 94. In the first two iterations of the antiphon (on the verso), a dot of division breaks up the phrasing of *Regem cui omnia vivunt*, assisting the user's performance, while a subtle splash of yellow through the capitals (*pied-de-mouche*, a scribal marking to be discussed in Chapter 4) signals either the shift of genre or the antiphon's phrasing (on the recto), or both. Clues thus abound to engage the noble owners with these crucial texts; death was quite literally staring them down if their eyes wandered into the margin in the reenactment of the liturgy for the deceased.

Marian antiphons

The Marian antiphons are a distinct category of sacred song drawn from liturgical practice. The repertory is small and did not emerge together as a unit, but rather over the course of centuries. These stand-alone chants honoring the Virgin are sometimes called "votive," suggesting their use beyond the proper liturgy. From the thirteenth century onward, the Marian antiphons were prescribed at the end of the Compline liturgy, no matter the feast. In many books of hours, they are usually placed after the service of Compline in the Office of the Virgin. There are some exceptions to this positioning, and by no means do all books of hours include a Marian antiphon. The Office of the Dead lacks the Compline service, so therefore it does not carry the antiphon. Within the subgenre of Marian antiphons, four larger-scale melodies deployed seasonally have commanded attention: *Alma redemptoris mater* (CAO 1356); *Ave regina caelorum* (CAO 1542), *Regina caeli* (CAO 4597) and *Salve regina*.[31]

The *Salve regina* was (and is) undoubtedly the best known of these four Marian antiphons. Liturgically, this melody was stipulated for the largest span of the year—from Trinity Sunday until the start of Advent. Known as a processional chant in Cluny as early as 1135,[32] the *Salve regina* could be heard year-round in processions of both Dominican and Franciscan orders by the first half of the thirteenth century. Like the other Marian antiphons, it is an independent melody with no accompanying psalm recitation; neither does it have traditional characteristics of an office antiphon. For users of books of hours observing the liturgical day, the *Salve regina* was usually the "last word" of the Office of the Virgin. As such, the omnipresent tune must have been held securely in the memory by lay and religious alike. We have already noted its use by seafarers in the fifteenth century. Despite its length and uneven lines, the *Salve regina* lends itself to relatively easy retrieval as a mode I melody (Example 2.6). David Rothenberg has called the opening four notes (*a-g-a-D*) a "motto of Marian devotion"; this deeply ingrained, clarion opening became the subject of several important works of Renaissance polyphony.[33] The first two phrases of the *Salve regina* are nearly parallel,

Figure 2.5 Invitatory antiphon, *Regem cui omnia vivunt* with Psalm 94. New Haven, Yale University, Beinecke Rare Book and Manuscript Library, MS 411, fols. 95v–96r. Photo credit: Beinecke Rare Book and Manuscript Library, Yale University.

Figure 2.5 (Continued)

56 *Music of the Offices*

making it distinct from typical office antiphons. Further, more than half of the phrases return to the *D* final and the vowel sound [e], creating consistent musical and poetic assonance (lines 1–4, 7, 9). These features provided aids to memory and allowed the lengthy melody to proceed without hesitation.

Marian antiphons on the whole are generally marked by short phrases—attributive or exclamatory—but none is more striking than the three poignant "O"s reserved for the conclusion of the *Salve regina*—"O clemens, O pia, O dulcis virgo Maria" ("O clement, O

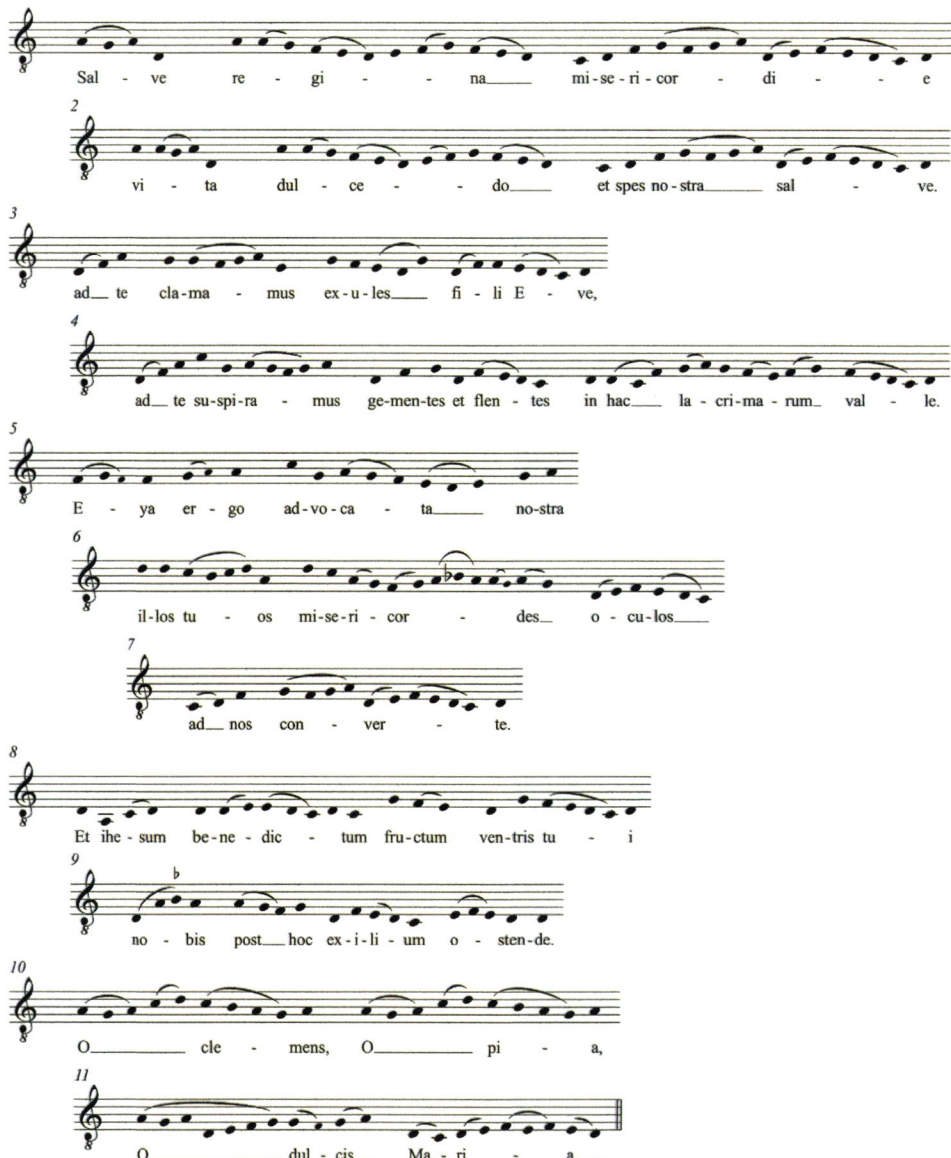

Example 2.6 Antiphon, *Salve regina*. Transcribed from BnF, lat. 15182, fol. 313r-v.

Figure 2.6 Salve regina. LBL, Add. MS 35214, fol. 84v. © The British Library Board.

loving, O sweet Virgin Mary"). At this point in the antiphon (lines 10–11 in Example 2.6), the moderately flowing melody yields to decorative flourishes on the vocative "O" for each of the cries to the Virgin. Regional variances were rampant in the *Salve regina*, more than most antiphons, a byproduct of its heavily oral transmission. Despite the slight melodic differences, it would have been recognized that the first two O's are nearly identical, circling around *a*. The third "O" ("O dulcis") takes a dramatic leap down toward the home *D* before climbing back in stepwise fashion toward a still-suspended destination of *a*. Only by naming the subject of the prayer—"Maria"—does the mode 1 melody return to its resting place on *D*.

In the many books of hours that write out the text of the *Salve regina*, scribes occasionally reveal traces of its envoicing. Notably, the concluding triple "O"s tend to be underscored in different ways. In LBL, Add. MS 35214, a book of hours in humanistic script prepared in the early sixteenth century for a member of the French royal family, the *Salve regina* falls not at the end of Compline in the Office of the Virgin but at the end of the Hours of the Holy Spirit (Figure 2.6). Despite its status as a melody, the antiphon is labeled "Oratio ad beatam mariam" ("Prayer for Blessed Mary"), reminding us of the blurred nature of prayer and song. In the unfolding of the prayer in this book, the *Salve regina* proceeds with regular phrasing marked by capitals drawn with yellow *pieds-de-mouche*. Most books of hours provide little clue as to the execution, probably reflecting an already firm grasp of this deeply embedded melody to the Virgin. In the example, dots of division intercede in the three Os as the spacing opens up relative to the poetry above, perhaps reflecting an awareness of the outpouring of melody at that moment.

While the four Marian antiphons that cycle through the year have been well studied, only the *Salve regina* and occasionally the *Regina caeli* (for use in Eastertide) appear in books of hours.[34] Sometimes construed as a Marian antiphon, *Sub tuum praesidium* (CAO 5041), the oldest known melody for the Virgin, appears in fifteenth-century books of hours with regularity. The text was part of the Ambrosian liturgy, surviving from as early as the third century.[35] The mode 7 melody is largely syllabic, its compass spanning a seventh in most renderings.[36] In medieval service books, *Sub tuum praesidium* was assigned to various Marian feasts (for example, Assumption, Annunciation, Nativity, and Conception) and in an array of liturgical positions (even extraliturgically). Users of books of hours only encountered the antiphon within the Compline service from the Office of the Virgin, not at its conclusion but in a more prestigious position than the *Salve regina*. In Roman usage, *Sub tuum praesidium* is the framing antiphon for the "Nunc dimittis," or Canticle of Simeon, the cornerstone of Compline. The liturgical day thus concludes with at least one Marian antiphon— *Sub tuum praesidium*—and, oftentimes, two (*Salve regina*).

Antiphons for the Cross and Spirit

The Hours of the Holy Cross and the Hours of the Holy Spirit are supplemental offices regularly found in books of hours, though without a fixed position. They were abbreviated services that could be experienced in two ways. More commonly, these devotional hours were grouped together, one after the other, following the Office of the Virgin. However, occasionally the Hours of the Cross and the Hours of the Holy Spirit appear "mixed," meaning their individual services follow the respective hours within the Office of the Virgin.[37] Each "hour" of these auxiliary devotions is highly compressed, most offering a few versicles and responses, a hymn verse, an antiphon, and a prayer. In both offices, a single antiphon was

Example 2.7 Antiphon, *Adoramus te*. Transcribed from BnF, lat. 15182, fol. 355v.

assigned to every service, set to familiar texts associated with each topic (Cross and Spirit). Repeated in each of the seven hours, the antiphon for the Hours of the Cross is *Adoramus te* ("We adore you"); the Hours of Holy Spirit feature *Veni sancte spiritus* ("Come Holy Spirit"). Both antiphons follow the hymn verse.[38] Inconsistent labeling and rendering of these items sparks uncharacteristic confusion for one trying to retrieve the musical sound that the user of these ancillary offices might imagine or perform.

Categorized as CAO 1287, *Adoramus te* is an antiphon from the earliest layers of chant, occurring unsurprisingly in connection with the two principal feasts for the Holy Cross—the Invention (May 3) and the Exaltation (September 14).[39] The full text reveals two short parallel statements and a causal clause: "Adoramus te Christe et benedicimus tibi, quia per crucem tuam redemisti mundum" ("We adore you, O Christ, and we bless you, for by your Cross you have redeemed the world"). The antiphon is a mode 1 melody with some of the contour of the well-known antiphon *Ave Maria* (CAO 1539) rising the fifth *D* to *a* with neighboring *b*-flat (Example 2.7). A performative pause would be appropriate before the clause beginning *quia*, effectively parsing this antiphon into two phrases of medium length. Additional moments of brief repose might be made after the words *Christe* and *tuam*.

Many books of hours designate *Adoramus te* as an antiphon (rubricated "a" for *antiphona*) and continue with this text.[40] Other books of hours, however, classify the text as a versicle and response, the sentence separated after the word *tibi*.[41] Those familiar with the *horae* and liturgical sources more generally are accustomed to rubrication errors involving genre, but this particular common case is further muddled by the fact that a versicle and response do exist for the "Adoramus te" text, namely CAO 7936. This versicle is likewise found in the two offices for the Holy Cross in various liturgical positions. Unlike the antiphon, however, notation of the versicle is rare in service books. It is thus difficult to posit or imagine one particular sound when a book of hours user encounters the text "Adoramus te." The antiphon more commonly occurs, but the versicle-response categorization is too widespread to dismiss as scribal error.[42] A more perplexing situation arises with *Veni sancte spiritus* in the Hours of the Holy Spirit in books of hours.

The title *Veni sancte spiritus* recalls the popular liturgical sequence, a rhymed and rhythmical poem for the feast of Pentecost, which unfolds in musical couplets. Though sequences were to be found in books of hours (as we will see in Chapter 8), they were not appropriate for the short commemorations of the Holy Cross and the Holy Spirit. Indeed, compilers of books of hours were not referring to the sequence; rather, they rubricated *Veni sancte spiritus* specifically as an antiphon. Designated as such, *Veni sancte spiritus* securely maps to CAO

60 *Music of the Offices*

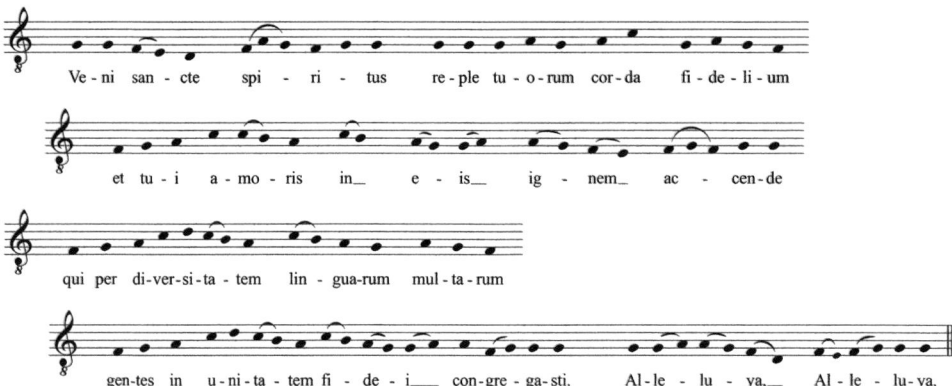

Example 2.8 Antiphon, *Veni Sancte Spiritus*. Transcribed from Chicago, Art Institute of Chicago, Mrs. William E. Kelley Collection, MS 1911.142b, fols. 57v–58r.

5327, a mode 8 melody found in differing liturgical positions in offices for Pentecost. The antiphon is centuries older than the sequence, rendering the latter a kind of gloss of the former in some of its recycled verbiage associated with Pentecost.[43]

In contrast to *Adoramus te* from the Hours of the Cross, we don't find nearly the genre confusion with *Veni sancte spiritus*. To be sure, liturgical books do not even show a versicle by that name. The text is almost always rubricated as an antiphon and consistently followed by a separate versicle and response (*Emitte spiritus/Et renovabis*). We are not out of the woods yet, though. When *Veni sancte spiritus* is compared to the melody CAO 5327, we find that the antiphon in liturgical sources presents a text that is noticeably longer than the version preserved in books of hours. The excess text given in italics: "Veni Sancte Spiritus reple tuorum corda fidelium et tui amoris in eis ignem accende *qui per diversitatem linguarum cunctarum gentes in unitatem fidei congregasti. Alleluia, alleluia*." In the absence of a link to the mode 8 melody (CAO 5327), the antiphon *Veni sancte spiritus* as found in books of hours does not seem to refer to any other known melody. It extends only to the command "accende."

Could the abbreviated *Veni Sancte Spiritus* in books of hours still "fit" with CAO 5327? Perhaps if there were a cadence on the final *g* of "accende," one could make the case that the melody from the *horae* was a truncated version of the antiphon sung at Pentecost. Indeed, the melody preserved in extant sources points in this direction. Example 2.8 shows the mode 8 *Veni sancte spiritus*, transcribed from a thirteenth-century antiphoner from an Italian convent. The three-syllable "accende" at the end of the second line is set to the notes *fgf-g-g*, suggesting a reasonable cadential gesture and arrival.[44] A similar cadential gesture—repetition of the final *g* coming from the *f* beneath—is also found at the end of this chant, at both the word "congregasti" and the final "Alleluia."

The repose on *g* connecting these moments is by no means confirmation that *Veni Sancte Spiritus* could have ended earlier. More importantly, this marks a rare instance when an antiphon in a book of hours would not match its liturgical counterpart precisely. A final point to consider is that while the antiphon *Veni sancte spiritus* survives widely in service books, it appears unknown in French liturgical sources.[45] France, though, was at the center of production for books of hours in the fifteenth century. It is possible that a lack of familiarity with *Veni Sancte Spiritus* in liturgical practice caused a branch of variance in the transmission of this antiphon in books of hours.

The issues uncovered with *Adoramus te* and *Veni sancte spiritus* in the Hours of the Cross and Spirit respectively may at first seem of little consequence. After all, these services are supplemental to the core offices for the Virgin and for the deceased. They are also unusually brief, nearly akin to a suffrage or commemoration. Illuminators, however, brought great attention to these services, often providing elaborate drawings for each of the seven hours. Further, unlike any antiphons surveyed in this chapter, *Adoramus te* and *Veni sancte spiritus* were prescribed multiple times in the liturgical day. In a "mixed" arrangement, users of books of hours would encounter the auxiliary Hours of the Cross and the Spirit with each passing service for the Virgin. In the more common consecutive arrangement, the antiphons would be repeated so regularly as to become a mantra for these supplemental devotions. Either way, *Adoramus te* and *Veni sancte spiritus* would each greet the owner seven times over the course of the book of hours. Every encounter meant some kind of performance of these short antiphons. For antiphons heard with this level of frequency, far more than any office antiphon, it is astonishing that sonic referents for these cannot rest on more secure terrain.

Notes

1 Fulton, *Mary and the Art of Prayer*, 103–235. The sources of the antiphons vary from Old Testament texts to newly written texts naming the Virgin Mary.
2 BnF, lat. 1156B, fol. 69v.
3 Helmut Hucke identified three stylistic categories for the melodies of antiphons based on the degree of flexibility in accommodating other texts. See Hucke, "Untersuchungen zum Begriff 'Antiphon' und zur Melodik der Offiziumsantiphonen"; Hucke, "Musikalische Formen der Offiziumsantiphonen," 7–33.
4 For example, François Gevaert (*La mélopée antique*, 230–381) identified 47 "themes" among the 1,000 opening formulas of antiphons for the Divine Office recorded by Regino of Prüm (ca. 900).
5 Zieman, *Singing the New Song*, 36–37.
6 Dillon, *The Sense of Sound*, 220.
7 Luke 1:28, 42. For a review of the complicated history of the two-part form of the devotion and the role of music in promoting it, see Anderson, "Enhancing the Ave Maria."
8 Hughes, "Modal Order and Disorder in the Rhymed Office."
9 Baltzer, "The Little Office of the Virgin."
10 On the brevity and memorability of the antiphons in the Office of the Dead, see Schell, "The Office of the Dead in England," 203–204.
11 The exceptions are *Omne quod dat* (VAM), *Regem cui omnia vivunt* (MI), and *Ego sum resurrectio* (LAB). Antiphons drawn from the assigned psalm sometimes undergo slight modification.
12 The precise calculation depends on whether MA9 is considered a mode 8 or mode 2 chant. *Sitivit anima* exists in two different versions, preventing a single modal determination.
13 For a notated example of *Beata dei genetrix*, see the early twelfth-century antiphoner from the Monastery of St. Maur-des-Fossés (BnF, lat. 12044, fol. 174v).
14 The custom is driven not only by a prescription in *LU*, lxi, but also by other resources. See, for example, Hiley, *Western Plainchant*, 89; Burkholder et al., *A History of Western Music*, 50–51.
15 Another example of this phenomenon is found in Walters Art Museum, MS W.289, fol. 37r.

16 The practice extends to antiphons accompanying psalm-like liturgical recitations such as the Benedictus of Lauds. See, for example, the antiphon *Ego sum resurrectio* surrounding an abbreviated Benedictus in the Office of the Dead (BnF, n.a.l. 3204, fol. 126v).
17 The full psalm 121 is found in BnF, n.a.l. 3258, fol. 53r.
18 Götz, *Liber quare*, 87–88. For another witness to the practice, see Sarbak and Weinrich, *Sicardi Cremonensis episcopi Mitralis de officiis*, 229–30 (Bk. IV, ch. I, 153).
19 Beleth, *Summa de ecclesiasticis officiis*, 51. See also the anonymous *Speculum de mysteriis ecclesiae* in *PL* 177: col. 343C (Ch. III). Migne wrongly credited this treatise to Hugh of St. Victor.
20 Durand, *Rationale divinorum officiorum*, 2: 26 (Bk. V, Ch. II, 28–29). The practice is described in Nowacki, "The Latin Antiphon," 26.
21 Semiduplex rank required doubling of the antiphons only at the major hours (i.e., Vespers, Matins, and Lauds).
22 The *Liber usualis* thus reflected a change with the revision of the rubrics in 1960, when it was prescribed that all antiphons should be sung complete before and after the psalm.
23 For example, the word *In* serves as the incipit for the antiphon *In odorem unguentorum* in the service of Sext in the Office of the Virgin in Montpellier Méditerranée Métropole, MS 332 (fols. 55bis-v). In the preceding service of Terce in the same manuscript (fol. 54v), the single syllable *Ma-* signals the beginning of the antiphon *Maria virgo assumpta est*. The manuscript on the whole is pressed for space; five words or fewer per line is common.
24 CAO 1041 is found in six of the earliest sources (E, M, H, R, D, and F), while CAO 1042 is found in just G and S. Descriptions of the early antiphoners may be found in Hesbert, *Corpus antiphonalium officii*, 1: XVII–XXIII and 2: VI–XXIV. Melodically, the two could not be more different: CAO 1041 is cast in mode 7, whereas CAO 1042 varies in its modal classification in the few sources that contain it.
25 Dyer, "The Singing of Psalms," 540.
26 Hanssens, *Amalarii Episcopi Opera Liturgica Omnia*, 3: 24 (*Liber de Ordine Antiphonarii* 3.4).
27 Different than most psalms, Psalm 94 grouped its 11 verses mostly into pairs (1–2, 3–4, 8–9, 10–11, with the exception being 5–7), instead of unfolding verse by verse. Interjections of the antiphon occurred after each grouping.
28 For a description of this book, see Deuffic and Booton, *Le livre d'heures enluminé en Bretagne*, 412–14.
29 In many sources, only the incipit "Ave Maria" appears after the odd-numbered verses, but it is meant to cue the full recitation of the invitatory antiphon.
30 Fulton, *Mary and the Art of Prayer*, 454.
31 The melody is not assigned a CAO number, as it was not part of the early antiphoners cataloged by Hesbert. The Cantus Index database online lists *Salve Regina* with the identification number 204367.
32 Snow, "Salve regina," in *NCE* 12:1002. The earliest surviving manuscript to transmit the plainchant is a mid-twelfth-century Cistercian antiphoner from the abbey of Morimondo, outside Milan (BnF, n.a.l. 1412, fol. 42v). On the history of the melody, see Chapter 1, fn. 1.
33 Rothenberg, *The Flower of Paradise*, 133–141.
34 An exceptional placement of all four Marian antiphons following the Hours of the Holy Spirit can be found in BnF, Ars. 434, fols. 136v–139r.
35 Hiley, *Western Plainchant*, 105.
36 For a notated medieval source of the melody (with the range f–e), see BnF, lat. 12044, fol. 178r.
37 The service of Lauds is omitted in these auxiliary offices. Their first service of Matins begins after Lauds in the Office of the Virgin.
38 Exceptionally, the antiphon *Adoramus te* is prescribed on either side of the hymn verses in the Hours of the Cross in BnF, lat. 1184, fols. 124r–128r.
39 *Adoramus te* is recorded in 7 of the 12 early antiphonaries as cataloged by Hesbert.
40 See, for example, BnF, lat. 9471, fol. 137r.
41 See, for example, BnF, n.a.l. 3187, fols. 63v, 69r. In BnF, lat. 923 (fol. 31v), the text *Adoramus te* is parsed as a versicle and response following the hymn verse. The hymn verse is preceded by the antiphon *Salve crux* (CAO 4694), an antiphon that occasionally is found in place of *Adoramus te*.
42 While most scribes rubricate *Adoramus te* as an antiphon, BnF, lat. 9473 classifies the text as a versicle-response pair for all but one of the Hours of the Cross (fols. 97v–100v).

43 The first three words are of course identical. The antiphon's command *reple tuorum corda fidelium* corresponds with the *reple cordis intima* in the sequence. Further shared commands include *accende* and *fove*, both meaning "inflame" or "warm up."
44 A medial cadence on *f* can be imagined after the word *fidelium*. One book of hours marks the division of the text with a colon at this halfway point. See Bethlehem, Lehigh University, Special Collections, Codex 18, fol. 74v.
45 Of the 44 sources in the Cantus Index that contain CAO 5327, none of them is of French provenance.

3   Hymns

*

Like psalms, hymns were a crucial component of one's early education and experience in the Christian faith. The medieval hymn corpus includes some of the earliest chants on record, dating from the fourth century. Assigning hymns to the celebration of offices was the task of the sixth-century Rules of Caesarius of Arles and Aurelian of Arles, the Rule of Isidore of Seville, and the well-known Rule of St. Benedict.[1] Monastic communities preserved hymn singing, which was only later incorporated in the secular Roman liturgy. Unfolding in strophic form, hymns set nonbiblical texts and deploy a single, recurring melody as new rhythmic poetry unfolds. Usually no more than three notes are assigned per syllable of text. Hymns retain a formal simplicity in line length, suitable to memorization; later examples added further mnemonics of rhyme and accent. With hardly a need for musical notation, hymns had strong influence on Christians at a young age.

In books of hours, hymns tend to occur with a noticeably larger script than antiphons and are comparable to that of the psalms, the other "pedagogical" genre of the book of hours. Large scripts also can also be found in lections and in various prayers (*orationes*). In this light, it is hard to generalize about the meaning of the large script. From an aural perspective, it is tempting to propose that a different sound should be imagined or performed when the writing is enlarged, but the texture of that sound will vary. Imputing a sense of greater importance or specific type of performance from genres with enlarged script likewise seems ill advised.

There is scant testimony on the performance of the medieval hymn to inform our understanding of the user's possible sound encounter with the genre. Despite any glimpses we might get from centuries of oral transmission, we can only guess about how the poetic meters might have been delivered in song. It is conceivable that hymns were envoiced mensurally with the alternation of long and short notes. (Iambic tetrameter was common.) A different kind of alternation is also visible in books of hours with hymns. Similar to psalms, hymns also display decorative capitals with rotating color schemes. The practice of alternation in groups appears to be one method of execution of the hymn, in contrast to a uniform choral performance. Bede (d. 735) affirmed that hymns were sung by alternating choirs, and fifteenth- and sixteenth-century polyphonic hymns further suggest a culture of alternation around the hymn corpus.[2] In books of hours, the revolving use of red and blue ink backgrounds in the decoration of hymn verses could have offered a prompt for the user's memory to rehear an exchange of voices from liturgical practice.

Books of hours offer a surprisingly narrow set of hymns, allowing more focused investigation in this chapter. Four hymns with strikingly different histories permeate the Office of the Virgin in the *horae*. *Quem terra pontus aethera* leads off the group in the service Matins, followed by *O gloriosa domina* at Lauds and the well-known *Ave maris stella*, which sits near the liturgical high point in the office of Vespers. The enigmatic *Memento salutis auctor* appears multiple times, located in each of the four minor hours of the liturgical day plus Compline. The auxiliary Hours of the Cross and Spirit offer hymn verses at each of their seven services, in a special type of presentation. Likely owing to its antiquity, the Office of the Dead does not present any hymns.[3] This chapter centers on the principal Marian hymns, those for the auxiliary Hours of the Cross and Spirit, and the versatile hymn Te Deum.

Quem terra pontus aethera

One of the major frustrations with studying the hymn involves linking text to melody. Fewer than 30 hymns are conclusively known to have circulated with text and melody together in medieval Europe. More often, popular hymn texts could be paired with any number of common hymn melodies.[4] The number of stanzas might differ from source to source, and occasionally, a stanza might take on a life of its own, migrating to another hymn. As with tune indices found in modern hymnals, a shared syllable count and pattern of accentuation allowed texts and tunes to "mix and match" in practice. The interchangeability has consequences in studying hymns in books of hours, beginning with *Quem terra pontus aethera* (CAO 8375), the hymn assigned to the opening service of Matins in the Office of the Virgin. Sometimes attributed to the sixth-century poet and bishop of Poitiers Venantius Fortunatus, *Quem terra pontus aethera* is usually the first hymn a user would encounter in a book of hours. The hymn typically contains four verses plus a paraphrase of the doxology as its fifth strophe, all set in lines of eight syllables.

Quem terra, pontus, aethera colunt, adorant, praedicant, trinam regentem machinam claustrum Mariae baiulat.	The one whom earth, and sea, and sky adore, laud, and proclaim, ruling over the threefold scheme, the Virgin's spotless womb carries.
Cui luna sol et omnia deserviunt per tempora, perfusa caeli gratia, gestant puellae viscera.	He whom the moon, sun, and all things serve in their appointed times, within the virgin's womb is borne clothed in heavenly grace.
Beata Mater, munere, cuius supernus artifex, mundum pugillo continens, ventris sub arca clausus est.	O blessed Mother, by your gift, the heavenly Creator, holding the world in his hand, was protected under the refuge of your womb.
Beata caeli nuntio, fecunda sancto spiritu, desideratus gentibus, cuius per alvum fusus est.	Blessed by the divine messenger, fertile by the Holy Spirit, desired by the peoples, He was cast in the womb.
Gloria tibi Domine, qui natus es de virgine, cum patre, et sancto spiritu, in sempiterna saecula. Amen.	All glory be to you, O Lord, born of the Virgin, with the Father and the Holy Spirit, forever and ever. Amen.

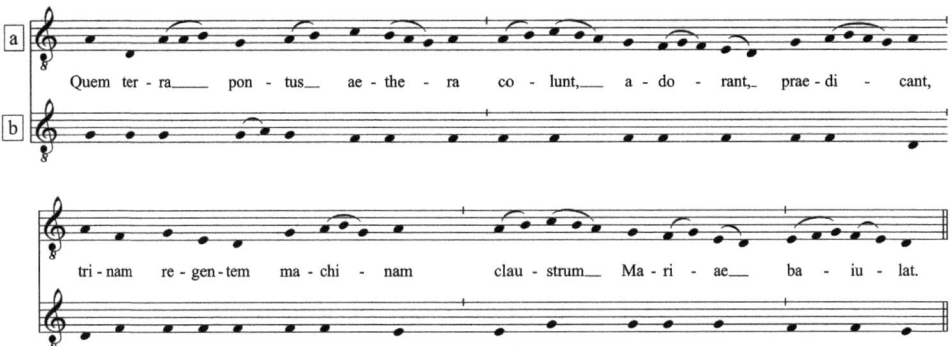

Example 3.1 Two versions of the hymn *Quem terra pontus aethera*, after Paris, Bibliothèque Sainte-Geneviève MS 113, (a) fol. 162r and (b) fol. 162v.

Bruno Stäblein identified a dozen melodies in connection with *Quem terra pontus aethera*.[5] The differences are stark, creating a range of melodic possibilities for this text. Although modal assignments were not formally recognized in medieval sources, the twelve melodies appear to span six of the eight melodic modes (not modes 6 and 7). All four medieval finals (*D*, *E*, *f*, and *g*) are witnessed, though more than half melodies end on *D*. Mode 2 is more prevalent than mode 1. Determining the priority of any of the twelve is not easy. In one early fifteenth-century French psalter-hymnal, for example (Example 3.1), *Quem terra pontus aethera* appears with two contrasting melodies—one on a recto (mode 1), another on the following verso (mode 4).[6] The former is decorated, undulating, and stretched, while the latter is almost entirely syllabic and confined to a fifth in its vocal compass.

While hope of tracing a given user's preferred melody for *Quem terra pontus aethera* is fraught with challenges, books of hours do reveal other musical and performative clues with the hymn repertory. In BnF, lat. 1157, for example, the scribe placed colons within the stanzas of *Quem terra pontus aethera* as an aid to parsing its phrases (Figure 3.1). Colons and other dots of division are occasionally found in hymns, but were by no means a norm. These marks are somewhat more common in psalms. The colons in the hymn, curiously, do not mark each verse. Here, the colon may mark the halfway point of a verse (vv. 1, 4, 5) or may follow the first and third lines of each stanza (vv. 2, 3). Rhyme is not a uniformly governing feature of *Quem terra pontus aethera*, though vowel assonance would provide some assistance in phrasing and memorization in the absence of punctuation.

The number of verses of *Quem terra pontus aethera* is not fixed in books of hours; occasionally an extra verse may be placed before the concluding doxology verse: "Maria mater gratie, mater misericordie, tu nos ab hoste protege, et hora mortis suscipe" ("Mary mother of grace, mother of mercy, shield us from the enemy, and receive us at the hour of death").[7] This supplemental verse of course fits the poetic rhythm of *Quem terra pontus aethera*, with each of the four eight-syllable lines ending with a proparoxytone, or final accent on the antepenultimate syllable. The "Maria mater gratie" variant was hardly a surprising verse to integrate into a Marian hymn. As we will see shortly, users met this verse elsewhere, and often, in the *horae*.

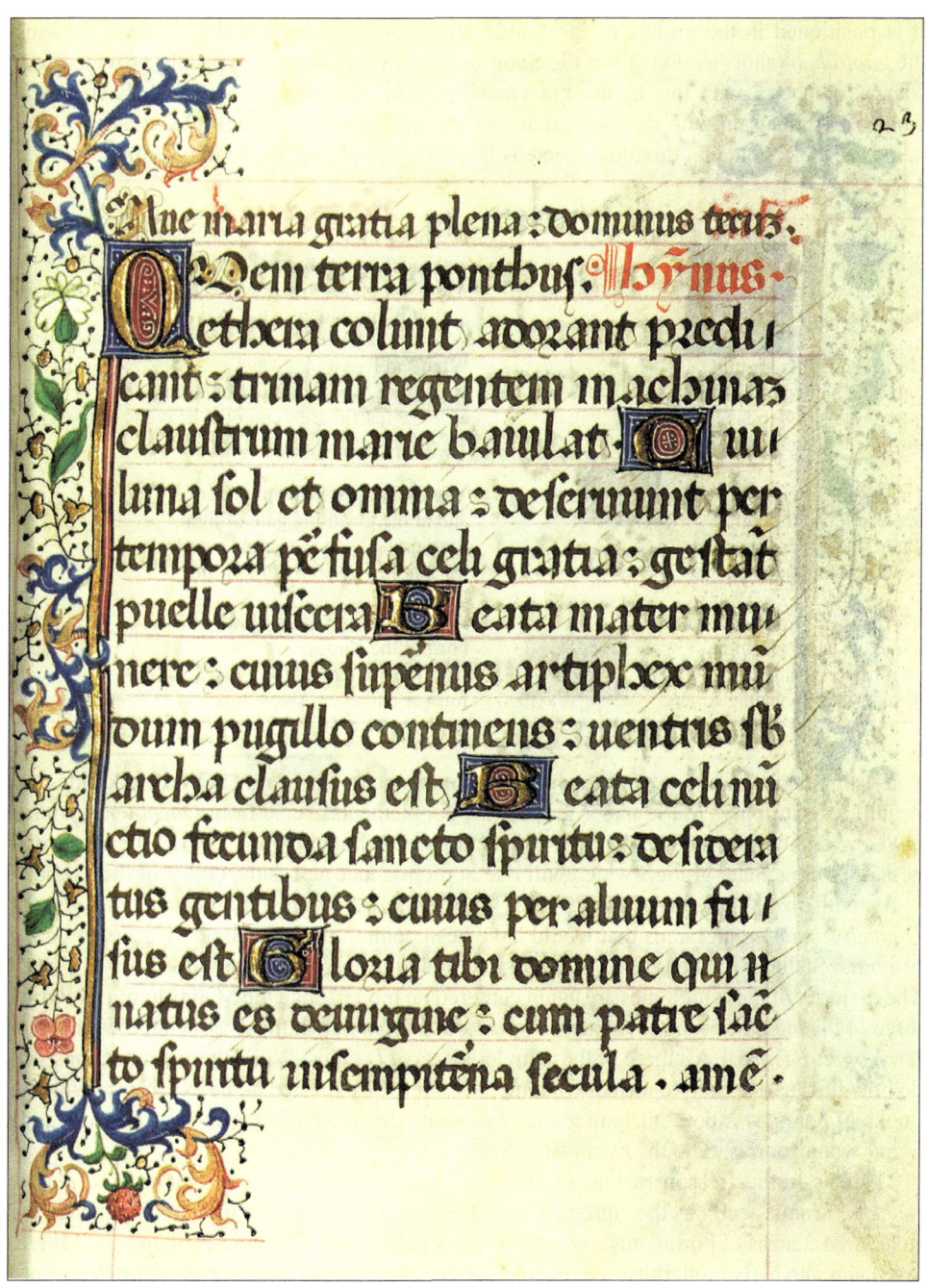

Figure 3.1 Hymn, *Quem terra pontus aethera*. Paris, BnF, lat. 1157, fol. 23r.

O gloriosa domina

The hymn *O gloriosa domina* is usually the second hymn encountered in the book of hours. It is positioned in the middle of the Lauds service in the Office of the Virgin, following the *capitulum* (short lection) from the Song of Songs (6:8). Scribes typically provided four stanzas of poetry with this hymn, but variants could of course be expected. Each stanza comprises a quatrain with rhythm and accent mirroring the structure of *Quem terra pontus aethera*. The concluding doxology verse is likewise shared with the Matins hymn.

O gloriosa domina excelsa super sidera, qui te creavit provide, lactas sacrato ubere.	O glorious Lady, enthroned above the stars, with your breast you produce holy milk providently.
Quod Eva tristis abstulit, tu reddis almo germine; intrent ut astra flebiles, sternis benigna semitam.	What sad Eve took away, you return by your kindly offspring; as those tearful ones enter the heavens you generously open up the path.
Tu regis alti ianua et porta lucis fulgida; vitam datam per Virginem, gentes redemptae plaudite.	You rule at that heavenly door and at the gleaming gate of light. Sing praise, you redeemed people for that life given by the Virgin.
Gloria tibi Domine, qui natus es de virgine, cum patre, et sancto spiritu, in sempiterna saecula. Amen.	All glory be to you, O Lord, born of the Virgin, with the Father and the Holy Spirit, forever and ever. Amen.

In some books of hours, *O gloriosa domina* expands to five verses with the addition of a penultimate strophe, "Maria mater gratie," the supplemental verse from *Quem terra pontus aethera*.[8] Although this addendum was uncommon in the Lauds hymn, it shows the pervasiveness of "Maria mater gratie," which will rise in prominence across the Office of the Virgin.

As with the hymn from Matins, it is impractical to suggest a universal melody for *O gloriosa domina* in Lauds that would have been commonly understood by users of books of hours. Stäblein tracked down five possible melodies in connection with the hymn text.[9] The majority of these melodies are again centered on mode 2, like the Matins hymn. Notably, three of the melodies sung to the text *O gloriosa domina* match those associated with *Quem terra pontus aethera*. All three of these melodies have *D* finals. While these connections still do not allow us a definitive idea of what melody could be expected in the experience with the books of hours, it is both intriguing and reasonable that the melody conjured for the Lauds hymn would simply echo the hymn from Matins.

There is further reason to link *O gloriosa domina* with the hymn *Quem terra pontus aethera*. From as early as the eighth century, the text "O gloriosa domina" accounted for the final three stanzas of Fortunatus's *Quem terra pontus aethera*.[10] Moreover, in the late Middle Ages and into early modernity, the offices of Matins and Lauds were sometimes merged into a single morning service.[11] The connection of these two offices might have been behind the apportioning of Fortunatus's hymn when the services separated. This testimony supports the idea that the same melody might be imagined or envoiced for the hymns of Matins and Lauds in the Office of the Virgin.

Memento salutis auctor

The offices of Prime, Terce, Sext, None, and Compline in the Office of the Virgin offer a single hymn, *Memento salutis auctor*. In the four minor hours, the hymn follows the versicle *Deus in adiutorium* and precedes the antiphon that will frame three psalms. In the aparallel service of Compline, *Memento salutis auctor* is positioned after Psalms 128–130 and before the chapter reading. As found in books of hours, *Memento salutis auctor* usually unfolds in two verses plus the poetic rendering of the doxology found in the other hymns in the Office of the Virgin. Each stanza bears a quatrain with eight-syllable lines and mainly proparoxytonic stress. While the opening strophe, "Memento salutis," addresses God as Creator (*auctor*), the following "Maria mater gratie" verse issues a direct plea to the Virgin and mentions the "hour of death" so crucial to the faithful.

Memento salutis auctor,	Remember, O Creator of salvation,
quod nostri quondam corporis,	that you once took on
ex illibata Virgine	the form of our flesh,
nascendo formam sumpseris.	By being born of the undefiled Virgin.
Maria mater gratie,	Mary mother of grace,
Mater misericordie,	mother of mercy,
Tu nos ab hoste protege	shield us from the enemy
Et hora mortis suscipe.	and receive us at the hour of death.
Gloria tibi Domine . . .	Glory to you O Lord . . .

The migrant stanza "Maria mater gratie" roamed beyond the Office of the Virgin as a stand-alone devotion, particularly in northern and central Italy. The poetic verse was a favorite prayer of Galeazzo Maria Sforza, the duke of Milan (d. 1476), and his chapel of singers performed this verse in four different sets of *motetti missales* by eminent composers of that time including Josquin des Prez.[12] In Siena, the general populace sang "Maria mater gratie" on different occasions; the hymn verse represented a song of civic pride in the city, dubbed "the true *Te Deum* of the Sienese."[13] The prevalence of this verse in books of hours cannot be overstated. In some respects, it flies under the radar as an interior verse, neither opening any of the hymns of the canonical hours and nor bearing an oversized initial. But the sheer number of appearances of "Maria mater gratie" across the liturgical day puts this stanza into an elevated category. *Memento salutis auctor* is assigned to a minimum of five services in the Office of the Virgin, but the detachable "Maria mater gratie" could be found in Matins and Lauds too. Only the iconic Marian hymn *Ave maris stella* from the service of Vespers does not accommodate the pervasive "Maria mater gratie" verse; the poetic rhythms do not match.

As for the melody associated with *Memento salutis auctor*, the possibilities are not only manifold but also shrouded an additional layer of mystery. In liturgical books, *Memento salutis auctor* is not the title of a stand-alone hymn; rather, the text appears as one of the verses of the Vespers hymn, *Christe redemptor omnium/ex Patre*, for the feast of the Nativity of the Lord, a hymn that carries up to eight verses. A widespread melody for *Christe redemptor omnium/ex Patre* is no easier to identify than the other hymns we have surveyed. Stäblein lists 15 hymn melodies to which *Christe redemptor omnium/ex Patre* corresponds in liturgical sources.[14] While it is again difficult to posit a dominant melody, it must be noted that one melody common to the three hymns of the Office of the Virgin mentioned to this

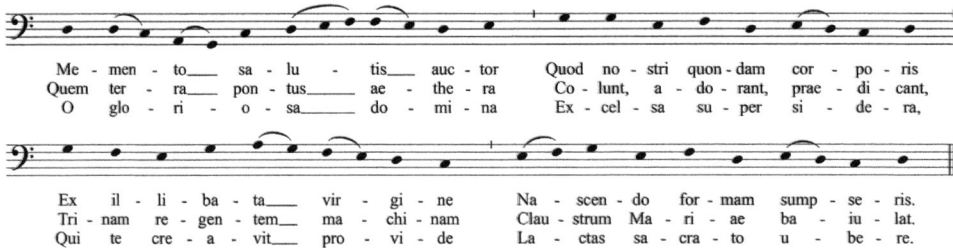

Example 3.2 First verses of the hymns *Memento salutis auctor*, *Quem terra pontus aethera*, and *O gloriosa domina*, set to Stäblein melody 16, after Milan, Biblioteca Trivulziana, MS 347, fols. 109v–111v.

point is Stäblein's no. 16, an Ambrosian hymn tune.[15] Example 3.2 sets the first verse of all three hymn texts to this melody.

Observing this link among *Quem terra pontus aethera*, *O gloriosa domina*, and *Memento salutis auctor* by no means settles the question of which melody a user of the book of hours may hear or utter. However, the presence of the verse "Maria mater gratie," encountered as a potential stanza in all three hymns, offers an opportunity to consider whether a universal melody might have been applied to as many as seven of the eight canonical hours in the Office of the Virgin. The office antiphons of Chapter 2 have already provided a clue that a narrow set melodies could be widely applicable for those who prayed these texts from books of hours. Perhaps the same principle is at work with the hymns.

A complicating factor in locating a sound referent for *Memento salutis auctor* is its unexpected relationship to the hymn for Pentecost, *Veni creator spiritus*. In a book of hours from just before the turn of the sixteenth century prepared for the northern French nobleman Louis de Roncherolles (BnF, Ars. 1191), the four minor hours of the Office of the Virgin reveal the text *Memento salutis auctor*, but only as the second verse of the well-known hymn for Pentecost *Veni creator spiritus*.[16] This manuscript is by no means alone among French books of hours in presenting *Veni creator spiritus* in connection with the more stable hymn for the minor hours in the Office of the Virgin.[17] As Rebecca Baltzer has shown, the hymn for Pentecost is also found in service books at the Cathedral of Notre Dame of Paris, the institution at the forefront of observing the daily office for Mary.[18] Even though *Veni creator spiritus* is not the usual hymn one finds in the minor hours of the Little Office, we can at least settle on a single tune for that hymn, one that is still well known today.[19] This variant is clearly an outlier, however, with no intersections among the potential hymn melodies stated earlier in the Office of the Virgin. There is some bit of comfort that a firm melody can be posited for the few books of hours that thread the highly fixed *Veni creator spiritus* through at least half of daily services for Mary. Yet, for the majority of users, the sound experience attached to the dominant text *Memento salutis auctor* remains hard to pin down.

Ave maris stella

Were it not for the celebration of the Mass, the evening hour of Vespers would be considered the apex of the liturgical day. With its five psalms and antiphons, Vespers mimics the office of Lauds, but the solemnity of Mary's Magnificat sets the eventide service apart from its equivalent at daybreak. The service of Vespers in the Office of the Virgin prescribes the popular hymn *Ave maris stella* (CAO 8272) after the five psalms and the capitulum but before Mary's canticle. Its opening nautical imagery inspired many a theologian to remark on meaning of the striking metaphor.[20] The hymn unfolds in seven quatrains with three trochaic feet in each line. *Ave maris stella* is both the longest of the continuous metrical hymns in books of hours and the only one to use the "short" meter.

Ave, maris stella,	Hail, star of the sea,
Dei mater alma,	loving Mother of God,
Atque semper virgo,	and also always a virgin,
Felix coeli porta.	Blessed gate of heaven.
Sumens illud Ave	Taking up that Ave
Gabrielis ore,	from Gabriel's mouth
Funda nos in pace,	confirm us in peace,
Mutans Evae nomen.	reversing Eve's name.
Solve vincla reis	Break the chains of sinners,
Profer lumen caecis,	bring light to the blind,
Mala nostra pelle,	drive away our evils,
Bona cuncta posce.	ask for all good.
Monstra te esse matrem,	Show yourself to be a Mother,
Sumat per te preces	may he accept prayers through you,
Qui pro nobis natus,	he who, born for us,
Tulit esse tuus.	chose to be yours.
Virgo singularis,	O unique virgin,
Inter omnes mitis,	mild above all,
Nos culpis solutos	make us gentle and chaste,
Mites fac et castos.	absolved from sin.
Vitam praesta puram,	Keep life pure,
Iter para tutum;	make the journey safe,
Ut videntes Jesum	so that, seeing Jesus,
Semper collaetemur.	we may always rejoice together.
Sit laus Deo Patri,	Let there be praise to God the Father,
Summo Christo decus,	glory to Christ in the highest,
Spiritui Sancto,	and to the Holy Spirit,
Tribus honor unus. Amen.	one honor to all three. Amen.

Musicologists, particularly those working in fifteenth- and sixteenth-century studies, have assumed that *Ave maris stella* maps to a single melody, and with good reason.[21] Their work tends to be entrenched in the study of polyphonic music, and the source melodies of polyphonic pieces titled *Ave maris stella* tend to point to the same well-known plainchant (Stäblein no. 67).[22] This mode 1 melody rises a fifth before reaching the octave all in the first phrase. Regional and institutional melodic variants of this version of the *Ave maris stella* are to be expected. There were, however, eight discrete melodies associated with the Marian Vespers hymn, spanning finals on *C*, *D*, *E*, and *g*.[23] While it is tempting to declare Stäblein's no. 67 the dominant form of *Ave maris stella* throughout Europe, a study of French books of hours teaches one to be more cautious. At least three of the melodic traditions associated with this hymn text (nos. 149, 174, and 208) surface in French sources.[24]

Hymn for the Holy Cross

In the spirit of the wandering "Maria mater gratie" verse, hymns for the auxiliary Hours of the Cross and the Hours of the Holy Spirit feature disassembled verses resituated in various services. The hymns texts slated for these supplemental hours—presented with almost no variation—are systematically dispersed, one verse surfacing in each of the seven services of these highly abbreviated offices. In the context of these compressed liturgies, the hymns remain a focal point. Not only do they appear in large script, but they are never truncated nor given an incipit, as their verses differed with each change of hour.

We may begin with the hymn for the Hours of the Cross, *Patris sapientia veritas divina*. The first verse unfolds in Matins, the opening "hour" of the Cross. Like other hymns, *Patris sapientia veritas divina* unveils rhythmic and rhymed poetry arranged in quatrains, but now cast in the goliardic meter. Each line divides into two parts of seven and six syllables, respectively.[25] The concluding line of a four-line stanza is sometimes hypermetric (extended by an extra syllable). Successive stanzas include references to the daytime hours to which they were assigned, mirroring the events of the Passion within the context of the brief office. Users thus mark the passage of time in connection with Christ's agony in the performance of these metrical texts.

Patris sapientia veritas divina	The wisdom of the Father, divine truth,
Deus homo captus est hora matutina	God made man, was captured at the morning hour,
A suis discipulis cito derelictus	Quickly abandoned by his disciples,
A Iudeis traditus, venditus, afflictus.	Betrayed by the Jews, sold and tormented.
Hora prima ductus est iesus ad pilatum	At the hour of Prime, Jesus was led to Pilate,
Falsis testimoniis multum accusatum:	Much accused by false witnesses;
In collo percutiunt manibus ligatum	They strike him on the neck with his hands bound,
Vultum Dei conspuunt lumen celi gratum.	And spit upon the face of God, the dear light of heaven.
Crucifige clamitant hora tertiarum	"Crucify him," they cry at the hour of Terce;
Illusus induitur veste purpurarum.	The one they mock is clothed in purple.
Caput eius pungitur corona spinarum:	His head is pricked with a crown of thorns;
Crucem portat humeris ad locum penarum.	He bears the Cross to the place of punishment.
Hora sexta iesus est cruci conclavatus,	At the sixth hour, Jesus was nailed to the Cross,
Et est cum latronibus pendens deputatus.	And was left hanging with thieves.
Pre tormentis sitiens felle saturatus,	Thirsting from his torments, he was satisfied with gall;
agnus crimen diluit sic ludificatus.	The lamb thus ridiculed washed away sin.
Hora nona Dominus iesus expiravit,	At the ninth hour, Jesus died,
Hely clamans animam patri commendavit.	Crying "Eli," he commended his spirit to his father.
Latus eius lancea miles perforavit,	A soldier pierced his side with a spear,
Terra tunc contremuit et sol obscuravit.	Then the earth trembled and the sun darkened.

De cruce deponitur hora vespertina Fortitudo latuit in mente divina. Talem mortem subiit vite medicina. Heu corona glorie iacuit supina.	He is taken down from the Cross at the hour of Vespers; Strength hid itself in the divine mind. The medicine of life suffered such a death. Alas, the crown of glory lay supine.
Hora completorii datur sepulture Corpus christi nobile spes vite future. Conditur aromate complentur scripture Iugis sit memoria mors hec michi cure.	At the hour of Compline he was laid in the tomb; The noble body of Christ, the hope of future life, is embalmed with spices; the Scriptures are fulfilled. May this death be perpetually in my memory.[26]

Because the origin of *Patris sapientia veritas divina* is traceable to a poem by Egidius of Rome (1247–1316), there has been little said about a musical tradition for the hymn text.[27] There is no CAO melody attached to the hymn, nor did Stäblein catalog it, strengthening the assumption that it was in circulation only as a poem or spoken prayer.[28] Giacomo Baroffio theorized that the instability of the poetic verses—both hypermetric and hypometric verses—may further indicate that it was to be read and not sung; however, the goliardics appear correct in the most common verses of the hymn shown here.[29] While a fixed tune does not appear in conjunction with hymn for the Holy Cross at its original conception, a melody fitting the syllable count was in circulation.

One monophonic setting with an *E* final has survived from around the middle of the fifteenth century. The evidence comes from a piece of polyphony for the Mass Ordinary found twice in the Trent Codices, which transmit a large repertory spanning the middle third of the fifteenth century. A Gloria-Credo pair with the tenor labeled "O patris sapientia veritas divina" indicates the Latin text in that voice (Example 3.3).[30]

The triple meter and diminution of this melody cloud what may be a skeletal song lying beneath it. However, the reappearance of a similar tenor in a hymn setting from the north German "Apel Codex" at the turn of the sixteenth century dispenses with the diminution and recasts the melody in duple meter, leaving us closer to a likely foundational tune

Example 3.3 Tenor from anonymous Gloria "O patris sapientia." Transcribed from Trent, Biblioteca Capitolare/Museo Diocesano di Trento, MS BL (Trent 93), fol. 192r.

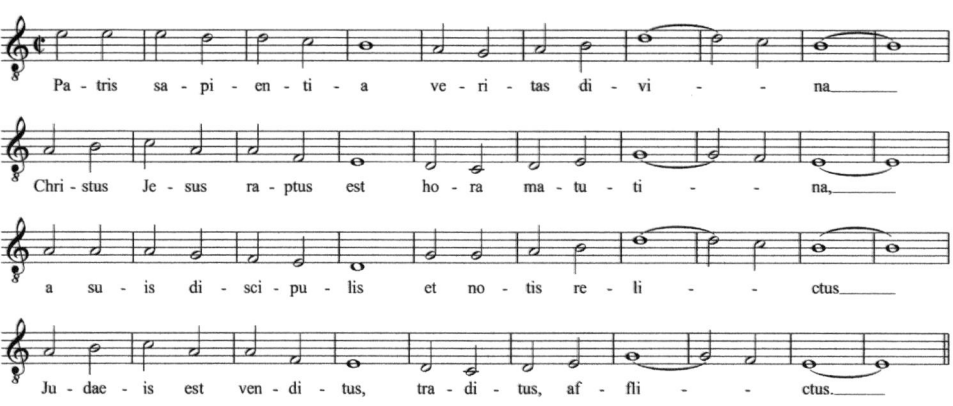

Example 3.4 Patris sapientia veritas divina (tenor). Transcribed from Leipzig, Universitätsbibliothek, MS 1494, fol. 61v.

(Example 3.4). Set with slight textual variants, this tenor is situated in an anonymous four-voice setting of *Patris sapientia veritas divina* in a manuscript dominated by hymn settings and motets.[31]

This cantus firmus was clearly centered on *E*, beginning an octave above the final. Almost entirely syllabic with regular, chorale-like phrase structure and internal cadences on *b*, there is no chance this melody is a decorated version of a plainchant. The tune promoted easy retrieval from its reinforcing features. The slightest embellishment occurs on the accented penultimate syllable of the phrase, and the rhythm and contour of that cadential figure is consistent for each phrase. The rhythms of all four phrases of *Patris sapientia* in the Apel Codex are in fact identical, and the second and fourth line match both rhythm and melody, condensing the material one might have to recall. It is possible that a melodic tradition had formed in Protestant Europe in connection with the seven-stanza hymn. Equally important, Czech, German, and English poetic translations of *Patris sapientia* also emerged by the end of the fifteenth century, a phenomenon in step with the increasing ownership of books of hours.[32]

Even with these traces of a melody for the Holy Cross hymn, there is still some room for comment on its performance, though cues for user engagement tend to be infrequent for *Patris sapientia veritas divina*. Despite the enlarged script used by scribes, the lines of the quatrain are rarely isolated, appearing as prose to the eye. The rendering of the hymn for the Holy Cross in the Hours of Louis of Savoy offers a welcome exception (Figure 3.2). As expected, the hymn's oversized script keeps it visually distinct from the *Adoramus te* beneath it, which is structured as a versicle and response, a problem described in Chapter 2. The performance experience with the hymn is enhanced with decorated letters and line breaks for the opening stanza of Matins. The four line-fills for the hymn's first verse, one for each line, are fairly uncommon to see with any hymn in a book of hours. The length of the line-fill in this example is visually arresting, isolating the rhythm and rhyme of each line. Noticeably extended, the line-fills accommodate the hymn's goliardic meter, which offers far more syllables than a standard hymn.

Unlike most hymns, *Patris sapientia veritas divina* offers a final stanza not tied to the doxology. The verse "Has horas canonicas" has a summarizing quality, looking back on the

Figure 3.2 Hymn, *Patris sapientia veritas divina*. Paris, BnF lat. 9473, fol. 97v.

services already enacted and turned inwardly with use of the first person singular (*recolo*, used in similar prayers of contemplation).

Has horas canonicas cum devotione	I recall these canonical hours with devotion
Christe tibi recolo pia ratione	To you, Christ, with the faithful understanding
Ut qui pro me passus es amoris ardore	That you who suffered for me, with the flame of love,
Sis michi solacium in mortis agone.	Might be a solace to me in the agony of death.

Although it retains the goliardic meter of the hymn's stanzas, the verse sits outside of the concluding office of Compline, which already bears a hymn verse. In books of hours, the genre of this concluding hymn-like postscript is not usually labeled as a "hymnus" but rather as a "recommendatio."[33] Alternatively called a "commendatio," a recommendatio is a concluding prayer sometimes found at the end of abbreviated offices for saints. It signals not just a closing but also a final entreaty for succor at the time of death, a ceaseless and central concern for all medieval Christians, especially one rehearsing the Hours of the Cross. "Has horas canonicas" may well fasten to the melody we have already identified, falling squarely into metrical profile established for the Holy Cross hymn.[34]

Hymn for the Holy Spirit

The hymn for the Office of the Holy Spirit, *Nobis sancti spiritus*, follows the structure of the preceding Hours of the Cross. Seven verses again fit into each of the seven appointed hours (except Lauds), although the corresponding hours are not named within the stanzas as in the Passion-oriented Hours of the Cross. *Nobis sancti spiritus* reveals the goliardic meter again, and rhyme maintains through each of the quatrain's lines, a sure aid to memory.

Nobis sancti spiritus gratia sit data,	May the grace of the Holy Spirit be given to us:
De qua virgo virginum fuit obumbrata,	From which the virgin of virgins was overshadowed,
Cum per sanctum Angelum fuit salutata,	When greeted by the angel,
Verbum caro factum est, virgo foecundata.	The Word was made flesh became, the virgin made fruitful.
De virgine Maria Christus fuit natus,	Christ was born of the Virgin Mary blessed
Crucifixus, mortuus, atque tumulatus:	Was crucified, died, and was buried:
Resurgens discipulis fuit demonstratus,	Rising he revealed himself to his disciples,
Et ipsis cernentibus, in caelis elevatus.	And to those observing, he rose to the heavens.
Suum Sanctum Spiritum Deus delegavit.	Then God sent his Holy Spirit
In die Pentecostes Apostolos confortavit.	and it comforted the Apostles on the day of Pentecost,
Et de linguis igneis ipsos inflammavit:	And it inflamed them who fiery tongues.
Relinquere orphanos eos denegavit.	And refused for them to be orphans.
Septiformem gratiam tunc acceptaverunt,	Then they accepted the sevenfold gift.
Quare idiomata cuncta cognoverunt.	And whatever the language they recognized them all.
Ad diversa climata mundi recesserunt:	Then they went out to the diverse corners of the world,
Et fidem catholicam tunc praedicaverunt.	And they were the first to make known the catholic faith.

Spiritus paraclitus fuit appellatus,	The spirit was called the Paraclete,
Donum Dei, caritas, fons vivificatus,	Gift of God, Charity, living fount,
Spiritalis unctio, ignis inflammatus,	Spiritual anointing, inflamed with fire,
Septiformis gratia, charisma vocatus.	Called charisma with a sevenfold grace.
Dexterae Dei digitus, virtus spiritalis,	May the finger of God's right hand, a spiritual
Nos defendat, eruat ab omnibus malis.	strength, defend us, rush us away from all evil.
Ut nobis non noceat daemon infernalis:	So that the infernal devil may not harm us:
Protegat, et nutriat, foveat sub alis.	Rather, protect, nurture, and cherish under his wings.
Spiritus paraclitus nos velit iuvare,	May the Spirit, the Paraclete, want to help us,
Gressus nostros regere et illuminare:	To illuminate and rule our steps
Ut cum Deus venerit omnes iudicare,	So that when God comes to judge all,
Nos velit ad dexteram omnes appellare.	He will want to call everyone to his right hand.

BnF, Ars. 638, one of two manuscripts illuminated by the Master of Flowers, positions the Hours of the Holy Spirit as the first office in the book, following the readings of the evangelists.[35] In the opening service of Matins (Figure 3.3), the antiphon *Veni sancte spiritus* is here denoted incorrectly as an "invitatorium" (in blue) and precedes the hymn verse *Nobis sancti spiritus*. (The antiphon's positioning before the hymn verse may occasionally be seen in the supplemental hours.[36]) Although the size of the hymn text is just a little greater than the surrounding antiphon, versicle, and response, the ornate capital letter distinguishes the hymn on the folio, occupying two lines of text and twice the width of the capitals around it. Crucially for the user, the hymn has not only provided ample space for the eye to absorb, but faint dots of division break up the poetry for sense-making in execution. Notably, the periods do not articulate the four verses of the quatrain, but rather divide it further into its eight constituent parts, each line separated into its heptameter and concluding hexameter. The accentuation of the Latin and the anticipation of the end rhyme emerges even more strongly in this atypical but performance-oriented scribal rendering.

There is little scholarship on the texts of the Hours of the Holy Spirit, from its origins onward. References here or there tend to surface as part of art-historical studies.[37] Though the Hours of the Cross inspired sorrowful depictions of Jesus's crucifixion (sometimes one for each hour), the visual imagery for the Hours of the Holy Spirit was limited, featuring the dove descending on, or hovering above, a scene. As for the hymn *Nobis sancti spiritus* in particular, only Alexander Agricola's polyphonic setting of the text has drawn attention among music historians. As William Prizer has shown, the piece may be situated in the context of Philip the Fair's patronage of music for the Order of the Golden Fleece.[38] Despite the fact that most of Agricola's settings of devotional texts refer to plainchant models, no known model has been identified for his *Nobis sancti spiritus*, which sets only the first verse of the hymn.[39] This text was elsewhere prescribed for the Hours of the Holy Spirit in Burgundian circles, namely in a breviary for Philip the Good, but again no melody is indicated.[40] Though the search for a musical correlate comes up empty, surely any melody that fit *Patris sapientia veritas divina* in the Hours of the Cross would be fair to take up with the goliardic hymn for the Spirit. The two hymns even converge in their concluding stanzas, betraying their textual (and possible musical) affiliation with the matching incipit "Has horas canonicas cum devotione" and first-person supplication.

Figure 3.3 Hymn, *Nobis sancti spiritus*. Paris, BnF, Ars. Ms-638 réserve, fol. 21v.

Has horas canonicas cum devotione	I have said these hours canonical hours with devotion
Tibi Sancte Spiritus pia ratione	and faithful prudence to you O Holy Spirit,
Dixi, ut nos visites inspiratione,	That you might visit us with the breath of life,
Et vivamus iugiter caeli regione. Amen.	And that we might live in the heavenly realm forever.

Medieval texts in the goliardic meter have traditionally been linked to nonliturgical repertories of the Goliards, the itinerant poets of the late tenth through the mid-thirteenth centuries, better known for their ribald than their moralizing verse. The *Carmina burana* is the most famous of goliardic examples. The poetry was almost certainly designed to be sung;[41] thus, it is not inconceivable that a goliardic tune could be used for one or both of the prominent hymns of the supplemental hours that carry that meter. In the Hours of the Cross and Spirit, the user returns to the hymn numerous times, no matter if the hours are mixed or gathered together in succession. In the Office of the Virgin, the hymns are connected to various melodic referents, with *Memento salutis auctor* returning several times in the liturgical day. Should users of books of hours recite *Patris sapientia veritas divina* and *Nobis sancti spiritus* with the aid of one or two popular melodies, they would likewise have numerous opportunities to interact with a fixed song throughout the day.

Te Deum

The Te Deum is perhaps the most popular melody of the Christian faith and was a staple in the *horae*. Liturgically, it was prescribed at the conclusion of Matins on Sundays and most feast days, though omitted in penitential seasons. Its lengthy psalm-like recitation had wide circulation outside the office too, functioning as a general song of praise and thanksgiving. Hundreds of laypeople could sing the Te Deum in processions or as part of liturgical dramas and coronations; sometimes it was heard on the battlefield. The origins of the Te Deum are not known, but it has been attributed variously to Church Fathers Ambrose and Augustine in the Middle Ages.[42] Though structurally resembling an ancient psalm, the Te Deum is widely considered a "hymn" of praise, akin to the text of the Gloria from the Mass Ordinary. Arranged in prose verses, the text unfolds neither in stanzas nor in rhythmically consistent lines. Instead, the Te Deum offers a pastiche of texts, presented in three broad sections. The first ten verses praise God the Father; a second section (vv. 14–23) directs glory to Jesus; and a final section (vv. 24–29) repurposes verses directly from the Psalter. A doxology-like insertion in vv. 11–13 appears to reflect a late addition to the prayer.

Situated after the Matins service in the Office of the Virgin in books of hours, the Te Deum customarily appears in large script, the same size used for psalms and hymns. Capital letters may further be drawn with varying levels of decoration consistent with these same genres in a given book of hours. (The adorned letter "T" for "Te" and "Tu" predominates among the verses.) An abundance of line-fills usually populates the Te Deum as well. All of these visual prompts inspire the user to recall how the song progresses over more than two dozen verses. As we have seen, scribes were attentive to the question of liturgical genre throughout books of hours, noting antiphons, versicles, and responses as they fell—and occasionally in error. Especially with its length and formidable position at the end of Matins, the Te Deum demanded that scribes provide an indication of its genre. But there was wide disagreement on what kind of "piece" this was. While Te Deum might be called a hymn today, scribes of books of hours rarely referred to it as such. The song did not fit conventional liturgical

80 *Music of the Offices*

categories, and scribes reflected the uncertainty we might expect from an unclassifiable song *sui generis*.

In French *horae* from the fifteenth century, the Te Deum is most often called a "canticum." This categorization is used similarly for gospel canticles such as the Magnificat, the Benedictus, and the Nunc dimittis. Other books of hours go further, calling the song a "canticum sanctorum ambrosii et augustini," a credit that perpetuated the authorship by both Church Fathers.[43] The mélange of texts in the Te Deum does not resemble a canticle, though the musical style might argue in favor of it, similar to that of a psalm. Indeed, a few books of hours will refer to the hymn as a "psalmus."[44] Sometimes, scribes abandoned the familiar categories of "canticum" and "psalmus" and opted for an unconventional tag such as "laus angelorum" ("praise [song] of the angels"),[45] a description usually reserved for the Gloria of the Mass, with which the Te Deum was closely associated.[46] At least one book of hours gestures more firmly toward the musical realm, rubricating the Te Deum as a "canticum angelorum" ("song of the angels").[47]

In medieval liturgical sources, musical notation rarely accompanied the Te Deum, likely because the song was so pervasive. Mercifully, there is only one melody connected with the text, though it holds many variants. Psalm-like formulas, reminiscent of the earliest Christian hymnody, dominate the Te Deum. It is officially a mode 4 melody, most verses finishing on *E*, with *a* as the prevailing tone for recitation (Example 3.5). The formulas shift, however, when a new section of text begins, possibly suggesting that the assigned tone is coeval with the text. After the grand opening statement, the succeeding verses of the Te Deum cling to a formula that begins and ends on *g*, despite the recitation on *a*, given in open note heads ("A" in the example). After an interruption of vv. 11–13 not captured in the example, a new tone emerges, beginning and ending on *E*, again with *a* as a reciting pitch (labeled "C"). At v. 21 ("Aeterna fac"), the recitation jumps a fourth lower, establishing a new tonal space (labeled "D").[48]

In the experience of the Te Deum, one of the most striking musical moments, now or then, is the invocation of the trifold "Sanctus" (Greek: *Trisagion*) from the celebration of Mass, which is quoted in verses 5 and 6 ("B" in Example 3.5). At this arresting moment in the

Example 3.5 Melodic formulas of the Te Deum

chant, the flow of the verses is abandoned, and the goal of each line is halted for the short outbursts of the angelic song. The text of verse 4 prepares the heavenly proclamation, setting the psalmodic formula ("A") to the words "To You cherubim and seraphic cry out with unceasing voice." The triple repetition of the celestial "Sanctus" follows with a special musical character.[49] The first two statements are identical; the final "Sanctus" then adds a single pickup note (E) to the gesture and continues with the text "Dominus Deus Sabaoth," a phrase elided with the third Sanctus in most books of hours.[50] Each Sanctus acclamation rings out the melodic substance of most of the Te Deum, captured in the notes (E)-g-a-b-c-b-a. The thrice-declared gesture is further distinguished by a customary lengthening on the final two notes of each Sanctus, another means of delineating the Trisagion, as the tradition has come down in practice.

The angel's outburst of "Holy, Holy, Holy" bears a distinct appearance in books of hours. In one example from the 1470s, we witness the visual interruption of the Sanctus in the context of the Te Deum that is characteristic of the *mise-en-page* (Figure 3.4). In the middle of the verso, the scribe devotes a single line to each acclamation of the Trisagion, forcing not just a longer line-fill, but a more crowded appearance of the "S" capitals, in contrast to the staggered appearance of the colored capitals for the rest of the hymn. The capitals of the "Sanctus" even appear fused, forming a unit and reinforcing the idea that the trifold Sanctus sits outside of the Te Deum visually as much as aurally. Other manuscripts signal the Trisagion's exceptionality with three decorative capitals in a single line.[51]

It can be useful to think about the thrice-declaimed Sanctus as referring to its correlate in the Mass. Peter Williams distinguishes these Sanctus relatives as the "separate and the incorporated" forms of the acclamation.[52] The invocation of the Sanctus "incorporated" in the Te Deum may prompt the user of a book of hours to recall other hallowed sounds associated with this song of the angels. The singing of the Sanctus in the Mass, for example, is generally accompanied by bells at the moment of consecration; likewise, the Te Deum at Matins was sometimes supplemented with bell-ringing and perhaps with organ. By the fourteenth century, the organ participated regularly in the performance of the Te Deum, even in the context of a procession.[53]

Performance considerations and extraliturgical use proliferate with the Te Deum. Medieval liturgical dramas, notably the *Play of Daniel*, often concluded with the singing of the Te Deum, presumably by all gathered. Other special occasions and celebrations made the song of the angels a strong candidate to be set in vocal polyphony or faburden.[54] The familiar practice of alternation also developed in the presentation of the Te Deum, similar to the exchange of verses found in psalmody, encouraging us to consider stereophonic implications of the sound.[55] For the laity, the Te Deum would most likely be encountered in town processions. Reinhard Strohm conjectured that, in the context of a procession, the song might have been expressed in a "walking rhythm" of a duple meter, connecting it with other public processional music such as hymns and litanies.[56] Rhythmicized plainchant was not unheard of in the fifteenth century, not only guiding one's steps but also securing one's recollection of texts. Sonic recall of the Te Deum might have included far more than human voices in unison when users encountered it in books of hours.

*

Hymn texts are among the more conspicuous cues for sound swirling in books of hours, present in every hour of the Office of the Virgin and the auxiliary offices of the Cross and Spirit. While ingrained in the memory of the faithful, the melodies also showed a great

82 *Music of the Offices*

Figure 3.4 Te Deum (excerpt). Paris, BnF, n.a.l. 3187, fols. 46v–47r.

Figure 3.4 (Continued)

84   *Music of the Offices*

"mix-and-match" versatility with texts that makes the genre hard to grasp, except for a few chants like the Te Deum. If tunes were applied to office hymn texts, it was possible to move through the hours with a limited number of melodies to fit the recurring poetic meters. The enlarged writing of hymns in books of hours calls special attention to the text as other scribal techniques further orient the eye to aid the ear. In the genre of responsories, we see a new "look" that both tests musical memory and reminds the user that repetition of texts is central to performing the liturgy.

Notes

1. Boynton, "Hymn. II. Monophonic Latin," *NG* 12: 19.
2. Bede, *Beda Venerabilis opera Didascalica*, 113, with translation in Boynton, "Glossed Hymns," 189. The alternation in the fifteenth and sixteenth centuries contrasts polyphonic verses with those in plainchant, possibly envoiced by different groups.
3. Cabrol, "Office of the Dead," in *CE* 11:220.
4. Hiley, *Western Plainchant*, 140.
5. These melodies correspond to 16, 52, 62, 116, 118, 145, 187, 205, 206, 414, 723, and 752, using Stäblein's numbering system in *Hymnen*. *Quem terra pontus aethera* is known from three of the earliest service books (B, S and L) as cataloged by Hesbert.
6. These correspond to Stäblein melodies 205 and 206, respectively.
7. See, for example, BnF, n.a.l. 3213, fol. 21r–v and BnF, n.a.l. 3114, fol. 30r–v.
8. For example, BnF, n.a.l. 3117, fol. 50r–v and BnF, Ars. 575, fols. 67v–68r.
9. Using Stäblein's numbers again, the five melodies are 16, 187, 551, 646, and 723.
10. See *AH* 50:86–87 for a variant version. *Quem terra pontus aethera* is also cross-listed with *O gloriosa domina*, for example, in Chevalier, *Repertorium Hymnologicum*, 2: 197 [no. 13042].
11. Robertson, *Guillaume de Machaut and Reims*, 37.
12. Macey, "Galeazzo Maria Sforza and Musical Patronage in Milan."
13. Falassi, "Le Contrade," 107.
14. Stäblein, *Hymnen*, 666.
15. *Quem terra pontus* and *Christe redemptor omnium / ex Patre* also have in common melody 116.
16. The hymn in this form occurs in the hours of Prime (BnF, Ars. 1191, fol. 28v), Terce (32r), Sext (34r), and None (37r). The third verse in this formulation is the migrant "Maria mater gratie," preceding the doxology.
17. See, for example, BnF, Ars. 434, fol. 84v. The reversal of the verses ("Veni creator" followed by Memento salutis") can be found in the minor hours of BnF, Ars. 644, beginning fol. 50r.
18. Baltzer, "The Little Office of the Virgin," 473.
19. This is cataloged as CAO 8409.
20. See, for example, Conrad of Saxony, *Speculum seu salutation beatae Mariae virginis*, 184–185.
21. See, for example, Van Orden, "Children's Voices," 216.
22. Stäblein, *Hymnen*, 40.
23. Stäblein (*Hymnen*) lists the melodies as 67, 149, 174 (mode 5 transposed to *C*), 191, 208, 507, 737, and 1031.
24. Melody 149 can be found in BnF, lat. 1235 (fols. 160v–161r), a twelfth-century gradual from Nevers; no. 174 comes from a thirteenth-century breviary from Caen in Normandy (BnF, Ars. 279, fols. 448v–449r); no. 208 is located in a later source from Normandy (Paris, Bibliothèque Sainte-Geneviève, MS 113, fol. 169r).
25. Proparoxytonic accent is found in the first part of the line and a paroxytone in the second part.
26. Translation from Boynton, "From Book to Song," 136–137.
27. Eastman, "Die Werke des Aegidius Romanus," 225.
28. The hymn is listed in Mone, *Lateinische Hymnen des Mittelalters*, 1:106–107, but without notated sources. The text is also cataloged among the *pia dictamina* (private devotional hymns) in *AH* 30: 32.
29. Baroffio, "Testo e musica," 45. Susan Boynton ("From Book to Song," 123) has also noticed that hypometric and hypermetric lines are scarce in liturgical hymns and thus not as well suited to

musical setting and performance as most Office hymns. She further notes that in some manuscripts, *Patris sapientia veritas divina* is rubricated as a reading (*capitulum*) rather than as a hymn.
30 Strohm, "Late-Medieval Sacred Songs," 134–136. The pair is found both in Trent, Biblioteca Capitolare/Museo Diocesano di Trento, MS BL (Trent 93), fols. 191v–193v (Gloria), 293v–295r (Credo), and again in MS 1377 (Trent 90), fols. 160v–162v (Gloria), 221v–223r (Credo).
31 For an edition, see Gerber et al., *Der Mensuralkodex des Nikolaus Apel*, 1: 70.
32 The Lutheran hymn text *Christus, der uns Selig macht* (composed by Michael Weiss, later harmonized by J. S. Bach) is one such translation of the Holy Cross hymn. For other settings of both German and Latin, see Strohm, "Zur Rezeption," 30–32. On poetic translations of the hymn into Middle English, see Pezzini, "Le 'Ore della Croce'," 675–678.
33 An exception would be BnF, lat. 9473 (fol. 101r), where the stanza is rubricated *hymnus*.
34 Boynton ("From Book to Song," 125) prefers to call this concluding verse a "reflection on the Crucifixion in a discursive framework borrowed from the Divine Office, rather than as a sung component of a liturgical service."
35 Both the Hours of the Cross and Spirit customarily preceded the Office of the Virgin in Flemish books of hours.
36 For another example, see Philadelphia, Free Library of Philadelphia, Rare Book Department, Lewis E 110, fol. 131v.
37 See, for instance, Wieck, *Time Sanctified*, 89–93.
38 Prizer, "Music and Ceremonial in the Low Countries," 129.
39 Edited in Agricola, *Opera Omnia*, 4: XI, 36–37. The motet survives in only one source, the "Rusconi Codex." Bologna, Museo Internazionale e Biblioteca della Musica di Bologna, MS Q 19, fols. 4v–5r.
40 Brussels, Bibliothèque royale, MS 9848, fol 33r.
41 Anderson, rev. Payne, "Goliards," *NG* 10: 112. For the goliardic meter in the motet, see Wolinsky, "Hocketing and the Imperfect Modes," 407.
42 Niceta of Remesiana was put forward as the author of the work by both Morin, "Nouvelles recherches," and Burn, *The Hymn 'Te Deum'*.
43 See, for example, BnF, n.a.l. 3120, fol. 39r and BnF, Département Arsenal, 4-T-934, image 31 (unfoliated).
44 See, for example, BnF, lat. 1184, fol. 24v and Montpellier Méditerranée Métropole, MS 332, fol. 38r.
45 See, for example, BnF, lat. 1363, fol. 34r and BnF, n.a.l. 3213, fol. 36r.
46 "Laus angelorum" can found in the twelfth century along with "laus angelica" to denote the Te Deum. See H. T. Henry, "Te Deum," in *CE* 14: 469.
47 See BnF, n.a.l. 3229, fol. 31r.
48 Hiley, *Western Plainchant*, 68. Tonal discrepancies around the use of *f*-natural and *f*-sharp have been noted by Steiner et al., "Te Deum," *NG* 25: 192.
49 For a proposed Byzantine origin of the "Sanctus" of the Te Deum and other Sanctus melodies assigned to the Mass, see Levy, "The Trisagion in Byzantium and the West."
50 For an exceptional case that breaks the line between the third Sanctus and its continuation, see BnF, n.a.l. 3117, fol. 39v.
51 See, for example, BnF, n.a.l. 3213, fol. 36r.
52 Williams, *The Organ in Western Culture*, 89.
53 Strohm, *The Rise of European Music*, 272.
54 This was particularly the case in Bruges where nine polyphonic Te Deum settings were noted in a register of endowments for St. Donatian from 1470 to 1471. See Strohm, *Music in Late Medieval Bruges*, 29–31. On the use of faburden for counterpoint to the Te Deum, see Harrison, "Faburden in Practice," 22.
55 Williams, *The Organ in Western Culture*, 93.
56 Strohm, *The Rise of European Music*, 304–05.

4 Responsories

*

Some of the more florid melodies of the liturgical day are found in the genre of the responsory. Compared to other genres, though, the common appearance of responsories in smaller script in books of hours can seemingly diminish the experience of these texts. But because signs of engagement still remain, it may be more prudent to consider the condensed look of responsories as simply differentiated. The Night Office of Matins is the locus for responsories, which occur as meditative postludes to prescribed readings with a musical style that can feature several notes per syllable of text. The most extravagant melismatic liturgical melodies with the responsory structure are found in the Mass. The long-winded quality of office responsories produced a subgenre of *responsoria prolixa* (or "great responsories"), as opposed to more modest *responsoria brevia* found after the lessons of the daytime liturgical hours,[1] a genre not encountered in the *horae*. Richard Crocker has described the profile of responsories as avoiding "clear location, direction, [and] goal" and featuring a "free play with tone" that breaks with the hierarchical pitch structures and formulaic nature of other liturgical genres.[2] The sonic liberty and elaborate melodies are hardly communicated, though, in the *mise-en-page* of books of hours. Most noticeably, the reduced size of script compared to the surrounding lections of Matins presents a conspicuous difference in layout, reminiscent of the scribal distinction made between antiphons and psalms.

In Chapter 2, we saw that antiphons yield a ternary structure, beginning with the incipit, advancing to the declamation of the psalm, and finishing with the antiphon in full. Responsories likewise have a tripartite shape, but operate somewhat in reverse. The opening section—itself called the responsory or choral respond—is sung in full; a verse then intervenes; and the concluding material is a partial repetition of the responsory, called a repetendum. Liturgically, the vocal texture of the responsory contrasts with that of an antiphon, which was largely built for a monastic choir, outside of its incipit. Within the responsory's three-part construct, the full choir airs the initial respond (the incipit likely coming from the cantor for locating pitch), and a soloist intones the verse, usually a single psalm verse. While the cantor would normally be called to sing a virtuosic passage, the verse of a Matins responsory is often more recitational and formulaic than the respond reserved for the choir.[3] The choir then resumes at the indication of the repetendum, typically singing through a grammatically and musically complete statement. Users of books of hours who had recollection of these responsories could reimagine the oscillation of forces when journeying through these melodies, from a full sound to a thinner tone of a single voice returning to the choral complement.

DOI: 10.4324/9781003140511-6

Taking a wider view of Matins, we find vocal exchanges of sound witnessed on a broader platform. A group of three responsories will alternate with a group of three antiphons in the unfolding of Matins in both the Office of the Virgin and Office of the Dead. As a single nocturn, the Office of the Virgin presents only one set of three responsories, though, while the Office of the Dead presents the more extensive menu of nine Matins responsories—three sets of three responsories across three nocturns, each paired with lections. This chapter surveys the texts and melodies for the responsories encountered in the Use of Rome in both major offices in books of hours. It continues with remarks on the repetendum, from both a visual and aural perspective. The chapter concludes with focus on the most extraordinary and variable structure of the responsory *Libera me Domine*, which follows the final lection of Matins in the Office of the Dead.

Responsories for the Office of the Virgin

Following the opening three antiphons and psalms of Matins in the Office of the Virgin (varying by day of the week), three responsories are assigned: *Sancta et immaculata virginitas* (MR1), *Beata es Maria* (MR2), and *Felix namque es* (MR3). Together with the prescribed readings, this set precedes the Te Deum to close the service of Matins. The three readings allocated to the responsories of the Night Office are drawn from nearly continuous verses from the Book of Ecclesiasticus (or the Wisdom of Sirach, 24:11–13, 15–16, 17–20), which are broken up by the musical interjections of the responsories and their attendant verses. Ecclesiasticus is also the source of the brief chapter reading in the hours of Terce, Sext, None, Vespers, and Compline. The trend thus continues of pulling texts from the Old Testament rather than from the Gospels for the Office of the Virgin.[4] That Mary is the unstated subject of these and other Old Testament readings is confirmed in medieval commentary. In the *Biblia Mariana* attributed to the polymath Albertus Magnus (d. 1280), teacher of Thomas Aquinas, the author avows that references to the Virgin are found in most books of the Old Testament, and most especially in Tobit, Judith, Wisdom, and Ecclesiasticus.[5] The great mystery surrounding the Virgin Mary was here and elsewhere bound up intimately in these particular Old Testament verses of the Office of the Virgin that place her in the familiar role of personified Wisdom.

The musical postlude to the first reading of Matins—*Sancta et immaculata virginitas* (CAO 7569)—doubles as a Matins responsory on the feast of Christmas, where it is almost always situated in the second or third nocturn liturgically. Widely found in the earliest layers of surviving plainchant, this responsory could also be heard in Matins for the octave of Christmas and occasionally on the Marian feasts of Annunciation and Purification. Composers of the sixteenth century and onward had high regard for this text, setting *Sancta et immaculata virginitas* with great frequency.[6] As monophony, the responsory also appeared unadorned and without a verse among Christmas office responsories cited in the early fourteenth-century *Roman de Fauvel* with musical insertions.[7] The prayer's first-person address to Mary's virginity makes it especially fitting for private recitation, presenting what Rachel Fulton has called "the principal mystery upon which the medieval devotion to the Virgin depended"—the enclosed womb containing the one whom the heavens (and the earth) could not contain.[8] The verse of *Sancta et immaculata virginitas* features Elizabeth's words from the Visitation (Luke 1:42), familiar from the "Ave Maria" prayer that infused Christian life.

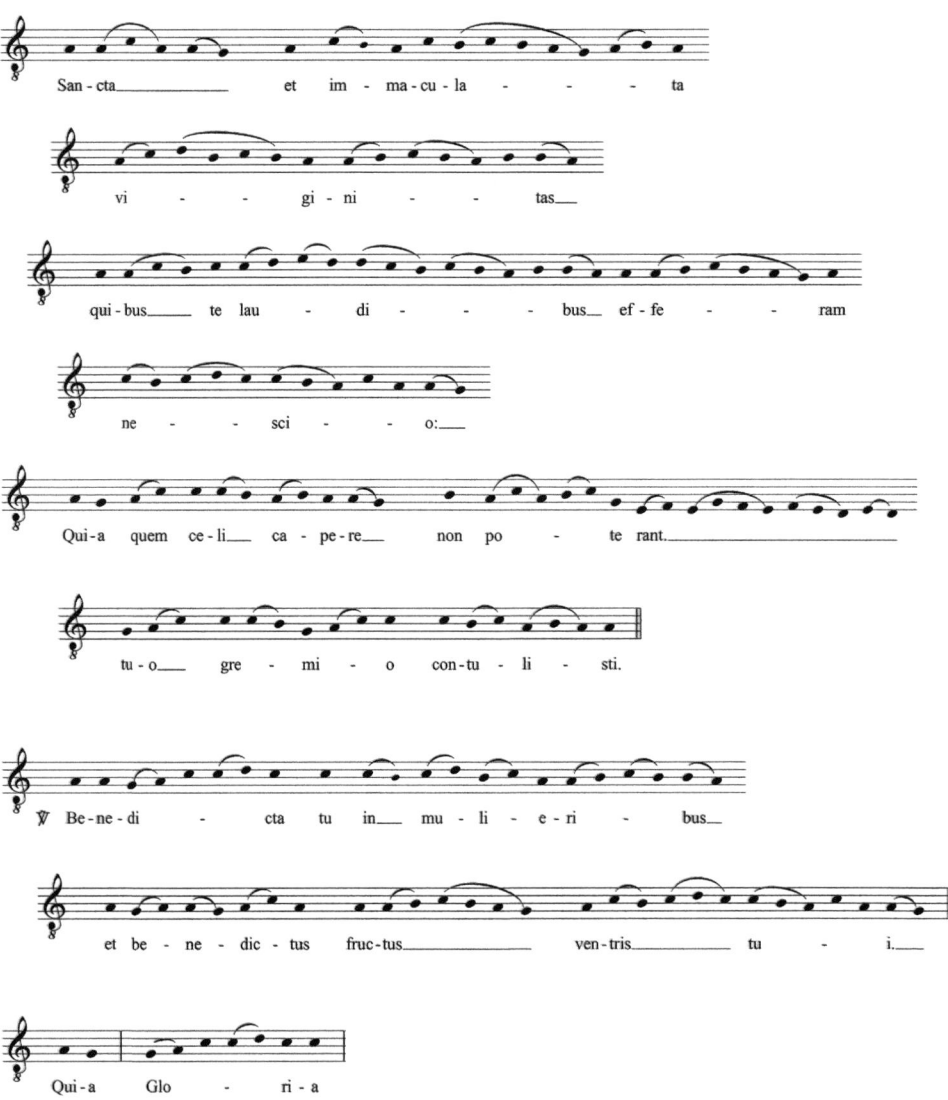

Example 4.1 Responsory, *Sancta et immaculata virginitas*. Transcribed from BnF, lat. 15181, fol. 147r.

Sancta et immaculata virginitas quibus te laudibus efferam nescio | quia quem caeli capere non poterant tuo gremio contulisti.	O holy and immaculate virginity, I know not with what praises I should extol you, for he whom the heavens could not contain, you bore from your womb.
℣ Benedicta tu in mulieribus, et benedictus fructus ventris tui. Quia quem . . .	℣ Blessed are you among women and blessed is the fruit of your womb. For he whom . . .

Almost invariably across the plainchant repertory, the melody connected to *Sancta et immaculata virginitas* occurs in a transposed mode 2, beginning and ending on *a*, a fifth above the traditional modal center of *D* (Example 4.1). The transposition reflects a practical awareness of the range traversed in the responsory. While part of the beauty of the unaccompanied chant corpus lies in its adaptability to human voices so long as they preserve the intervals of the melody, some pieces required a more drastic shift to place the voices in a more comfortable vocal register for execution. *Sancta et immaculata virginitas* would typically span a ninth in its melodic compass (*G-a*) if destined for the conventional final of *D*. Descending a fifth below the final to the bottom of the gamut is relatively uncommon in chant and may well have prompted the kind of transposition that was transmitted in many liturgical sources. With *a* as the starting and ending point instead of *D*, the responsory would be heard and performed in a register of higher frequency—interestingly, closer to the natural speaking pitch of adult females than that of males.[9] The soloist assigned to the verse *Benedicta tu in mulieribus* might have been acquainted with different verses for the responsory text, each with distinct melodies, but only one melody corresponds to the one heard on Christmas and in the Office of the Virgin (CAO 7569a). This verse bears slight melodic variants in surviving sources, but followed the customary mode 2 formula for responsories from the Gregorian repertoire.[10]

The second responsory of Matins in the Office of the Virgin, *Beata es Maria* (CAO 6163), was dispatched in the second or third nocturn of Matins of two Marian feasts, the Purification and the Assumption. There are two notable connections to the previous responsory. Across both respond texts, the supplicant addresses the Virgin Mary in the second person, establishing her presence to grant aid and mercy. The verse of *Beata es Maria* links directly to the salutation of the angel Gabriel but also to the Ave Maria prayer glimpsed in the verse of *Sancta et immaculata virginitas*. Together, these verses comprise (in reverse) the "first part" of the Ave Maria prayer, before the appended entreaty "Sancta Maria . . ." crystallized as part of the devotion in the late sixteenth century.[11]

Cast in mode 1, the melody of *Beata es Maria* principally covers a sixth in its range, with upper neighbor on *b*-flat, and cadences on the note beneath the mode's final (*C*), called the *subtonium modi*. The stepwise undulation throughout the respond and verse with the occasional leap of a fourth (*C-f*) may spark problems of musical retrieval for a book of hours user. A melody of this sort exemplifies Crocker's "free play with tone" that could strike one as nearly improvisational (Example 4.2).

Felix namque es (CAO 6725), the final Matins responsory in the Office of the Virgin, could be heard on various Marian feast days, most commonly on the celebrations of the Nativity of Mary and the Assumption. A number of extant liturgical books also assign the responsory to the feast of All Saints. The verse of *Felix namque es* presents the last half of a short prayer attributed to Bishop Fulbert of Chartres (d. 1029), which begins "Sancta Maria succurre miseris."

Echoing the preceding responsory *Beata es Maria*, *Felix namque es* (Example 4.3) retains a mode 1 profile and navigates the *C-a* tonal space mainly by step, but it ascends to the mode's theoretical upper limit of *d* on the cipher for Christ (*sol iustitiae*), before coming to rest a ninth lower at its lower boundary (*C*). The verse hews closely to *a* with neighboring support of *b*-flat to strengthen the mode's reciting pitch a fifth above the *D* final. The reinforcement of *a* creates anticipation for the descent to the repetendum at "Quia ex te . . ." Remarkable among responsories, the final word of the verse could vary according to the feast. "Commemorationem" was changed to "assumptionem" when sung on the Assumption, and to "conceptionem" for the Feast of the Conception, and so on. The melodic flourish on this ultimate word provided plenty of room for whatever syllables needed accommodation.

90   *Music of the Offices*

Example 4.2 Responsory, *Beata es Maria*. Transcribed from BnF, lat. 12044, fol. 56v.

Beata es Maria quae Dominum portasti creatorem mundi | genuisti qui te fecit et in aeternum permanes virgo.	Blessed are you, Mary, who brought forth the Lord, the creator of the world. You gave birth to him who made you, and you remain a Virgin forever.
℣ Ave Maria gratia plena Dominus tecum. Genuisti …	℣ Hail Mary, full of grace, the Lord is with you. You gave birth …

While they generally move stepwise and with some predictability, the three responsories for the Office of the Virgin present a complexity of sound seldom summoned in books of hours. If users heard these melodies in public or if they had currency outside the Matins liturgy, they might be more inspired to hear the sounds of these responsories by the

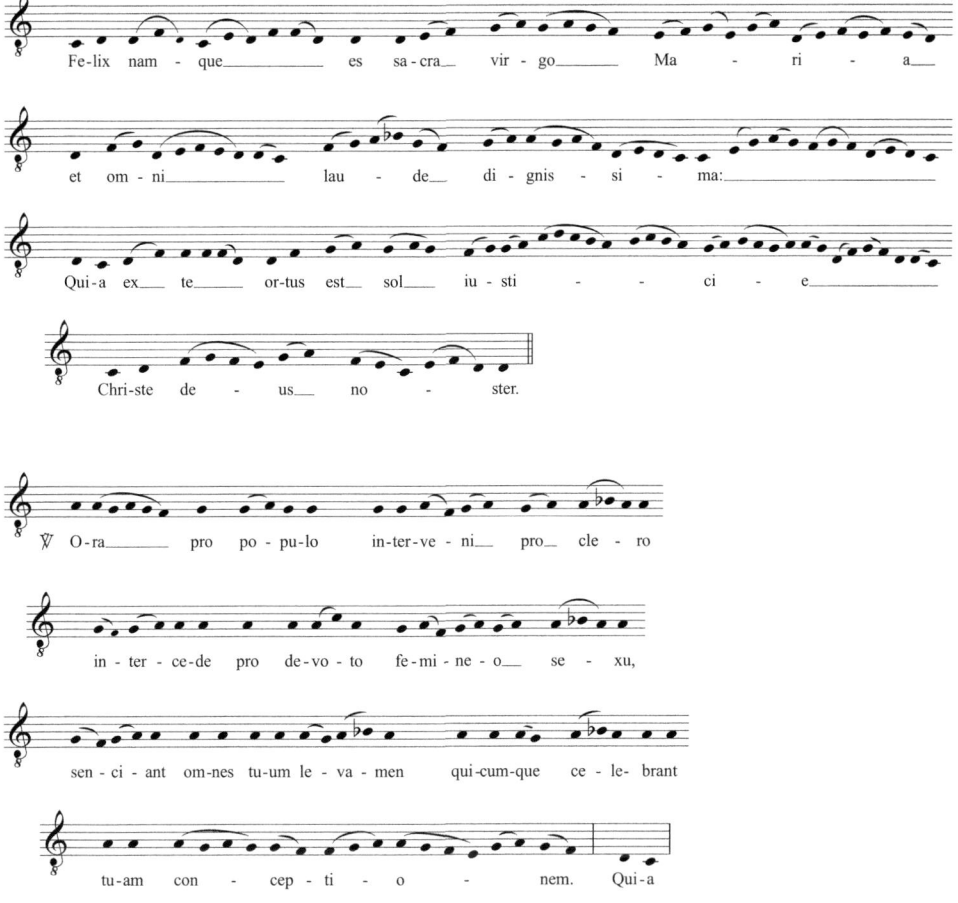

Example 4.3 Responsory, *Felix namque es*. Transcribed from BnF, lat. 15181, fols. 381r-v.

Felix namque es, sacra Virgo Maria, et omni laude dignissima | quia ex te ortus est sol iustitiae, Christus Deus noster	Blessed are you, holy Virgin Mary, and most worthy of all praise, for out of you arose the sun of justice, Christ our God.
℣ Ora pro populo interveni pro clero intercede pro devoto femineo sexu sentiant omnes tuum iuvamen quicumque celebrant tuam commemorationem. Quia ex te . . .	℣ Pray for the people, intervene on behalf of the clergy, intercede for all devout women; may all who celebrate your commemoration feel your assistance. For out of you . . .

sight of the text. Two bits of evidence suggest the Marian responsories migrated to more outward-facing positions. An endowment for French King Charles V (r. 1364–1380) at Reims Cathedral established various commemorations in his memory centered on the Virgin Mary and the Holy Spirit. Among the final provisions is a bequest for the singing of three items following Compline during the season of Lent: the prose *Inviolata integra et casta*; the antiphon *Salve regina* or the responsory *Sancta et immaculata virginitas*; and a special collect.[12] Given the towering reputation of the *Salve regina* in the late Middle Ages, it is striking to witness the Marian responsory *Sancta et immaculata virginitas* listed as an alternative to a melody that was scarcely written down because of its pervasiveness. The responsory *Felix namque es* also had a life outside the Office of the Virgin. In a book of processions prepared in the mid-fifteenth century for Barbara Pfintzing, a young woman who entered a Dominican convent in 1441, *Felix namque es* was chant to be sung first on the feast of the Assumption, arguably the most exalted of the annual Marian feasts celebrated at the time.[13] That this responsory and just two others were selected from all of melodies for the Virgin to sing outside the liturgy in procession further speaks to their exceptional status.[14]

Responsories for the Office of the Dead

Charged with remembering their deceased brothers, sisters, and patrons, monastic communities sang the Office of the Dead every weekday and sometimes on Sundays or feast days when a death had just occurred. The office could also have taken the place of a wake preceding the Requiem Mass for the soul of the departed. The texts were presumably known by heart and could be recited or sung. Relative to the Office of the Virgin, the more public nature of the Office of the Dead meant that the responsories might be more familiar to layfolk who experienced the service—often in procession—and could relive the sounds of those regular events in a book of hours. The standard progression in fifteenth-century *horae* with French provenance is found in Table 4.1.[15] Ordering may slightly differ from book to book, though a clear norm emerges for the Use of Rome.

The responsories provide musical reactions to the nine lessons of Matins, which were all taken from the book of Job. Two responsory texts likewise use Job as a source (MR1, MR4) while others draw from the psalms or have no biblical connection. As the table reveals, all but two of the Matins responsories (MR7, MR9 [I]) are in an "even" plagal mode, emphasizing the lower and more compressed collections of notes in a melodic mode. Modes 2 and 8 dominate the responsories. The ninth responsory of Matins is inconsistent in books of hours. Not infrequently, scribes will provide two possibilities for a responsory in this position, both with the title *Libera me Domine*. This substance of these concluding responsories will be examined at the end of this chapter.

Table 4.1 Matins responsories for the Office of the Dead

Position	Title	Mode	CAO no.	Verse	CAO no.
MR1	Credo quod redemptor meus	8	6348	Quem visurus sum	6348a
MR2	Qui Lazarum resuscitasti	4	7477	Qui venturus est	7477b
MR3	Domine quando veneris	8	6507	Commissa mea pavesco	6507a
MR4	Memento mei deus	2	7143	De profundis clamavi	7143a
MR5	Heu mihi Domine	2	6811	Anima mea turbata	6811a
MR6	Ne recorderis	6	7209	Dirige Domine	7209a
MR7	Peccantem me quotidie	1	7368	Deus in nomine	7368a
MR8	Domine secundum actum meum	8	6512	Amplius lava me	6512a
MR9	Libera me Domine (I)	1	7092	Clamantes et dicentes	7092a
MR9	Libera me Domine (II)	2	7091	[multiple, varies]	

Repetendum and the *pied-de-mouche*

In this study of books of hours, the responsories are distinct for having partial repetitions of earlier material built into their structure. The phenomenon concerns the aforementioned repetendum, the part of the responsory that must be repeated. The end of the verse in a responsory will often send the user back not to its beginning, as would be expected in an antiphon following the recitation of a full psalm, but to a specific place within the respond, somewhere around its midpoint at the start of a musical phrase. The repeated text from the respond may connect both sensically and grammatically with the sentiment of the verse, perhaps with the help of a conjunction. Other times, the connection between the verse and the repetendum is tenuous and more mechanical. The repetendum may also occur twice, the latter time following the doxology at the end of a nocturn. In these cases, the point of musical connection from doxology to repetendum remains identical, but any sense is lost returning to the responsory because of the doxology's generic text.

Occasionally, the repetendum was written out in full, such as in BnF, lat. 1188 (Figure 4.1). In the first Matins responsory from the Office of the Virgin, *Sancta et immaculata virginitas*, the scribe of this book of hours provides a red capital "Q" for "Quia," following the verse *Benedicta tu*. It refers to a word found midway through the responsory. Although the "Quia" from the respond likewise carries a red capital, it was unnecessary for the user to retrace to locate the earlier text because all words of the repetendum words had been supplied after the verse.[16] The second red "Q" could alert the user to recall the melody at that matching position from above or to imagine the change of vocal forces and texture at the "short repeat." Namely, there is a sounding exchange between the soloist, who completes the verse, and the choral atmosphere that resumes at the respond.

Offering the repetendum in full was by far the exception in books of hours. While scribes were known for providing full texts of a liturgical item (even when they are repeated), they also economized in many places in the offices, notably in the repetenda of responsories. In books of hours, copyists use various methods of abbreviation coupled with visual flagging to promote users' saccadic eye movement, allowing them to "jump" to the correct text in the process of executing the repetendum. These performance cues, both visual and aural in nature, are a kind of notation to prompt the eye and the ear. The scribe will usually provide a few words (between one and three), compelling a return within the choral respond just a few lines earlier. The longer the incipit given, the more time the user could spend hunting back in the text in the act of transition. Sometimes there was no need to go back. The textual cue alone could have stimulated the user's sonic memory of the complete repetendum, eliminating the need for the eye to retrace to the middle of the respond.

Among the common visual cues a scribe may deploy to draw the users' attention and ease them backwards toward the repetendum were capital letters. In some rare cases, a large decorated capital could be used to make the distinction between the end of the verse and the beginning of the repeat.[17] Usually, scribes provided more modest points of reference to indicate the transition. An example can be seen in the first Matins responsory from the Office of the Dead in a books of hours from Tours ca. 1500 (Figure 4.2). In the cue to return to the middle of the responsory *Credo quod redemptor* from the end its attendant verse *Quem visurus sum* at the words "Et in," the scribed aided the shift backward by ensuring that capital letter prompting the repetendum matched the corresponding capital in

Figure 4.1 Responsory, *Sancta et immaculata virginitas*. Paris, BnF, lat. 1188, fol. 30r.

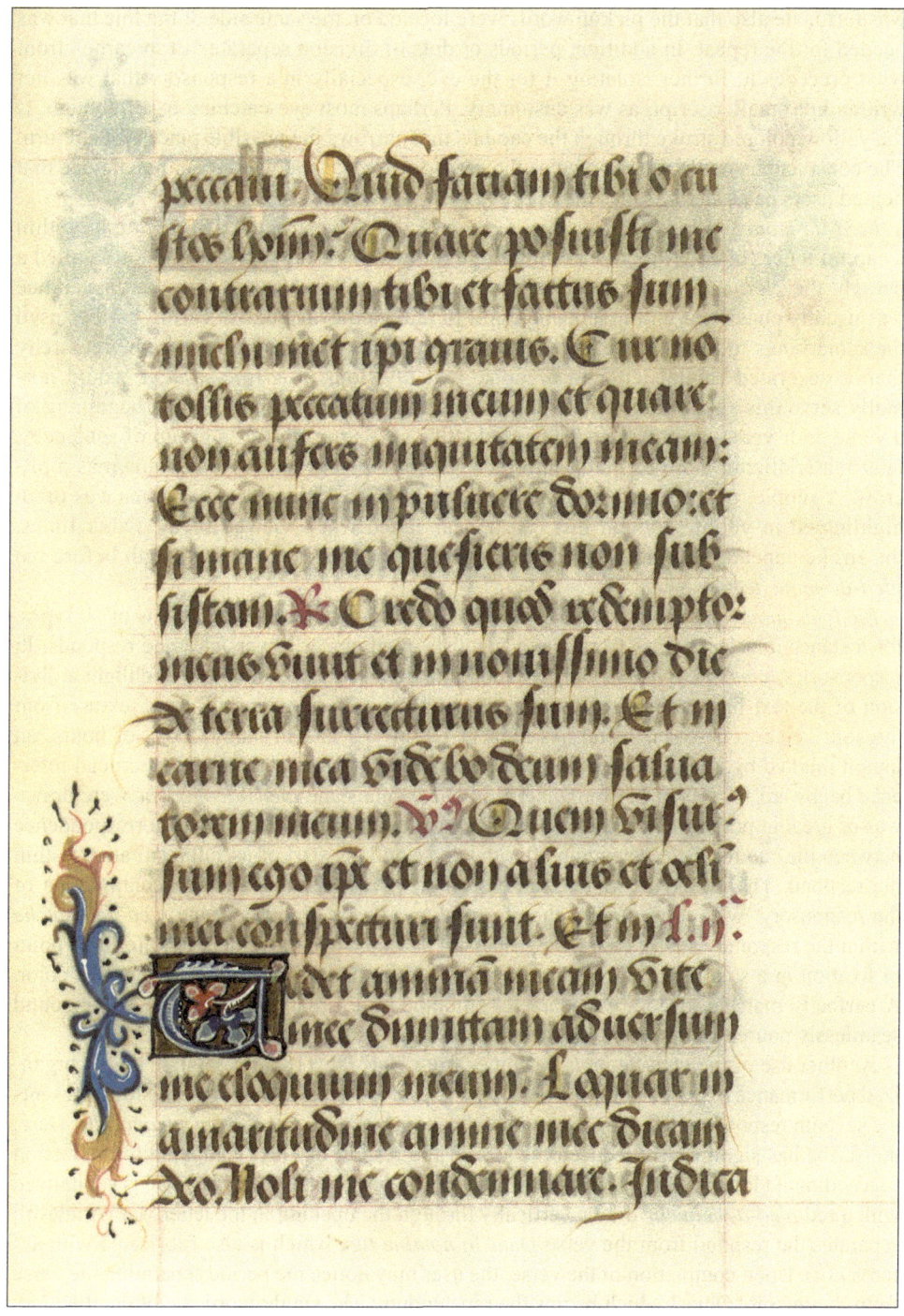

Figure 4.2 Responsory, *Credo quod redemptor*. Bethlehem, Lehigh University, Special Collections, Codex 17, fol. 114r. Image: Bibliotheca Philadelphiensis.

the choral respond. The user needed to scan up only four lines to retrieve the repetition, but was fortunate also that the pickup words were located on the same side of the line that was needed for the repeat. In addition, periods or dots of division separate "Et in carne" from what precedes it, further isolating it for the eye, especially in a responsory that was not written in a smaller script, as was customary. Perhaps most eye-catching of all, though, is the yellow-colored stroke through the capitals that narrows the possible places for a return. The conspicuous marking is known as the *pied-de-mouche* and was a common device that helped users navigate passages of text.

Pied-de-mouche is a paleographical term describing the stroke drawn before or within a capital letter (often with color) to highlight a division of the text.[18] Sometimes called a paraph, the *pied-de-mouche* could be represented in different ways, but the appearance was usually consistent within a manuscript. In late medieval English carols, scribes used these markings to indicate the beginning of a burden or stanza.[19] Lower in the hierarchy than a decorated capital letter to organize text divisions, *pieds-de-mouche* would normally serve this single text-centric purpose, merely calling attention to the beginning of a verse, half verse, or sentence. They could also stress the start of a group of sentences, later materializing more formally into the sign for a paragraph (¶), also known as a pilcrow. A simple, undecorated *pied-de-mouche* beside or within a capital letter was often highlighted in yellow, though this can appear faded when viewed today. Other times, the stroke appeared in red. In execution, one expects a pause of some length before the *pied-de-mouche*.

Pieds-de-mouche were used throughout books of hours to mark distinctions of all types, for instance in select verses from the evangelists' readings or in versicles and responds. In responsories, *pieds-de-mouche* had an added function. They do not simply highlight a division of the text or a moment of prominence, showing the transition of sonic texture from the solo verse to choral respond. As seen in Figure 4.2 and in many books of hours, an incipit marked by a *pied-de-mouche* after the responsory's verse signaled that crucial reference backward for proper performance. How the capitals and *pieds-de-mouche* were drawn was of great importance. Artists and scribes typically aimed for close visual correspondence between the cue for the repetendum after the verse and the start of its full restoration within the respond. The closer the match, the more quickly the user located the continuation of the responsory. With the sound of the repetendum already a constant, the *pied-de-mouche* within the respond visually eased the process of saccadic eye movement by offering a point of fixation in a small field of text that is otherwise limited in (or void of) the use of color. A perfectly matched decorative character smoothed the ritual action further as the sound seamlessly poured forth to conclude the responsory.

Another use of the *pied-de-mouche* comes from BnF, lat. 1184, revealing a highly organized performance experience for the observant user (Figure 4.3). The top of the folio presents the seventh responsory of Matins from the Office of the Dead, *Peccantem me quotidie*. Here, the scribe has significantly reduced the size of the responsory text compared to the lection succeeding it (Job 19:20–27).[20] Halfway through the respond, the word "Quia" is capitalized with a red *pied-de-mouche* drawn vertically through the opening in the letter "Q." A line-fill separates the respond from the verse *Deus in nomine tuo*, which is also rubricated with a ℣ for *versus*. Upon completion of the verse, the user may notice the period separating the verse from the incipit "Quia," which begins the repetendum. The single-word cue offers the *pied-de-mouche* just as it appeared in the respond. Not only do the similarly drawn "Q"s assist in a quick return up four lines, but again the position of the repetendum on the right side of the folio limits the saccadic eye movement.

Figure 4.3 Responsory, *Peccantem me quotidie*. Paris, BnF, lat. 1184, fol. 171r.

Clerics and perhaps some lay owners of books of hours would have been familiar with the melodies of the responsories, especially those in the Office of the Dead. Top of mind in one's memory of the responsory would have to be the repetendum, since it is traversed at least twice in performance. Other users needed signposts for execution of the responsory's short repeat, which scribes provided in myriad ways. A survey of *horae* reveals anything but a hasty run-through of the often minuscule responsory. Scribes strove for clarity in rare times like this in which the user needed to retrace for a dutiful performance of the texts. The most complex responsory that sent users retracing in books of hours awaited at the end of Matins in the Office of the Dead—the *Libera me Domine*.

Libera me Domine

The ninth and final Matins responsory of the Office of the Dead merits special attention. In many books of hours, there are two final responsories to conclude the Night Office, both with the title *Libera me Domine* (CAO 7091 and 7092). The two diverge structurally, if not stylistically. When the responsory CAO 7092 was assigned, it carried a single verse (*Clamantes et dicentes advenisti*, CAO 7092a), though occasionally the familiar text *Requiem aeternam* supplied a doxology substitution, constituting an additional verse and repetendum.

Libera me Domine de viis inferni qui portas ereas confregisti et visitasti infernum et dedisti eis lumen ut viderent te qui erant in penis tenebrarum.	Deliver me O Lord from the ways of hell. You have broken the towering gates, you have visited hell, and you have given light to them, so that they who were in the pains of darkness might see you.
℣ Clamantes et dicentes advenisti redemptor noster. Qui portas . . .	Crying out and saying, you have come our redeemer. You have broken . . .
℣ Requiem aeternam dona eis Domine, et lux perpetua luceat eis. Qui portas . . .	Eternal rest grant unto them O Lord, and may perpetual light shine upon them. You have broken . . .

A later developing mode 1 chant known from the ninth century, CAO 7092 ascends to *b*-flat within its first six notes, reinforcing that note several times as the upper neighbor that prepares the intermediate cadence on the mode's reciting tone *a* (Example 4.4).[21] At least part of this elaborate opening section shows musical economy through the repeated material bracketed in the example, both words beginning with the syllable "vi" (*visitasti/viderent*). The verse, which assumes the reciting pitch *a*, makes a steady fall down to *C*, the *subtonium modi*. This momentary resting point on *C*, which the soloist hands back to the choir, provides smooth access to the continuation of the melody in that same tonal space (*C-D*) at the repetendum from "Qui portas," itself a faint echo of the responsory's incipit.[22] If a Requiem verse were included, it would follow the pattern of the previous verse.

The other *Libera me Domine* responsory (CAO 7091) appears regularly in fifteenth-century books of hours, either by itself or with CAO 7092. When both are slated together, CAO 7091 almost always follows CAO 7092, both occurring in the position of the ninth responsory with no intervening material.[23] In contrast to CAO 7092, CAO 7091 will vary more in its structure and number of verses; each verse proceeds to offer a new melody as well. CAO 7091 also finds an important liturgical occasion besides the end of Matins in the Office of the

Example 4.4 Responsory, *Libera me Domine* (I), CAO 7092. Transcribed from BnF, lat. 15182, fol. 426r.

Dead: *Libera me Domine* (II) was also assigned to the absolution ceremony that followed the Requiem Mass.[24] Here, several drama-filled verses could be also appended, of varying lengths.[25] In liturgical books, the number of verses assigned to the *Libera me Domine* (II) was not standardized and could reach as high as 30. Local communities were known to contribute their own verses.[26] In books of hours, the norm is three verses (inclusive of the final "Requiem" verse), but occasionally, up to seven may appear. The ordering of the less common verses will sometimes differ among sources. The seven verses of *Libera me Domine* (II) most often encountered with the respond are given here:

Libera me Domine, de morte eterna in die illa tremenda, quando celi movendi sunt et terra, dum veneris iudicare seculum per ignem.	Deliver me, O Lord, from eternal death on that terrible day, when the heavens and the earth shall be shaken, when you come to judge the world by fire.
℣ Tremens factus sum ego, et timeo, dum discussio venerit, atque ventura ira.	I am made to tremble, and I fear, until the judgment be upon us and the coming wrath.
℣ Dies illa, dies irae, calamitatis et miserie, dies magna et amara valde.	That day, day of wrath, calamity and misery, day of great and exceeding bitterness,

Less common:

℣ Quid ego miserrimus, quid dicam vel quid faciam; cum nil boni perferam ante tantum iudicem.	What will I, most miserable, what will I say, or what will I do, since I have accomplished nothing good to bear before such a judge?
℣ Tremebunt angeli et archangeli: impii autem ubi parebunt?	The Angels and Archangels shall tremble: but the wicked, where shall they appear?
℣ Vox de celis: O vos, mortui, qui iacetis in sepulcris, surgite! et occurite ad iudicium salvatoris.	A voice from the heavens: Arise, you dead, who lie in your tombs! And hasten to the judgment of the Savior.
℣ Vix justus salvabitur, et ego, ubi apparebo.	The just one shall scarcely be saved, and I? Where will I appear?
℣ Creator omnium rerum Deus, qui me de limo terre formasti, et mirabiliter proprio sanguine redemisti: corpusque meum licet modo putrescat, de sepulcro facias in die iudicii resuscitari: exaudi, exaudi, exaudi me Deus, ut animam meam in sinu Abrahe patriarche tui iubeas collocari.	God, creator of all things, you formed me of the filth of the earth, and wondrously redeemed me with His own blood: though my body should now rot, you shall revive it from the tomb on the day of judgment. Listen, listen, listen to me, O God, that you might command my soul to be placed in bosom of your father Abraham.

Concluding:

℣ Requiem aeternam dona eis Domine, et lux perpetua luceat eis.	Eternal rest grant unto them O Lord, and may perpetual light shine upon them.

Libera me Domine (II) is usually classified as a mode 2 melody, though the respond bears a mixed modal profile. This opening section is conservative in placing all but one of its cadences on the final *D*, but the normally compact tonal space and relatively low range one expects of a second-mode melody is steadily undone in the course of the responsory (Example 4.5). The interval space of the leaping fourth on "die" in the second line, already presaged in the same stepwise ascent on "de" in the first line, is expanded in a jarring run through a tritone on "mo-" of "movendi." The ambitus inches yet more widely in the succeeding phrase, reaching the *a*—a fifth above the final—and breaks into the range above *a* which usually defines mode 1 melodies. The verse *Dies illa, dies irae* is notable among those for the soloist: the opening phrase beginning *f-E-f-D* provides an aural hook to the eponymous liturgical sequence, an extensive melody growing out of this responsory verse, which was added to the Requiem Mass in French missals in the later fifteenth century.[27]

Beyond its multiple verses, the *Libera me Domine* (II) is further remarkable among the Matins responsories in the Office of the Dead—or any responsory in the book of hours—because of its unusual scheme of repetenda, not exploited in the source for Example 4.5.[28] The respond is in fact set up for multiple points of return after the verses. The two principal repetenda of the *Libera me Domine* begin at "Quando celi" and "Dum veneris." A common unfolding of the verses and repetenda of *Libera me Domine* (II) in books of hours may be witnessed in BnF, n.a.l. 3110 with rubrics and yellow *pieds-de-mouche* for navigating the execution (Figure 4.4). The responsory follows the ninth reading of Matins, but the script size remains relatively consistent, not diminished. Following the most common verses *Tremens factus sum* and *Dies illa, dies irae*, the scribe instructs the user to return to different points in the respond, first to "Quando celi" and next to "Dum veneris." Falling more or less in the middle of the responsory, the "Quando celi" repetendum should be sung only until the beginning of the next part of the respond at "Dum veneris." Though only the incipits are given in this manuscript, some books of hours include

Example 4.5 Responsory, *Libera me Domine* (II), CAO 7091 (two verses only). Transcribed from BnF, lat. 15182, fols. 426r–427r.

the full text of the repetendum to clarify how far to continue once restarting at "Quando celi."[29] After the verse *Dies illa, dies irae*, the user is required to return to "Dum veneris," a shorter repeat sung through the end of the respond. In this example, the lowercase "d" of "dum" after the verse matches its corresponding lowercase "d" in the respond. More often, there are capital letters. A *pied-de-mouche* falls only on the latter "d" instead of on both letters for the eye to jump, but by now the user would presumably have narrowed the general location of the repeat.

Figure 4.4 Responsory, *Libera me Domine* (II). Paris, BnF, n.a.l. 3110, fol. 137v.

Following the concluding "Requiem" verse (itself abbreviated) in Figure 4.4, the prescription now points to a full recitation of the *Libera me Domine* respond. The repeat of the choral respond in its entirety was traditionally a sign of the relative importance of that responsory within a feast. That this was the only responsory to command a full repeat with some regularity reinforces its stature in the Office of the Dead. In some cases, scribes will write out the full respond after the "Requiem" verse, sparing the user another backward reference. The length of the *Libera me Domine* (II) may also have been adjusted in liturgical situations. As a chant also prescribed in the absolution ceremony after the Requiem Mass, *Libera me Domine* (II) shows different configurations of verses and repeats across books of hours and service books, suggesting that it was customizable in response to ritual action in context.

*

It is ironic, to be sure, that such melodious works as the responsories often appear suppressed in the *mise-en-page* of books of hours. The relatively small script size in many manuscript sources may be signaling not only a difference in genre but a distinct vocal texture, or perhaps an alternation of types of voices. Despite the isolated nature of this chapter, the responsories do not operate alone; they are set in dialogue with the lessons of the offices in books of hours. Each responsory allowed the supplicant to ruminate in the sound world prompted by a resplendent musical postscript to the Word of God, a shapely melody contrasting with the lesson's relative monotone. The music to which responsory texts were set could even push the bounds of the traditional melodic modes. In the next chapter, we survey responses of a different sort, as well as the sonic realm of functional liturgical music that connects the more contoured genres we have traversed.

Notes

1 Hiley, *Western Plainchant*, 85.
2 Crocker, "Thoughts on Responsories," 82.
3 Edwards, "Dynamic Qualities," 51.
4 For the Office of the Virgin prescribed for Advent, the lessons were taken from Isaiah and Luke. For this version of the Marian office, see Catholic Church, *The Little Office of the Blessed Virgin Mary in Latin and English*, 75–105, 164–170.
5 Albertus, "Biblia Mariana," esp. 385–88, 402–407.
6 Even Lutheran composers set the text amid waning interest in Mariology. See Frandsen, "*Salve regina/Salve rex christe*," 181.
7 BnF, MS fr. 146, fol. 38v.
8 Fulton, *Mary and the Art of Prayer*, 258.
9 Adult male speaking voices tend to vibrate around 125Hz (pitch: B); females at 200Hz (pitch: g). See Titze, *Principles of Voice Production*, 185–188.
10 Cutter et al., "Responsory," *NG* 21: 224–225.
11 Anderson, "Enhancing the Ave Maria," 35–37.
12 The provisions of the endowment can be found in Archives de la Marne, dépôt annexe de Reims, 2G 1550, no. 1. This passage is discussed in Robertson, *Guillaume de Machaut and Reims*, 217–218.
13 New Haven, Yale University, Beinecke Rare Book and Manuscript Library, MS 205, fol. 54r-v.
14 The two other Assumption responsories were *Quae est ista* (CAO 7455) and *Sicut cedrus* (CAO 7657).
15 The Matins responsories and their attendant verses from the Office of the Dead were the subject of a massive study by Knud Ottosen (*The Responsories and Versicles of the Latin Office of the Dead*), who surveyed over 1,800 liturgical manuscripts from the ninth to the seventeenth century in search of local liturgical particularities.

16 A similar tactic is found in BnF, lat. 1414 (fol. 52r-v) for the responsory *Felix namque es*; however, here the repetendum is written out twice—once after the verse and again in full after the Gloria.
17 See the repetendum for the responsory *Credo quod redemptor* in BnF, n.a.l. 3181, fol. 149v.
18 My thanks to Ilya Dines for kind assistance with these markings.
19 Palti, "Singing Women," 366.
20 The lection is mislabeled as the seventh instead of the eighth in the Matins series. The preceding lection (fol. 170r) is likewise rubricated incorrectly as "lectio octava." The readings and responsories themselves, however, are correctly positioned in the service.
21 There is a variant melodic tradition (with *E* final) for this *Libera me Domine* in Hungarian sources. See Dobszay, "The Responsory," 10.
22 The start of the repetendum for CAO 7092 was split in the sources. Some restart at the text *qui portas*, others at *qui erant* in the respond. Both of course begin with a "qui," and both are musically viable as the start of melodic phrases. Beginning the repetendum at *qui erant* is less convincing grammatically, but would directly pick up the *C* from the verse, which also explains the likely confusion of the two possible repetenda.
23 For exceptions to this order, see, for example, BnF, n.a.l. 3114, fol. 158r-v and BnF, n.a.l. 3197, fols. 108v–109r.
24 Felix Fabri (*The Wanderings*, 1: 149) mentioned that this chant was sung part of the funeral rite on board his vessel. A book of hours owned by a family from St. Maur-des-Fossés suggests that CAO 7091 was used on more solemn occasions, namely on All Souls' Day and on days when the nine lessons of the Office of the Dead were sung (*cum nota*). See BnF, n.a.l. 3107, fol. 198v.
25 Hiley, *Western Plainchant*, 45.
26 Ottosen, *The Responsories and Versicles of the Latin Office of the Dead*, 16.
27 Caldwell and Boyd, "Dies irae," *NG* 7: 332–333. For the early history of the text and melody of the sequence *Dies irae*, see Vellekoop, *Dies Ire Dies Illa*, 29–96.
28 The verses are reversed in the source and switched here to preserve the order normally encountered in books of hours. BnF, lat. 15182 in fact presents all seven of the possible verses for the responsory, with no Requiem verse notated or signaled. All verses suggest a repetendum back to the text *Quando celi*.
29 See, for example, the *Libera me Domine* in BnF, n.a.l. 3187, fol. 175r and BnF, lat. 1408, fol. 110r.

5 Dialogues

*

"Dominus vobiscum" . . . "Et cum spiritu tuo" ("The Lord be with you" . . . "And with your spirit"). Anyone who grew up attending Catholic Mass before Vatican II or has attended a traditional Latin Mass in the present day knows the pervasiveness of this liturgical greeting and utterances like these that inhabit the liturgy. In the age-old salutation "Dominus vobiscum," the officiant intones the words not to a fixed formula, but to one reflective of the solemnity of the moment. The congregation listens to its degree of elaboration and responds by mirroring the precise formula established by the prompt with its assigned text. For those who knew these words, seeing them printed—then as now—summons a specific sound from experience, recalled at a certain intensity, resonance, pitch, tone color, and other sonic qualities. The melodic stimulus from a single voice in a middle range sets up a full and reverberant, though sometimes blurry, choral echo. While the exchange beginning "Dominus vobiscum" is the perhaps most familiar example of the genre of the versicle and response in the Mass, it is scarcely found in book of hours. Dialogues of this sort however are distributed across the *horae*. Edward Foley has noted the "indexical" purpose of short versicles and responses, introduced in various contexts to affirm that an action has happened or will happen.[1] In short, the versicle and response (*versiculus*, or "small verse," and *responsio*) function as the connective tissue of the liturgy.

As linking devices, versicles and responses can serve as overtures to more formal prayers and readings, or they may perform a punctuative purpose, leading the faithful listener out of a larger liturgical item and into a different texture, whether meditative, active, or narrative. In some books of hours, there is a well-known dialogue situated before the readings of the evangelists, in which the celebrant proclaims the author of the gospel excerpt, and the assembly replies "Gloria tibi Domine," perhaps signaled with different colored ink to separate the contrasting sounds.[2] In the service of Lauds in the Office of the Virgin, Elizabeth's greeting of Mary, *Benedicta tu in mulieribus*, forms a versicle and response (CAO 7971) in the textural shift from the hymn *O gloriosa domina* to the Benedictus led by the antiphon *Beata dei genetrix*.[3] Similarly, in the Office of the Dead, the Revelation-inspired versicle *Audivi vocem meam* (CAO 7957) and its attendant response *Beati mortui* enable a transition at the apex of the eventide liturgy of Vespers; they join the end of the opening series of antiphons and psalms with the Canticle of Mary and its framing antiphon *Omne quod dat*.[4] Dialogues like these are found elsewhere in the liturgies, whether at the beginning of offices or following chapter readings in the minor hours. Versicles and responses were also placed outside the offices and may be organized in a more extended series of exchanges. Some pairings repeat in the liturgies and in accessory texts throughout books of hours.

DOI: 10.4324/9781003140511-7

In notated service books, it is rare to see music provided for a versicle and response. Often, the scribe will provide only the text of the versicle and not the response. Even more likely, just the versicle's incipit will be indicated. For example, in a late twelfth-century Benedictine antiphoner from south Germany, staff lines appear above the incipit of the versicle *Audivi vocem meam*, simply continuing the ruling of the page. Musical notation fills the page, but no pitches are given above that incipit.[5] The solemnity of a feast would have dictated differently shaped versicle formulas. But the glaring absence of musical detail for versicles and responses should not surprise us. Not only did the dialogues offer melodic simplicity and flexibility in their unvarnished musical formulas, but also the response expected of those gathered needed no written cue. No doubt the statement of the versicle, with its textual prompt fastened in the sound world with a plain formula, generated a near-mechanical response from congregants. Psychologists may refer to this phenomenon as implicit memory, a type of long-term memory that is unconscious. While most implicit memory tends to fall into procedural tasks that have become automatic (like riding a bicycle), the involuntary recall of texts, music, or images when given a prompt belongs to a branch of implicit memory known as priming.[6] The versicle and response as they appear in liturgical sources and in books of hours represent a clear case of priming.

The modest intonations of versicles and responses are matched in other parts of the liturgy that were captured in books of hours. Readings (*lectiones*) and prayers (*orationes*) had sound equivalents in the sung liturgy of the Mass and Office and thus could be received as sounds remembered or even intoned when interacting with books of hours, similar to the other genres surveyed to this point. Their length, however, far exceeds versicles and responses; dialogues may in fact surround them. In books where scribes use differentiated script sizes, the stretches of prose found in lessons and prayers are uniformly cast in a larger script, perhaps reflective of different factors, from the nature of the text (narrative or contemplative) to the texture of the sound, namely the direct and relatively inflexible tone of a single voice. This chapter surveys two key prefatory versicles in the office, before probing the sounds that might be expected with the dialogues. It concludes by considering how the Pater noster is represented as a kind of dialogue in the *horae*.

Salutatory versicles

The most urgent versicle-response pair to discuss is the one that dominates the Office of the Virgin—*Deus in adiutorium*. This salutation of most services in the Marian hours presents the second verse of Psalm 69: "O God, come to my assistance; O Lord, make haste to help me" ("Deus in adiutorium meum intende; Domine ad adiuvandum me festina"). The prescription to initiate offices in this fashion is traceable to the Rule of St. Benedict, but was also included in other rites to follow.[7] In many usages outside of Rome, all eight services of the Divine Office in the liturgical day began with this psalm verse as a call to worship. In the Roman rite, Psalm 69:2 opens every office except two: the initial service of Matins features Psalm 50:17 (*Domine labia mea aperies*), and the concluding hour of Compline begins with Psalm 84:5 (*Converte nos, Deus*). In both cases, Psalm 69:2 follows the alternative opening verse. For Christians who did not know the offices, the recitation of *Deus in adiutorium* was part of at least one recommended regimen that provided a suitable remedy.[8]

Psalm 69:2 was more than a formality to inaugurate six of the eight services in the Office of the Virgin. The verse had transcended liturgical usage and was woven into daily life. Augustine identified recitation of the psalm verse as a means of protection from the dangers of evil and the threat of sin, an idea echoed by later medieval writers from Iohannes Beleth to Guillaume Durand.⁹ The resolve inherent in the plea became a kind of amulet to be uttered when faced with difficult tasks, distressing moments, or emergency situations. It also could serve as a mind-centering motto in the course of one's regular labor or life at home. Following the Pauline edict of unceasing prayer, Christians seem to have embraced Psalm 69:2 as part of a means to that end. The impulse to imbue devotional life with the psalm verse is supported as early as the fifth century in John Cassian's *Collationes patrum* (Conferences with the Fathers), which may have influenced Benedict's Rule. In Cassian's conversation 10 on monastic prayer with Desert Father Abbot Isaac, the latter confirms the unparalleled plasticity of Psalm 69:2: "Not without reason has this verse been selected from out of the whole body of scripture. For it takes up all the emotions that can be applied to human nature, and with great correctness and accuracy, it adjusts itself to every condition and every attack."¹⁰ Unique for a psalm verse, the recitation of *Deus in adiutorium* was often accompanied by the gestural Sign of the Cross, a ritual action that no doubt reinforced the power of the verse through physical embodiment. Mary Channen Caldwell concludes that the verse served as "an all-purpose, utilitarian petition that served countless functions in the everyday life of the faithful, refrain-like in its constant reiteration."¹¹

Beyond the pure reflection of the Roman rite, the extraliturgical functions of Psalm 69:2 would have magnified its presence for those praying the hours. The subsequent repetition and salutatory role of this verse in the core Office of the Virgin and in the supplemental Hours of the Cross and Spirit further reminded users of the centrality of this verse among the numerous psalm verses that flooded their *horae*. The chance to recite Psalm 69 in full was not provided in the customary liturgies in books of hours. In about three-quarters of the fifteenth-century corpus, however, the complete psalm does appear following the Litany.

The versicle-response pair *Domine labia mea aperies* (Psalm 50:17) deserves special mention for its presence at the beginning of the Office of the Virgin in Matins: "O Lord, open my lips, and my mouth shall declare Thy praise." The opening of the "Little Office" was a destination page of sorts in books of hours. In illustrated books, it inaugurated the Marian cycle of events with an image of the Annunciation. If an owner was lucky enough to be depicted in prayer within her cherished book, the portrait would have most likely fallen within this image for Matins.¹² *Domine labia mea aperies* would usually lie prominently beneath this image. The versicle was also notable for its use at the beginning of the Hours of the Cross and Hours of the Holy Spirit. *Deus in adiutorium* will always follow the two half verses of *Domine labia mea aperies* in these cases.

Like Psalm 69:2, *Domine labia mea aperies* presents another command to the Lord: "open my lips" of Psalm 50:17 replaces "come" and "make haste" in the other decree. The directive is just as personal but here plainly involves the body of the supplicant, namely the lips, mouth, and ultimately the voice as instruments of praise. The vocal implications of *Domine labia mea aperies* are tempting to consider in light of this well-known verse. In their study of the Gualenghi-d'Este Hours from ca. 1470, Shephard, Ştefănescu, and Sessini assert that the act of opening one's lips and declaring God's glory, according to the psalm verse, "can *only* be read as breaking into song" (italics mine). They envision that, in the encounter of this verse, "the book's owner breaks into a song . . . about breaking into song."¹³ Though these authors emphasize figurative song over literal song in books of hours, the activation of the voice and sound is implicit in the experience.

The radiance of the human voice is not the only possibility for an auditory environment at the outset of the offices. In the "Malet-Lannoy Hours," prepared in the second quarter of the fifteenth century, the sounding aura in conjunction with the salutatory versicle is made more explicit (Figure 5.1). The extraordinary visual liftoff to Matins in the Office of the Virgin

Figure 5.1 Opening of Matins in the Office of the Virgin with versicle, *Domine labia mea aperies*. Walters Art Museum, MS W.281 ("Malet-Lannoy Hours"), fols. 30v–31r. Credit: The Walters Art Museum, Baltimore.

Figure 5.1 (Continued)

reveals a manuscript opening that is fully illustrated, not just with the expected imagery of the Annunciation on the recto, but also with the uncommon scene of the Marriage of the Virgin Mary on the preceding verso.[14] Kneeling with a prayer book open in the miniature on the right, Mary faces Gabriel, whose message ("Ave Maria [gratia plena] Dominus tecum") unfurls on a scroll around his shoulder. The banner presages the invitatory antiphon *Ave Maria*, the liturgical invitation to the Night Office that follows the opening versicles. Not an atypical accessory in Annunciation scenes, the angel's texted scroll stands in for a vocal proclamation to be recognized as such when beholding the depiction. In the Malet-Lannoy Hours, the power of Gabriel's decree is strengthened by a band of instrumentalists in the frame of this image and in the border of the facing page. This was an unusually reverberant beginning to the office as the owners Thomas Malet de Berlettes and his wife, Jeanne of Lannoy, ask God to "open my lips." Thomas's coat of arms is seen in the lower register of the recto.

The sounds across this manuscript opening move from loud to something more subdued, perhaps an intentional diminuendo headed into the liturgical core of the *horae*. A handful of angels surrounding the wedding on the verso blare the trumpet, commanding attention for a declaration. Four of the angels sound the unwieldy straight trumpet, while the angel in the upper right holds the variant S-curved trumpet. In the upper register of the miniature, there is yet more music: three singing angels are pictured centrally, flanked by pairs of cherubic instrumentalists.[15] Scanning toward the recto, the attentive supplicant may witness the marginal ruckus abating as the formal recitation of the versicle *Domine labia mea aperies* prepares the liturgical chants of Matins. The oversize angels are replaced by smaller figures situated in irregular medallions around the Annunciation scene. A single trumpet (or shawm) player remains in the upper left of the recto, joined by two musicians playing "soft" (*bas*) instruments—the harp and lute (or psaltery), in the lower left and upper-mid right, respectively.[16] A trio of singers in a medallion on the middle right gather around a book, like their counterpart on the verso. The versicle's imposing capital "D" likewise shrinks the Annunciation scene relative to the more public spectacle on the facing verso, further nudging the user toward the chanted texts that await.

As David Rothenberg has explained, consorts of soft instruments, which included flutes, harps, vielles, and the like, often accompanied scenes of the Virgin Mary's earthly life, communicating an atmosphere of secular song. The Annunciation qualifies as one of several terrestrial events in the Marian cycle, as opposed to the heavenly Assumption, which unleashed high and loud instruments in visual art. The wedding scene, however, was an earthly setting, which unexpectedly appears to emphasize the loud instruments over the diminutive band of "low" sounds, or an unruly confluence of the two. Appropriately, the progression toward softer sound and *bas* music in the scene, combined with the kneeling angel in the lower right modeling contemplative prayer, would allow the owner of this book to become awash in gentler sounds, reminiscent of the courtly chanson, while simultaneously readying for the official liturgical ceremony beginning with the versicle and response. Two of the three singers on the recto hold up their hands (one distracted from the book), as if to halt the clamor of the wedding or the lingering collage of sound, a potential signal to the user that the focus must be placed on the hallowed texts to come. While it was easy to become fixed on Gabriel's iconic message on the recto or the marriage ceremony that precedes it, the marginal images appear to have thrust the noble users into a complex world of sound, barreling toward the venerable versicle *Domine labia mea aperies*, adorned with the large capital, a reserved call to worship that tempers the intense visual and aural stimulation at the outset of the Night Office.

Sounds of the dialogues

The versicles and responses of the liturgy are fundamentally characterized by melodic simplicity and flexibility. Like psalm verses, the dialogues exhibit a two-part structure; as we have seen, versicles and responses were often psalm verses themselves. While the psalm tones offered many possibilities for musical execution, the tones of the versicles were apparently limited. The musical formulas for psalm verses across the different melodic modes were containers to be filled with text and offered minimal decoration of those words. The versicle tones are likewise recitational, with the capacity to accommodate a text of any length: on the level of elaboration, they sit closer to psalm tones and do not quite approach the more monotonous character of a chanted reading. The versicle was typically intoned by a celebrant with the response offered in full voice by the assembly. There were no doubt practical reasons for these part assignments. The community of participants in a liturgy cannot easily coordinate as a group musically, even for the simplest utterance. Pitch would need to be accurately communicated, and even if an opening note were fixed, starting a group together and keeping them together for an unmetered verse is a recipe for clumsy declamation.[17]

As mentioned, the music of the versicle-response pair varied according to the solemnity of the ceremony at hand. It is of course not possible to say which formula a supplicant or user of a book of hours had in mind in connection with a given versicle, but with the variants being minimal, one can quickly narrow the options. In the rare cases where versicles were notated in liturgical sources, there appear to be a couple of possibilities. In connection with a versicle incipit, a music scribe might simply have written a few repeated notes; importantly, these were placed on *f* or *c*, notes that have a half step located beneath them.[18] Versicle incipits are surprisingly rare in books of hours; scribes apparently wanted to be thorough with these texts, not relying on a user's implicit memory, even when the versicles were repeated in different parts of the book. The common melodic formula for the versicle was to chant on any comfortable pitch (theoretically mapping to the *f* or *c*) and "flex" down the minor third at the cadence (to *D* or *a*, respectively), usually lengthening and pausing at the end of that phrase.[19] The change of tone would be introduced directly following the ultimate stressed syllable of text. The response to the simple prompt assumes the reciting pitch and similarly flexes down after the final accented syllable. For monosyllabic words at the end of a versicle, the flex tone occurs on that final word. Books of hours often rubricate the response with ℟ corresponding to the vocal return of the chosen note of recitation. Occasionally, the division between versicle and response is not explicit; given the ubiquity of these sentences, the user likely knew exactly where the break occurred.

Solemn occasions commanded a more ornate tone for the versicle and response. In the exceptional case that a service book would notate a full versicle, a decorative cadence would be provided, for instance on Sundays and feast days during the major hours.[20] The response would again be omitted in these books. While the cadence ends on *D* or *a* like the simpler tone, a series of seven intervening notes fall on the ultimate syllable of the more elaborate tone, beginning with neighboring motion (*f-E-f* or *c-b-c*), as shown in Example 5.1. This example, *Diffusa est gratia* (CAO 8014), is found more than once in the course of the Office of the Virgin in books of hours.[21] The twelfth-century antiphoner from the Monastery of St. Maur-des-Fossés notates music for each syllable of the versicle in an office for St. Agnes. The response is not given in the manuscript, but is supplied for the sake of completeness. The half step beneath the recitation tone—an unstable pitch (here, *E*)—may be elongated in practice. The remaining pitches descend a fourth by step before rising and encircling the cadential

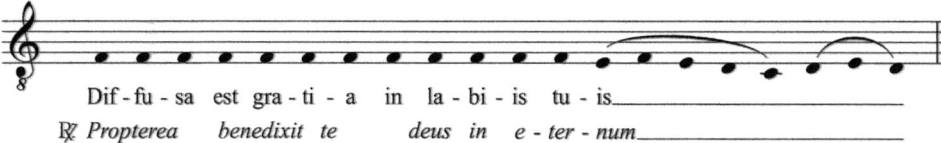

Example 5.1 Versicle, *Diffusa est gratia*. Transcribed from BnF, lat. 12044, fol. 46r.

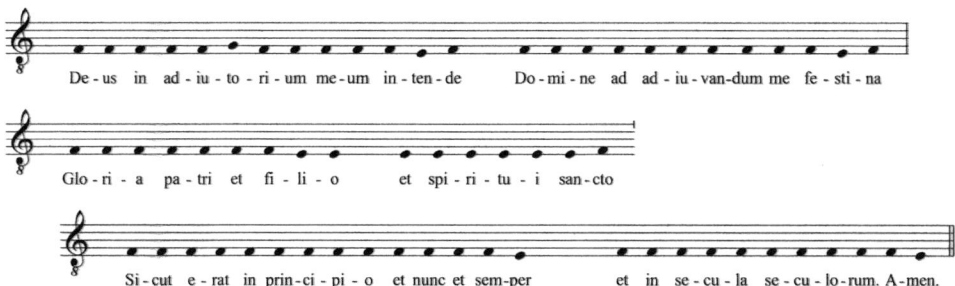

Example 5.2 Versicle and response, *Deus in adiutorium* and doxology, following LBL, Add. MS 23935, fol. 82v.

pitch. From its repetition throughout the year, the rhythmic freedom of execution of this flourish would have been familiar to cantors, monastic communities, and probably the laity.

Situated at the head of several services in books of hours, the prominent versicle *Deus in adiutorium* has a shadowy history as a chanted prelude. For its reconstruction in sound, Dominican master exemplars from mid-thirteenth-century Paris may transmit a possible tone that a lay supplicant recalled for Psalm 69:2 as expressed in song (Example 5.2).[22] These exemplars captured even the shortest and most incidental of liturgical chants in notation, including versicles and collects. For *Deus in adiutorium*, the exemplar mirrors the "ferial" tone for this versicle found in modern chant books. The more modest melodic shape was presumably suitable for the Office of the Virgin, which operated in the shadows of the daily office and celebration of feast days.[23] In this simple tone, once again a recitational pitch (*f* or *c*) must be established so that a half step lies directly beneath it. A whole step will sit above the reciting tone as well, implicit in the tones already mentioned because they were not accessed. The conservative melodic course of the versicle, which lacks a discernible melodic mode, reflects awareness for the accent of the phrases. The recitation takes the upper neighbor on the accented syllable of *adiutorium*; it returns to the reciting tone until the ultimate accented syllable of the half verse (*intende*), which falls to the lower neighbor before returning to the stable home pitch. The response is not identical, continuing the recitation and only repeating the lower neighbor motion on the accented syllable of *festina*. Sometimes abbreviated but rarely omitted in books of hours, the doxology *Gloria patri* takes a different course emphasizing the lower neighbor *E* for a longer stretch and making a final cadence on that note rather than the *f* from the versicle and response of Psalm 69:2.[24]

In the milieu of books of hours, it is impossible to impute a sonic experience to users with a verse that could be remembered differently depending on context. The ubiquity of Psalm 69:2 as a spoken verse in everyday life must also be seriously entertained—for example, when considering the performance of these words by the laity outside church walls. As an exhortation to prayer in the hours, *Deus in adiutorium* rarely attracted tropes or settings in medieval polyphony.[25] Among musicologists, it has thus tended to escape the attention it deserves as a sung and spoken prayer of its stature.

Voices of the Pater noster

Taught to the disciples by Jesus himself and relayed in the Sermon on the Mount (Matthew 6:9–13), the Pater noster remains one of the principal prayers of the faith, and medieval Christians committed it to memory at an early age. Like the Ave Maria, the mere sound of the words "Pater noster," after years of repetition, would have triggered implicit memory for the whole, one phrase flowing after the next. The same would presumably be true upon seeing those two-word prompts in books of hours. The Pater noster and Ave Maria were joined in the practice of praying the rosary, a fifteenth-century development that emphasized organized recitation of these devotions and eventually meditation on various mysteries based on sets of beaded prayers.[26] In books of hours, the two prayers could often be found together after various accessory prayers, or interleaved in devotions such as the Seven Prayers of St. Gregory or the Joys of the Virgin.[27] The Pater noster was recited in these cases, whether aloud or in silence. It does not represent a dialogue in the manner we have seen with the versicles and responses. The prayer appears by itself in yet more places in books of hours corresponding to its wide use in office liturgies. In the Office of the Virgin, it fell between the lections and the psalms and antiphons in each nocturn of Matins; later in the book, it was placed after the Litany, following a tripartite Kyrie eleison, typical in the Roman rite. In these instances, the expressly condensed "notation" of the Lord's Prayer merits examination, reflective of its execution.

In the transition between psalms and readings in Matins, the Pater noster was usually recited in a low voice (*privatim* or *secreto*) by the officiating priest. In this practice, the prayer was uttered quietly until the words "et ne nos inducas in tentationem" ("and lead us not into temptation"), which then emerged audibly in the speaking voice. Those gathered would supply corporately the final independent clause, "sed libera nos a malo" ("but deliver us from evil"). The unanimous participation of the supplicants at the vocal affirmation was essential; structurally, the prayer acts as a dialogue with the congregation at its conclusion. In the context of the Mass, the Lord's Prayer could be elevated to the level of plainsong, equally memorable for those who experienced it. The priest again shouldered much of the prayer. Unlike much of the Canon of the Mass, the music of the Pater noster is not set to a formula; it is a distinct, predominantly syllabic melody (Example 5.3). While this melody shows noticeable contour, it is notoriously constrained, limited to just a tetrachord in its range (g-c) for the majority of the text, drawing on the pitch content found in the Preface and the Collect at Mass. It is still the most "developed" of the priest's prayers.[28] Similar to the spoken recitation of the prayer, the text "et ne nos inducas" is marked for importance for the engaged listener or performer when it is intoned aloud. The initial "et" breaks the bounds of the established tetrachord and dips down to an E below the final g. This sonic shift to the tonal space beneath the final, in addition to the text cue, prompted congregants to complete the prayer at "sed," restoring the primary tonal space of the prayer.

Given the ubiquity of the Pater noster and its stronghold in the implicit memory of devotees (medieval or otherwise), the text of the prayer was unnecessary to include in books of hours. Still, Christians intent on emulating monastic liturgies needed to be aware of its positioning in the course of prayer; the ordering of prayer is, after all, something more easily

Example 5.3 Pater noster. Transcribed from *GR*, 812.

forgotten than the content of the prayers themselves. Important for this study, when scribes indicated the position of the Pater noster, they provided more than just the incipit; they frequently provided a cue for the concluding part of the prayer beginning "Et ne nos." These are the words to which supplicants would have been specially attuned in the liturgy. In written form, the juxtaposition of the beginning and end of the Lord's Prayer may appear incongruous at first glance. But when viewed as a reflection of practice, the notated apposition ("Pater noster"/"Et ne nos") makes sense, capturing the texture changes in the recitation of the prayer. As a spoken devotion, the sound quality transforms from murmuring to audible speech at the "Et ne nos" and gathers strength at the spoken choral retort "Sed libera." If a book of hours user regarded the prayer as song, on the other hand, the exchange of textures maintains, but in different vocal realms. The celebrant's execution of the chant transitions into the lower tetrachord at "Et ne nos" before the assembly responds to punctuate the Pater noster.

The "notation" of the key moments of the Pater noster differed across books of hours. Sometimes, the indication of the prayer depended on the space afforded on manuscript folio. Extremely limited space could mean that the only suggestion of the prayer was its incipit "Pater noster." The most common notation, however, was the first two prompts, "Pater noster" and "Et ne nos." These two utterances encapsulate the major vocal modification in the prayer when it is imagined to begin "in secret." A generously spaced *mise-en-page* could feature all three cues for the Lord's Prayer ("Pater noster"/"Et ne nos"/"Sed libera") consecutively. The three key textural shifts of the Lord's Prayer in practice are found in a mid-fifteenth-century book of hours (LBL, Add. MS 27697) prepared for a member of the House of Saluces of Piedmont, possibly Aimée (or Amadée) de Saluces (Figure 5.2).[29]

With its decorated capital "P," the Pater noster here falls in the service of Vespers in the Office of the Dead, following the recitation of the Magnificat and the full iteration of its framing antiphon *Omne quod dat* (CAO 4115) at the top of the folio. The tripartite Kyrie eleison precedes the Lord's Prayer, a common pairing in transitions. This extraordinary example

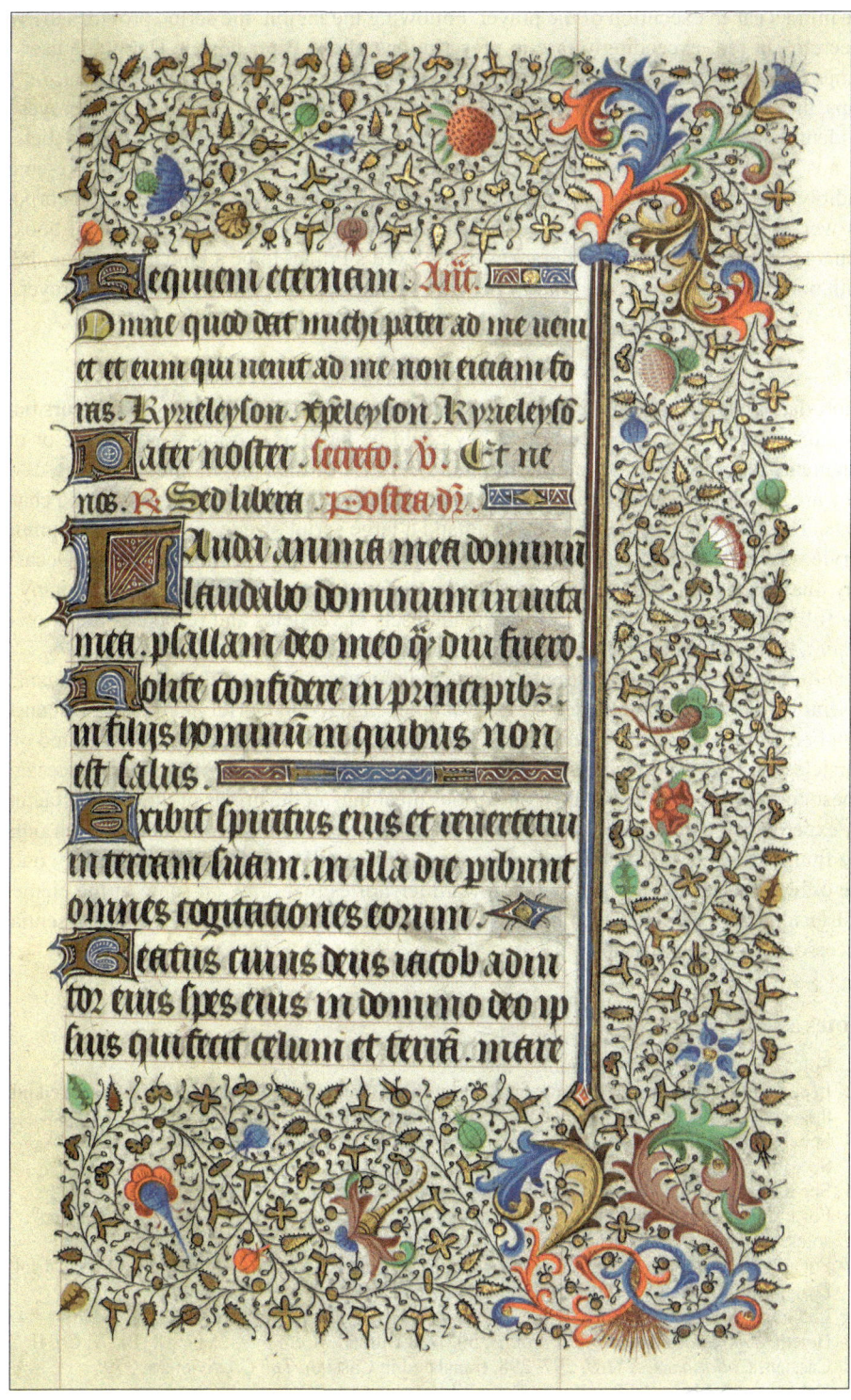

Figure 5.2 Pater noster. LBL, Add. MS 27697, fol. 123r. © The British Library Board.

uses rubrication to create designations for the parts of the Pater noster that are crucial for the mind's ear in execution of the prayer. Following the incipit, the scribe provides the word "secreto" in red, exceedingly rare in prescriptions of the Pater noster. The noble user was either to murmur the words of the Our Father, imitating the actions of a celebrant; or, perhaps, they were to imagine a priest doing the same. The plainsong rendition of the prayer was evidently not to be entertained here. As the prayer nears its conclusion, the scribe labels "Et ne nos" with a red ℣ for versicle, at the moment when the priest's words would re-emerge audibly in a liturgical setting. Correspondingly, a rubricated ℟ appears before the corporate answer "Sed libera nos." The scribe of LBL, Add. MS 27697 and other scribes of books of hours recognized the closing utterances of the Lord's Prayer to be a kind of dialogue, in line with our understanding of the change in vocal texture and force in the context of prayer.[30]

*

Short dialogues, usually in the form of versicles and responses, infuse books of hours but do not attract attention in their entirety. They could be familiar extracts from psalms or other fragments repurposed in a bipartite format.[31] Because of their function as a linking device, they are necessarily scattered in liturgies surrounded by different types of prayer and chanted texts. The dialogues further did not command a large script size, except at the beginning of services, where they sometimes mirrored the grandeur of an opening miniature. Occasionally, dialogues poured out in a more lengthy series, for example following the Litany and the full recitation of Psalm 69.[32] The extended sets of versicles and responses are known as *preces*, though the term is hardly found in books of hours.[33]

Different types of voices saturate liturgical dialogues, and not only between officiant and assembly. The officiant and a lector, for example, engaged in a brief interchange of benediction before the latter read lessons in the service of Matins. The benediction consisted of the versicle *Jube domne benedicere*, which bore a formula calibrated to the solemn occasion.[34] These formalities must have taken on various meanings in the minds of those manufacturing an experience of the office liturgies. The dialogues became a familiar device even outside the liturgy, for instance in the suffrages, as we will see. We now tread purposefully outside the office liturgies in books of hours, toward territories that draw on some of the elemental liturgical genres we have seen but now designated in sections that were either essential or accessorized for their owners.

Notes

1 Foley, "The Song of the Assembly," 204–205.
2 In each of the four gospel readings in BnF, lat. 1375 (fols. 17r–20r), the scribe provides red ink for the versicle sung as solo and blue ink for the congregational response.
3 See, for example, the versicle *Benedicta tu in mulieribus* in BnF, n.a.l. 3120, fol. 46r.
4 See, for example, this versicle and response in BnF, n.a.l. 3111, fol. 119v.
5 See Karlsruhe, Badische Landesbibliothek—Musikabteilung, Aug. LX, fol. 221r.
6 For introductions to the topic, see Alexopoulos, Grasso, and Palomares, "Social Cognition"; Marsolek, "What Is Priming and Why?"
7 For a brief overview of the liturgical verse, see Leclercq, "1. Deus in Adjutorium"; Cabrol, "2. Deus in Adjutorium," in *DACL 4/1*: cols. 697–699.
8 Le Grand, *Statuts*, 37–38.
9 Beleth, *Summa de ecclesiasticis officiis*, 50, 187; Durand, *Rationale*, 2: 17–18 (Bk. V, Ch. II, 7–8).
10 Cassian, *Collationes*, XXIIII, 297–298, translated in Cassian, *The Conferences*, 379.
11 Caldwell, "A Medieval Patchwork Song," 140.

12 Penketh, "Women and Books of Hours," 271.
13 Shephard et al., "Music, Silence," 492.
14 The wedding scene is neither biblical nor part of the traditional Marian cycle across the hours. On the cycle of visual imagery in the Office of the Virgin, see Wieck, *Time Sanctified*, 60–66. In a lower register of this folio, the young Mary is pictured weaving in the Temple, a symbol of procreation.
15 The instruments from left to right appear to be a bowed rebec, lute, harp, and portative organ.
16 My thanks to Laudon Schuett and Adam Knight Gilbert for assistance in deciphering these instruments.
17 Hughes, *Medieval Manuscripts*, 23.
18 See, for example, the *C*s written for the incipit of the versicle *Diffusa est gratia* in Wroclaw, Biblioteka Uniwersytecka, I F 401, fol. 178r.
19 The formula is no different for flex tones (not the mediant cadences) commonly found in modes 2, 3, 5, or 8.
20 For example, versicles would fall after the nocturns of Matins and after the hymns of Lauds and Vespers.
21 The texts of both the versicle and response are drawn from Psalm 44:3.
22 There is some risk in relying on Dominican service books to supply tones for Roman usage, as the Franciscan liturgy provided the template for the Use of Rome. My thanks to Rebecca Baltzer and Joseph Dyer for their counsel on these questions about the versicle.
23 Reflecting varying levels of solemnity, festal, solemn, and ferial tones for *Deus in adiutorium* are given in the *LU*, 250–51, 263–264.
24 The ferial tone in the *LU* (263–64) shows the doxology and the versicle cadences matching.
25 For a series of French monophonic and polyphonic tropes of the verse, see Caldwell, "A Medieval Patchwork Song." On key polyphonic settings of Psalm 69:2 in the thirteenth and fourteenth centuries, see Maschke, "*Deus in adiutorium intende* Revisited."
26 On the development and evolution of the rosary, see Winston-Allen, *Stories of the Rose*.
27 For an example linking the Pater noster and Ave Maria with the Seven Prayers of St. Gregory, see New Haven, Yale University, Beinecke Rare Book and Manuscript Library, MS 435, 111v–112r.
28 Mahrt, *The Musical Shape of the Liturgy*, 8, 136.
29 For a dedicated study of this manuscript, see Gardet, *Les Heures d'Aimée de Saluces*.
30 For another rubricated designation of the versicle and response at the end of the Pater noster, see BnF, lat. 1157, fol. 90v.
31 The "Ave Maria" salutation, for instance, was formulated as a versicle and response (CAO 7958) and sometimes placed after the antiphon *Salve regina* at the end of Compline in the Office of the Virgin. In these cases, a prayer always followed, thus giving a memorial-like shape to the devotion. See, for example, BnF, n.a.l. 3188, fol. 69r and BnF, lat. 923, fol. 52r.
32 A large series of consecutive versicles and responses prescribed after the Litany and Psalm 69 can be found, for example, in Philadelphia, Free Library of Philadelphia, Rare Book Department, Lewis E 214, fols. 99v–100r and BnF, n.a.l. 3120, fols. 99v–100r.
33 For an exception, see LBL, Add. MS 27697, fol. 171r.
34 For this benediction, see *LU* 119–120.

Part II
Music beyond the Offices

6 The Seven Penitential Psalms

*

Hailed by the mid-nineteenth-century Anglican priest and hymn writer John Mason Neale as the "seven companions" to the canonical hours of the liturgical day,[1] the Seven Penitential Psalms—namely, Psalms 6, 31, 37, 50, 101, 129, and 142—fall in a section between the Office of the Virgin and the Office of the Dead in the *horae*. The seven psalms form the first part of a sequence, which includes the Litany and the Office of the Dead. These sections focus the devotee on contritional prayer that could decrease the time the soul spent in purgatory.[2] The progression in books of hours was also known to be associated with funeral ceremonies. Some have pointed to the sixth-century Roman statesman, monk, and commentator Cassiodorus as the first to single out the seven psalms as being expressly penitential in the *Expositio Psalmorum*, a verse-by-verse expounding of complete Psalter with lessons for contemporary Christians.[3] Most agree, though, that the Carolingian champion of learning Alcuin of York is first to comment directly on the Seven Penitential Psalms as a distinct group.[4]

Medieval Christians encountered the Seven Penitential Psalms in different ways. Besides the integration into funeral rites, recitation of the group could also be assigned as penance in confession. However, the sacrament of confession for the laity might occur only once per year, as prescribed in the Fourth Lateran Council of 1215. Left to their own spiritual care in the absence of priest for most of the year, the faithful would have sought devices like the Seven Penitential Psalms to manage their purity and remediate their sins on an ongoing basis.[5] In addition to the act of penance itself, the group of seven psalms presented an opportunity for devotees to perform "supererogatory" duties known from eleventh-century monastic life. The act of supererogation constitutes the performance of good works beyond what God expects. For example, certain psalms were required as part of the daily cursus in monasteries and convents, while the Office of the Virgin and the Office of the Dead were part of an auxiliary devotional program that a monk or nun could undertake. The Seven Penitential Psalms as a group were further included among the supererogatory actions above the call of duty.[6] Supplemental psalms requiring a physical position to demonstrate contrition, sometimes known as prostrate psalms, also fell into the supererogatory category.[7]

Considered a particularly efficacious subset of the Psalter because of the emphasis on the acknowledgment of sin and the process of penitence, the Seven Penitential Psalms had inestimable value in prayer life, but they also constituted a component of children's primary education. In the *petites écoles* that local authorities set up to promote learning and basic literacy in French cities and towns, instructors focused attention on reading the texts of basic Latin prayers, which included the Seven Penitential Psalms in addition to the much shorter Pater noster and Ave Maria.[8] After the group of 7 were learned, the 15 Gradual Psalms (a

DOI: 10.4324/9781003140511-9

contiguous series, Psalms 119–133) represented another practicable step toward mastering the entire Psalter. That vernacular translations, paraphrases, and commentary on the Seven Penitential Psalms survive in significant numbers in the late Middle Ages is an indication of their centrality in devotional life.[9] In the early years of print in France, the Seven Penitential Psalms could be found in translation with French texts parallel to the Latin.[10] The popularity of these particular psalms for all ages did not wane in the age of Reformation. As it concerns engagement around these psalms in early modern England, Clare Costley King'oo has noted an "eruption of activity around the Penitential Psalms, as the series was translated, paraphrased, contested, fragmented, set to music, copied, printed, marketed, smuggled across the Channel, and so on." For centuries then, the effectiveness of these psalms of atonement made them a vital part of Christians' path to deliverance.

The style and structure of each of the penitential psalms differs, but Psalm 31 represents an anomaly for its use of the past tense, in contrast to the present tense employed by the other six. Further, it might better be classified as a song of praise or thanksgiving, rather than a uniform psalm of penitence, on account of its emphasis on rejoicing as much as adversity.[11] The remaining six psalms operate on something of a spectrum of lamentation. The plea of the psalmist may concentrate on the recognition of sin, a petition for God's clemency and pardon, or the resolve to strive for virtue, leaving entanglements with iniquity behind. Psalms 50 and 37 occupy more confessional ground, whereas Psalms 6 and 101 are more forward looking, approaching Psalm 31 for not being fully centered on repentance. Psalms 129 and 142 rest in between these pairs, pivoting between admission of guilt and the hope of redemption.[12] The journey through, and rewards of, the Seven Penitential Psalms was clear, though. In his commentary on the first penitential psalm (Psalm 6), the fourteenth-century English mystic Richard Rolle wrote, "The seuen psalmes of the whilk this is the first begynnys all in sorowand gretynge and bitternes of forthynkynge, & thai end in certaynte of pardoun" ("The seven psalms of which this is the first begin in sorrowing lamentation and in bitterness of repentance, and they end in certainty of pardon").[13]

Musicologists have paid scant attention to the Seven Penitential Psalms, despite the pervasiveness of these texts in medieval devotional practice. The series of psalms was rarely set in polyphony because of its length. Orlande de Lassus is probably the most famous composer of any period to render these memorable verses in an extended choral work.[14] The book of hours presents an important venue for studying the Seven Penitential Psalms from an "ear first" perspective. This chapter will explore three aspects of these widely practiced psalms of confession. First is a review of the musical backdrop associated with subject of David, whose image typically adorns the beginning of the series. The psalmist's instrument—the harp—plays no small role in the visual program, but its curious presence at once in the foreground and background of scenes deserves a closer look. We will then examine cues for performance, similar to the other psalms throughout books of hours. Finally, we note the enduring appearance and unusual structure of the antiphon *Ne reminiscaris Domine*, which traditionally frames the Seven Penitential Psalms.

David and the Seven Penitential Psalms

We have seen that David's name sometimes emerged in rubrics placed before psalms of the offices, but the belief in his authorship of the Psalms was all but assured when the Seven Penitential Psalms were isolated in books of hours. Illustrated psalters and *horae* almost always featured a portrait of the psalmist. In these depictions, David is drawn in various environments, but usually in the act of prayer.[15] His specific connection to the harp—conspicuously drawn in books of hours—may be traced to 1 Samuel 16, which presents the story of King Saul, who was troubled by an evil spirit from the Lord. To quell his agitation, Saul commanded his servants to search for an artful player of the harp. One servant suggests the valiant, wise, and handsome David, son of Jesse, who was talented on the instrument. The servants collect David from Jesse in exchange for bread, wine, and a young goat, and the young man plays for Saul, calming his anger. The evil spirit departs him after the therapeutic effects of the music.[16] David appears with his harp or a similar chordophone (such as the kithara) in imagery from as early as the eighth century, and his association with the instrument in visual culture lasted throughout the Middle Ages in different versions of the author portrait. Elizabeth Teviotdale has proposed that this pairing may reflect the ancient image of a poet accompanying himself on a stringed instrument.[17] We will see that, while David's association with the harp is very much present in books of hours, he is rarely if ever accompanying himself. Suzanne Wijsman views the harp more generally as broad signifier of the psalms as a genre.[18] Others have posited deeper significance of the stringed instrument. The author of the late fourteenth-century English *Book to a Mother*, a moral treatise and epistolary guidebook, compares David's harp to a righteous human soul in an extended analogy.[19]

Three different images from later fifteenth-century books of hours reveal the common positioning of the harp in illustrations of David kneeling in prayer at the opening of the penitential psalms. First, in a book of hours belonging to Marguerite d'Orléans (d. 1466), Countess of Étampes and granddaughter of French King Charles V, we find David away from the Holy City (Figure 6.1). Kneeling in the act of prayer, the aged king humbles himself before God the Father, who peers down from heaven. Cloaked in lavish fur-lined regalia with a gold purse, the crowned David has laid down his harp in the foreground, an instrument of seven strings, perhaps providing a subtle connection to the number of psalms that lie ahead in the book. With hands folded, the royal supplicant nearly establishes direct eye contact with his Maker. Still, the harp's size commands attention as one of the few prominent objects in the image. While the eye cannot ignore this conspicuous musical instrument resting on the ground beside the king, David's gaze directs us heavenward to the Almighty, pulling Marguerite's attention away from the instrument and into the king's entreaty.

A similar scene is found in BnF, Ars. 1194 (Figure 6.2), a book of hours from around 1460 with illuminations attributed to Antoine de Lonhy, who spent the early part of his career in Toulouse, around the time when this book was made.[20] The David miniature, again at the head of the seven psalms preceding Psalm 6 ("Domine ne in furore tuo"), features the artist's brilliant use of color and rendering of clothing with heavy folds. With arms crossed on his chest instead of hands folded, the king kneels in prayer with his eyes raised to heaven in submission to God the Father, likewise missing direct contact but making an unmistakable connection. Within the familiar wilderness backdrop, the harp—now 15 strings—once more lies in the foreground, though more prominently than in Figure 6.1. Antoine communicates the instrument's status by having the oversized harp rest on David himself in addition to a nearby rock.[21] The user would be amply assured that the king is a musician, who has set down his instrument for prayer.

In the "Chasteauneuf Hours" (BnF, n.a.l. 3210) prepared between 1483 and 1503 in northeast France's Lorraine duchy, David's harp appears in connection with a different scene at the beginning of the Seven Penitential Psalms—the king's encounter with Bathsheba. In this alternative setting, the harp is again not the center of attention but emerges in association with the wife of Uriah the Hittite, with whom the king would commit adultery and murder her husband. The narrative from 2 Samuel 11–12 set the stage for David's penitence, and the illustration of the event was increasingly prevalent in books of hours from the 1480s

124 *Music beyond the Offices*

Figure 6.1 Seven Penitential Psalms opening with David in prayer. Paris, BnF, lat. 1156B, fol. 179r.

Figure 6.2 Seven Penitential Psalms opening with David in prayer. Paris, BnF, Ars. Ms-1194 réserve, fol. 93r.

Figure 6.3 Seven Penitential Psalms opening with David and Bathsheba. Paris, BnF, n.a.l. 3210, fol. 63r.

onward.[22] In this miniature (Figure 6.3), the king spies the beautiful Bathsheba from his palace window, bathing in a pool. The scene captures the moment of ultimate temptation, before David sends out a servant to bring Bathsheba to him. Paul Saenger has noted that the erotic presence of Bathsheba in the later fifteenth century fits with a general shift to private experiences with reading in general—books of hours in particular.[23] He proposed that the titillating scenes on one hand illustrate the "vices for which penance was required" but at the same time are "consciously intended to excite the *voyeur* of the book."[24] On the face of it, Saenger's proposal might be difficult to reconcile with the fact that female ownership of books of hours increased dramatically in the late fifteenth century.[25] Clare Costley King'oo more strictly associates the Bathsheba scene to the act of penance, noting that these later images "participate in a reorganization of confessional practice around sexual concerns."[26] We may note in this image that the harp is not only peripheral and partially cut off by the artist's decorative border but also inaccessible to the psalmist himself, who rests on the windowsill well above ground level. Still one of only a few objects in the scene, the instrument lies upright against the palace wall, relegated to the status of a symbol of David's music and poetry.

In all three of these images, the harp and the sound it could make attracts some attention, but it is not the central focus of the scene preceding the texts of the Seven Penitential Psalms. The act of setting down the harp for prayer is nonbiblical, as is the instrument's role in the Bathsheba scene, making the consistent presence of the plucked chordophone across the corpus of books of hours all the more curious. Martin van Schaik suggests that when David is not actively playing or tuning the harp in visual imagery, the harp is merely an identifying attribute of the wise king.[27] The abandoned harp could very well be a straightforward reminder of the poet-musician, but we might dare to probe the phenomenon more deeply based on the stringed instrument's steady appearance in books of hours. The scene of David and the harp may for instance refresh the sonic world that has hovered over the book in general, encouraging users to be transported into an imagined sound-space while preparing for a solemn state of penitence. On the other hand, the unplayed harp separated from David may also signal to the user to seek silence before engaging with the psalms, just as the king's artistic activity is sidelined. Music in this case may be understood as an earthly temptation, as Augustine experienced, giving empty pleasure if received as raw sound.[28] Depictions of the nude Bathsheba bathing further confuse our understanding of the harp. She is an even greater temptation for the king, symbolizing the act of adultery and making musical performance seem hardly a sinful pursuit by comparison. A final image moreover complicates the question of the role of music in the Bathsheba scene and by association, across the group of seven psalms.

A Lyonnais book of hours from ca. 1500 (Walters Museum MS W. 447) bears miniatures from the circle of Jean Bourdichon, who served as official court painter to four French kings and worked in a variety of artistic media.[29] The scene with David and Bathsheba that opens the penitential psalms (Figure 6.4) has nearly the same orientation as that in Figure 6.3. From a similar window in the castle on the image's left side, David fixes his eyes on the young bathing woman. The old king is not alone, presumably attended by one of his servants, who would be commanded to bring her to the king. Bathsheba establishes her gaze away from the onlookers or is simply unsuspecting, as they are beyond the bushes that separate the pool from the palace.

In this version, David holds on to his harp, a rare occurrence for this scene in books of hours. He is, on the other hand, in no position to play it, as it hangs over the windowsill. Yet, it is the closest we might see the instrument to the king. In this unusual instance, we are challenged to consider whether the handheld harp is a distraction from the potential sin of

Figure 6.4 Seven Penitential Psalms opening with David and Bathsheba. Walters Museum MS W. 447, fol. 74r. Credit: The Walters Art Museum, Baltimore.

adultery in the making or whether the music is indeed a temptation in itself and a contributing agent toward sin.

Performing the Penitential Psalms

From the multilayered meanings of the harp at the head of the Seven Penitential Psalms, we may tread delicately into questions of performance of the psalm group in books of hours, exploring two key questions: (1) is there motivation for reciting the Seven Penitential Psalms versus, say, reading them silently? And (2) what clues may indicate physical or cognitive engagement in this set of psalms? The psalms in general are dramatic texts, pleading words of forgiveness and restorative action delivered or penned by their presumed creator, David. These seven as a set have been noted in connection with performative action. Writing about the duties of teenage boys training to enter the monastery, the eleventh-century Anglo-Saxon monk Ælfric Bata noted that the young men sang the Seven Penitential Psalms as they washed themselves in the morning before attending church.[30] Addressing the faithful at large, Pope Innocent III (r. 1198–1216) decreed that the Seven Penitential Psalms should be recited in Lent. At the start of this penitential season, on Ash Wednesday, there was also a tradition of inviting citizens who had sinned gravely to make a public penance at the celebration of ashes. A bishop would bless a penitential garment, known as a *cilicium* ("hair shirt," usually made from the hair of mountain goats), and sprinkle it with ashes made from palms of the previous year. The sinners would don the *cilicium* for the 40 days of Lent, and the laypeople gathered would sing the seven psalms framed by the antiphon *Ne reminiscaris Domine*, a melody about which more will be said later. During the singing of the penitential psalms, the penitents were dismissed from the church on account of their sins, mirroring Adam's fall from grace.[31] Despite the dramatic performance of the seven psalms in this annual public ceremony, Christians were more likely to encounter this grouping in the context of funerals.

The active recitation of the Seven Penitential Psalms, whether in private or public, was particularly efficacious, serving to remedy one's relationship with the Almighty through the promise to behave uprightly. As Annie Sutherland has written on the seven psalms, "[N]ot only was their recitation believed to have the potential to actively restore one to a right relationship with the divine, but they are also closely focused on the performance of God's will."[32] When voiced in the spirit of genuine remorse, these psalms may transform the standing of the penitent in the face of the creator in the hope of a lasting reconciliation.

Scribes of books of hours seem to anticipate some kind of performance of the seven psalm texts grouped together as a unit. These psalms are always written out in full in this important section before the Litany. Two of the penitential psalms—6 and 50—are repeated in the Office of the Dead and are occasionally abbreviated or cross-referenced in the latter case. Psalm 129 appears in both the Office of the Dead and the preceding Office of the Virgin. While this psalm is written out in full for the Marian office, it is always written out again for the Seven Penitential Psalms. The recopying tells us that compilers seem to have considered the seven psalms an inviolable set and were unwilling to send users elsewhere when engaged with this hallowed series. Visually, the seven psalms of penitence have the appearance of any psalm assigned to an office. Manuscripts reveal different clues to performance, similar to the psalms found in the offices in books of hours. At minimum, we would see a capital letter to articulate the beginning of each verse. The level of decoration and the positon of the capital will of course vary from there. Line-fills may further demarcate the poetic verses of the psalms and may alternate two color tones in different ways, evocative of the practice of alternation we witness in the long history of psalm singing.

The Lorrainese Chasteauneuf Hours, mentioned earlier for its image of David and Bathsheba, offers additional insight into cues to performance of the Seven Penitential Psalms. Figure 6.5 presents a snapshot of the series from just past its midpoint, in transition from Psalm 50 to Psalm 101. The line-fills are present for a few verses, differing in their use of color; however, the alternating use of red and blue in the decorative capital letters will remind us of the *alternatim* plainchant practice in monastic life. Within the psalm verses themselves, a colon indicates the medial distinction discussed in Chapter 1, causing either a pause (if read) or a simple cadential figure (if sung). Only one verse ("Sacrificium Deo ..." [Psalm 50:19]) lacks a colon; fortuitously, the line break between "contribulatus" and "cor" might be considered a kind of punctuation. As with the psalm verse above it, the scribe had already exceeded the text block, but placing a colon here might give a more sloppy appearance. In the second half of that same verse, the text again overruns the space. This time, the user is redirected by a red and gold *pied de mouche*, which cuts into the next line but allows clear separation of the verb "despicies" in completion of the psalm verse.

Books of hours are split on the question of including the *Gloria Patri* at the end of each of the Seven Penitential Psalms. The doxology customarily caps the end of any psalm, prompting the repetition of the antiphon stated at the outset. But groups of psalms framed by a single antiphon present a decision: provide the *Gloria patri* at the end of each psalm or offer it only at the end of the set? The scribe of the Chasteauneuf Hours opted to provide the doxology at the end of each psalm and moreover to truncate it to an incipit of four words. The decision to abbreviate the *Gloria patri* would do no harm to users engaged with the seven psalms; they knew the doxology, which was among the most frequently uttered texts in the *horae*, given the number of psalms it contained. In the Chasteauneuf Hours, the incipit for the *Gloria patri* left space for a rubric ("psalmus d[avi]d") to conclude that line, marking the beginning of Psalm 101 and a reminder of David's authorship. "Domine exaudi orationem meam" could thus begin flush on the left with a decorative capital spanning two lines.

Ne reminiscaris Domine

Invariably, the antiphon *Ne reminiscaris Domine* arrives at the end of the Seven Penitential Psalms in books of hours. Enclosing a group of psalms rather than one psalm, the antiphon seems to have acted like those one might find in the four minor hours of the Office of the Virgin. An incipit for *Ne reminiscaris Domine* however does not always appear before the series of psalms. When the incipit precedes the inaugural Psalm 6 in illustrated books of hours, it may occasionally be placed before the opening miniature, detached from the psalm and located alongside a rubric signaling the entire set.[33] Typically just the first two words "Ne reminiscaris" are given for the incipit when it occurs. The complete text of the antiphon, unveiled at the conclusion of the seven psalms, takes a verse from the Book of Tobit (3:3) as its model. The subject of a colorful historical narrative, Tobit was a virtuous and wealthy Jew who was struck blind. The particular verse is drawn from the larger opening section of the book concerning the main character's plight. Notably, the text of the antiphon inverts the biblical text, and the first-person singular ("mei," "meis," "mea," "meorum") becomes the first-person plural ("nostra," "nostrorum," "nostris"). The meaning is basically unaffected, but the latter alteration may remind us of the public nature of the Ash Wednesday service, for example, as well as the corporate spirit of the Litany, which is slated immediately after the conclusion of the antiphon *Ne reminiscaris Domine* in books of hours.

Figure 6.5 Penitential Psalms 50 and 101 (partial). Paris, BnF, n.a.l. 3210, fol. 67r.

Latin Vulgate (Tob 3:3)

Nunc Domine memor esto mei ne vindictam sumas de peccatis meis neque reminiscaris delicta mea vel parentum meorum.

And now, O Lord, think of me, and take not revenge from my sins, neither remember my offenses, nor those of my parents.

Antiphon

Ne reminiscaris Domine delicta nostra vel parentum nostrorum neque vindictam sumas de peccatis nostris.

Remember not, O Lord, our offenses, nor those of our parents, and take not revenge from our sins.

Because the Seven Penitential Psalms were not positioned together as a series in liturgical books, *Ne reminiscaris Domine* did not exist in connection with these sources. Rather, the antiphon (CAO 3861) appears in the office of Tobit, which was widely found across the European continent and in all 12 of the earliest sources of office chant as cataloged by Hesbert. There is no fixed feast day for the antiphon, as it falls in a variable period calculated after Pentecost.[34] In late medieval French breviaries and antiphoners in particular, *Ne reminiscaris Domine* is consistently prescribed in offices executed during the 20-plus weeks of summer. Sometimes it is designated as the antiphon for the Magnificat in a week assigned to readings from Tobit. In cases where *Ne reminiscaris Domine* is not specified to accompany the Magnificat, it may be encountered in a section of consecutive antiphons—sometimes 15 or 20 in a row—listed in the liturgical books designated for summer usage.

Several variants exist for *Ne reminiscaris Domine*, but the chant normally bears a mode 4 profile, unfolding in a few modest phrases (Example 6.1). In its first phrase, the melody begins and ends on a C, an unusual resting point in mode 4. The melody traverses the tonal space beneath the final without touching the notoriously unstable B that theoretically provides a boundary to the lower tetrachord. For the text "vel parentum nostrorum," the melody rises above the final, but only by two pitches (*f* and *g*), now spanning just a pentachord before reaching the midpoint of the antiphon on E, its eventual final. At the word "vindictam," the range creeps up another tone, touching *a* in its brief journey through the tetrachord above the final. The melody for the finishing words "de peccatis nostris" descends beneath the final from *g* before rising up to E to finish.

Performance indications are surprisingly rare for *Ne reminiscaris Domine* in books of hours. In BnF, lat. 1170, a book of hours prepared for Marie de Rieux (d. 1465), wife of Louis d'Amboise,[35] we can view the antiphon in context following the conclusion of Psalm 142, the last of the Seven Penitential Psalms (Figure 6.6). After the *Gloria patri* caps the psalm, the French rubric "Antiene" signals the genre of *Ne reminiscaris Domine* and prompts a reduction in the size of the script, a feature we have come to expect with antiphons. No punctuation

Example 6.1 Antiphon, *Ne reminiscaris Domine*. Transcribed from BnF, lat. 15182, fol. 124v with text emendations.

Figure 6.6 Antiphon, *Ne reminiscaris Domine*. Paris, BnF, lat. 1170, fol. 54v.

134 *Music beyond the Offices*

Figure 6.7 Antiphon, *Ne reminiscaris Domine*. Paris, BnF, n.a.l. 3210, fol. 70r.

or unusual spacing would guide Marie in the experience of this simply contoured melody. More details emerge in the Chasteauneuf Hours, though (Figure 6.7). The concluding antiphon for the seven psalms sets up similarly to that shown in Figure 6.6, prefaced now by the Latin rubric "Antiphona." In this example, the scribe provided colons to separate the phrases of *Ne reminiscaris Domine*. A tripartite division of the text unfolds across less than three full lines of the antiphon's text; pauses are suggested after the words "nostra" and "nostrorum." The partitioning shows sensitivity to the phrasing of the antiphon and its sense units when executed vocally. Using Example 6.1, the first phrase spans 19 notes; the second, 10; and the final phrase, 20. This seems persuasive, as a combination of the first two phrases could exceed a reasonable breath to accomplish in song.[36] Thus, the short second phrase preceded by a pause in a logical place grammatically—before the conjunction "vel"—would be necessary.[37]

In about three-quarters of the books of hours under review, the antiphon *Ne reminiscaris Domine* continues with additional text: "Parce Domine, parce pro populo tuo, quem redemisti precioso sanguine tuo; ne in eternum irascaris nobis" ("Spare, Lord, spare your people, whom you have redeemed with your precious blood; be not angry with us forever").[38] In these examples, the "Parce Domine" text elides seamlessly with the end of the antiphon *Ne reminiscaris Domine* to conclude the Seven Penitential Psalms—so seamlessly that they may even strike one as a single text, as in Figure 6.8. Scribes do not appear to have ever separated the texts with a rubric to indicate a new chant or change of texture. Occasionally however, there is some indication of a performative break between the end of *Ne reminiscaris Domine* and the *Parce Domine* extension, as in Figure 6.9. In this example, a capital letter "P" of "Parce" with yellow *pied-de-mouche* separates the distinct texts and matches the size and color of the "N" of *Ne*. Again, there is no shift in genre, suggesting that the additional text could be a part of the previous antiphon.

Ne reminiscaris Domine has already been shown to be a self-contained chant. So how did the "Parce Domine" addendum relate to the antiphon, particularly in musical practice? In fact, no clear liturgical tradition supports the fused appearance of *Ne reminiscaris Domine* and "Parce Domine" seen in books of hours. The appended text is not known to have ever followed *Ne reminiscaris Domine* in extant service books. The supplemental "Parce Domine" by itself corresponds closely to a distinct mode 5 antiphon *Parce Domine* (CAO 4219), which survives in a handful of notated sources, but was also an early processional chant of the Old Roman corpus, apparently prescribed by Gregory the Great for the Ember Days of Advent in Rome.[39] In the later Middle Ages, this nonbiblical text was sung on different occasions, from Ash Wednesday to Easter Sunday and beyond. Two melismatic Alleluias follow the chant in Eastertide, though these do not punctuate the text in books of hours. *Parce Domine* is also listed for processions and as part of the major Litany of Saints, which took place on the feast of St. Mark (April 25), a day that always fell in the Easter season and no doubt commanded the jubilant Alleluias.[40] This is significant as one or more antiphons occasionally preceded the Litany procession, and the "Parce Domine" text directly precedes the Litany in books of hours.[41]

If the texts of *Ne reminiscaris Domine* (CAO 3861) and *Parce Domine* (CAO 4219) flowed together in books of hours, the melody of the latter antiphon would have been no easy fit with the former. In the few sources that transmit *Parce Domine*, the mode 5 melody would boldly contrast with the mode 4 *Ne reminiscaris Domine*. The musically conservative host antiphon also carries no more than two syllables per note; whereas, ecstatic melismas reverberate throughout *Parce Domine*. CAO 4219 is therefore not likely to be the melody intended to attach to *Ne reminiscaris Domine* of the Seven Penitential Psalms. A modest

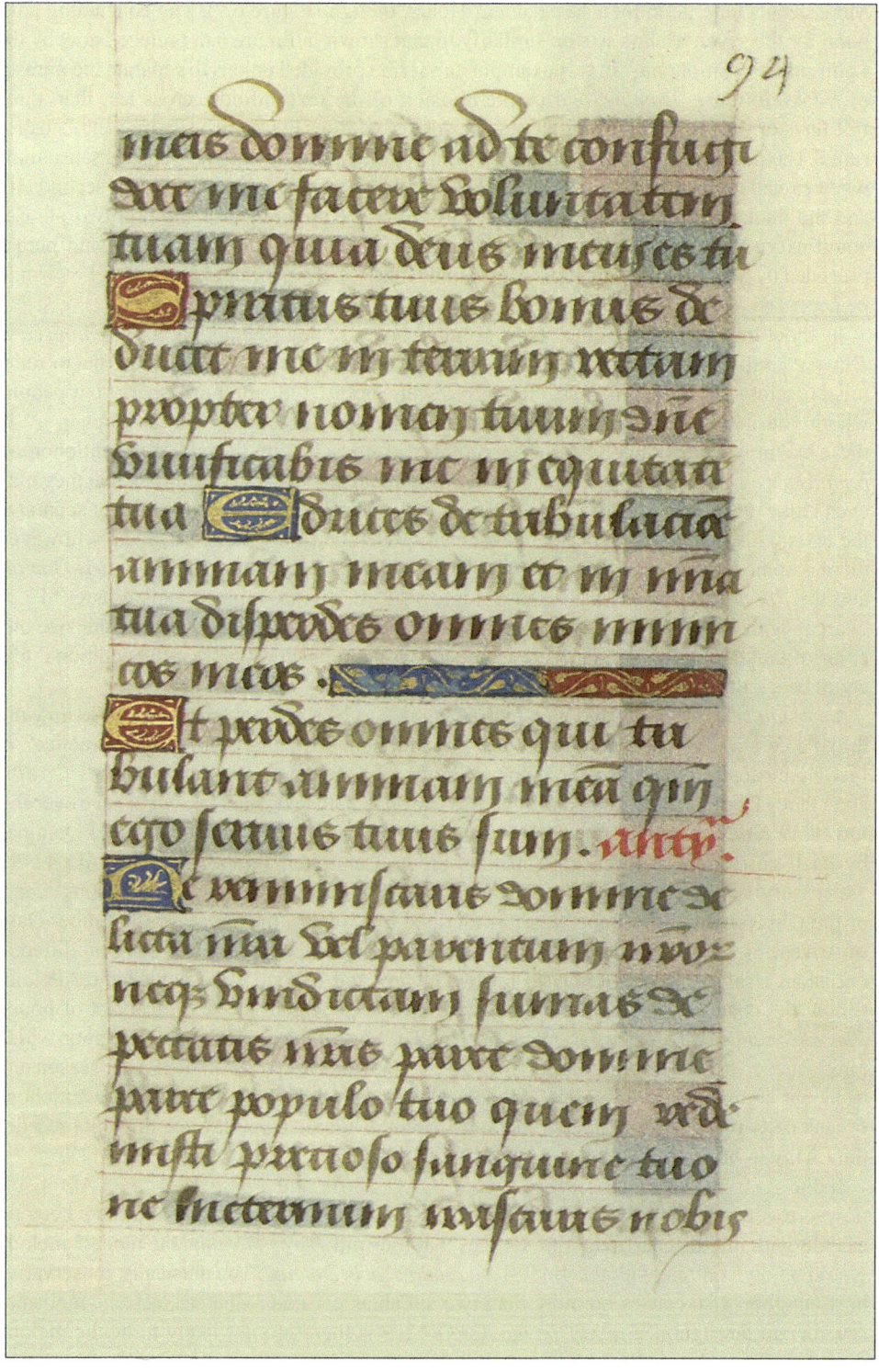

Figure 6.8 Antiphon, *Ne reminiscaris Domine*. Paris, BnF, lat. 1374, fol. 94r.

Figure 6.9 Antiphon, *Ne reminiscaris Domine*. Paris, BnF, Ars. Ms-637 réserve, fol. 105r.

antiphon for the text "Parce Domine," whose origin is unknown, is transmitted in the *Liber usualis*, but its modal final of *D* is likewise incompatible with *Ne reminiscaris Domine*.[42] With liturgical sources pointing toward use in processions and in connection with the Litany, it may be the case that "Parce Domine" was a chanted preamble to the opening Kyrie eleison of the Litany in books of hours, which always followed the seven psalms. If this is true, then scribes of books of hours have largely misled their users into thinking that "Parce Domine" is part of the ritual concluding the Seven Penitential Psalms. The misplaced assignment of the prayer text would indeed be a rare misstep in the transmission of ritual practice.

Tonal ambiguity and ethos

This chapter has navigated the periphery of the penitential psalms in books of hours. It established a context for the history and usage of Seven Penitential Psalms, examined David's harp in miniatures preceding the set of psalms, and considered the antiphon enclosing the entire group—*Ne reminiscaris Domine*. However, besides the cues to active engagement addressed earlier, nothing has been said about the sounds of the psalms themselves. By unlocking the music of the mode 4 antiphon *Ne reminiscaris Domine* that frames the series, it would not be unreasonable to assume that the psalms themselves could also be rendered in this plagal mode if performed aloud or relived with the mind's ear.

Because the Seven Penitential Psalms consume much space in books of hours and thus much time in the devotional experience, we might briefly consider what it would be like for users to experience an extended mode 4 orientation for the entire set. What effect could the infusion of dozens of mode 4 verses have? Modal affect or ethos is notoriously uncertain from the development of modal theory from the ancient Greek traditions onward. While it is tempting for example to equate mode 1 with a "minor" (and thus a sad- or serious-sounding) musical tonality, the "Dorian" mode had variable meanings throughout history, and nothing overtly lamenting. For classical theorists, mode 1 projected a "steadfast" or even "majestic" affect. In some late medieval ecclesiastical circles, it was considered a flexible tonality, suitable to all affections, according to theorists from Juan Gil de Zamora in the thirteenth century to Bartolomé Ramos de Pareja two centuries later. Similarly, mode 4 was perceived as austere and reflective of anger by classical authors, but by the late Middle Ages, others found this mode as "caressing," "chatty," bordering on "lascivious." Such descriptors fly in the face of the affect a supplicant might expect when reciting the Seven Penitential Psalms. By this time, however, modal affect became bound up with the practice of polyphony among theorists. The most important music theorist of the sixteenth century, Gioseffo Zarlino, lumped mode 4 into a group of others that had sad and languid qualities emanating from the minor third above the final.[43] Nicola Vicentino, another mid-sixteenth-century theorist, likewise regarded the fourth mode as "sad," with the potential of being "funereal."[44] Between these two later theorists, we at least come closer to an affect we might expect to be connected with the Seven Penitential Psalms.

Of course, there was nothing forcing the owner of a book of hours to hear or articulate a particular mode for recitation of this penitential series. The antiphon *Ne reminiscaris Domine* by itself suggests a ready mode for the seven psalms, but by no means did all books of hours present the antiphon at the head of the section to orient the layperson. Even if embarking on the Seven Penitential Psalms in mode 4, the user may recall any number of termination formulas, permitting a variety of musical experiences with the set. Some of the penitential psalms are also duplicated in the Offices of the Virgin and the Dead, paired with antiphons that would have steered users to other modes. As mentioned, Psalm 129 ("De profundis clamavi") appears not only in the Seven Penitential Psalms but also three other times in the principal offices for the Virgin and for the Dead. Although no antiphon encloses the psalm in two of the three occasions (Lauds of both offices), Psalm 129 is paired with the mode 8 antiphon *Si iniquitates observaveris* at the Vespers service in the Office of the Dead. The accompanying psalm could thus have been heard in connection with a mode 8 tone and termination formula. Psalms 6 and 50 likewise appear elsewhere in books of hours, both revisited in the Office of the Dead with mode 8 and mode 1 antiphons, respectively. Of course, any of these could also have been recited monotonously as text. Local practice might have also played a powerful role in how the penitential psalms were retrieved as voiced sound.

*

As shown in this chapter, the Seven Penitential Psalms present some difficulty in hearing music with consistency. Since the series does not occur as a group in liturgical books, we must look elsewhere for testimony about its performance. The psalm tones on which to envoice the seven psalms are by no means clear. The steady mode 4 antiphon *Ne reminiscaris Domine* surrounding the group of seven psalms might have dictated a formula in that mode throughout the recitation of these select psalms, but the disruption of that antiphon with a supplemental "Parce Domine" clouds the unnotated reception of these chants when prescribed in books of hours. The Litany of the Saints ensues after "Parce Domine" and is perhaps linked to it ritually. Like the penitential psalms, the Litany also remains modally ambiguous in some respects. But the musical content and performance traditions of the Litany are more assured in this part of the book of hours, as the spirit of penitence and concern about earthly plight and salvation gather momentum with the intercession of the heavenly throng.

Notes

1. Neale and Littledale, *Commentary on the Psalms*, 1: 125.
2. Costley King'oo, *Miserere Mei*, 18.
3. Cassiodorus, *Expositio psalmorum*, 97: 71. It is possible that Possidius's mid-fifth-century vita of St. Augustine recognized the penitential grouping even earlier (*Sancti Augustini vita*, 140). The author's intriguing reference, however, does not reveal the precise collection of psalms his friend had in mind. Augustine himself, who wrote at length on the Psalms, never called attention to this subset of seven.
4. Alcuinus, *Expositio in Psalmos Poenitentiales*, in *PL* 100: cols. 569–596.
5. Costley King'oo, *Miserere Mei*, 17.
6. Driscoll, "The Seven Penitential Psalms," 174.
7. *Psalmi prostrati* were said by monks at Cluny in the late eleventh century following several of the canonical hours in the winter. See Hunt, *Cluny Under St. Hugh*, 101–103.
8. Margolin, "L'apprentissage des éléments et l'education," 1: 73–104.
9. For example, see the fifteenth-century translation of an Old French commentary on the Seven Penitential Psalms into English by Dame Eleanor Hull, *The Seven Psalms*.
10. Reinburg, *French Books of Hours*, 96.
11. Gunkel, *Die Psalmen*, 135.
12. Costley King'oo, *Miserere Mei*, 6–7.
13. Text and translation from Bramley, *The Psalter of Psalms of David*, 21.
14. Lassus, *Psalmi Davidis poenitentiales*.
15. The Seven Penitential Psalms in books of hours from the thirteenth and fourteenth centuries were more likely to display the *Salvator mundi* image of Christ as Judge at the end of the world. See Wieck, *Time Sanctified*, 97.
16. 1 Samuel 16: 14–23.
17. Teviotdale, "Music and Pictures in the Middle Ages," 182.
18. Wijsman, "Silent Sounds," 317.
19. *Book to a Mother*, in which a cleric dispatches moral advice to his mother, survives as Oxford, Bodleian Libraries, MS Bodl. 416.
20. On the illuminator's period in Toulouse, see Elsig, *Antoine de Lonhy*, 33–44. On his connection to the manuscript, see details provided in the online finding aid (gallica.bnf.fr) for BnF, Ars. 1194.
21. For an even larger harp, nearly the size of David himself, see Philadelphia Museum of Art, Department of Prints, Drawings, and Photographs, MS 1945-65-8, fol. 110v. For a scene featuring musicians playing harp for David, in addition to the harp he has set down, see Philadelphia, Philadelphia Art Museum, Department of Prints, Drawings, and Photographs, MS 1945-65-13, 179.
22. Costley, "David, Bathsheba, and the Penitential Psalms," 1241–1244.
23. Saenger, "Reading in the Later Middle Ages," 146–147.
24. Saenger, "Books of Hours and the Reading Habits," 156.
25. Bell, "Medieval Women Book Owners," 746–748. Elizabeth Leesti suggests a negative attitude toward sexual themes ("A Late Fifteenth-Century Parisian Book of Hours," 46–47).
26. Costley King'oo, *Miserere Mei*, 36.
27. Van Schaik, *The Harp in the Middle Ages*, 38, 58.
28. Augustine, *Confessions*, 216–217 (Bk. 10, xxxiii).

140   *Music beyond the Offices*

29 On the manuscript, see Randall, *Medieval and Renaissance Manuscripts in the Walters Art Gallery, France, 1430–1520*, vol. 2, pt. 2, 414–418. For the attribution, see Hindman, "Review of 'Die illuminierten Handschriften'," 658.
30 Orme, *Medieval Schools*, 45.
31 Schiltz, "Gioseffo Zarlino and the 'Miserere' Tradition," 186–187. On public penance in France, with reference to the Seven Penitential Psalms and the hair shirt, see Mansfield, *The Humiliation of Sinners*, 173–175, 205.
32 Sutherland, "Performing the Penitential Psalms," 19.
33 See, for example, LBL, Add. MS 35214, fol. 85r.
34 Readings in the summer weeks are known as *historiae*, taken from "historical" parts of the Bible, such as Kings, Wisdom, Job, Tobit, Judith, Esther, etc. See Hughes, *Medieval Manuscripts*, 11, 61, 189–192.
35 BnF, lat. 1170, was one of four prayer books into which the original manuscript was divided in the seventeenth century. For details on the complex, see the entry for Marie de Rieux in Booton, *Manuscripts, Market and the Transition to Print*, 327–328.
36 For a rare two-part division of the antiphon before the word *neque* using a colon, see BnF, n.a.l. 3196, fol. 124r.
37 The *Liber usualis* (*LU* 992) suggests additional "quarter-bar" rests after the words *Domine* and *sumas*, producing five divisions of the antiphon text with additional lengthened notes. Late medieval notated sources, however, do not agree on internal divisions of *Ne reminiscaris Domine*.
38 A few variants may be found in connection with this appended text. See, for example, BnF, lat. 1160, fol. 130r.
39 Dyer, "Roman Processions," 123–125.
40 The melody is documented in the city of Rouen on Rogation Tuesday and also during prayers for favorable weather. See Morgan, "Chant and Urban Procession," 217, 226–228.
41 The texts of processional antiphons typically expressed the assembly's sorrow for their sins. Some processional antiphons are edited, with music and bibliography, in Colette, *Le Répertoire des Rogations*.
42 *LU* 1868. The occasion assigned to the chant is "at a time of penance."
43 Palisca, "Mode Ethos," 132–133.
44 Vicentino, *Ancient Music Adapted to Modern Practice*, 143.

7 The Litany

*

Saints are the noble heroes of the Christian faith and have infused culture since the early Middle Ages.[1] Whether through their bravery or their wisdom, saints ultimately won themselves a coveted residency in the kingdom of heaven and were stationed in a position to intercede powerfully on behalf of the faithful, whether personally or corporately as part of cities, institutions, or foundations. Details of the lives (*vitae*) of the saints reveal episodes and symbols that became intimately associated with these figures. Sanctoral imagery and talismans were far from idolatry; instead, they were potent reminders of the proximity of intercession for devotees. As members of societies preoccupied with calamity, death, and final judgment, late medieval Christians sought the efficacy and immediacy of the saints to improve their lives. Some saints fell into distinct areas of intercessory specialization, summoned for any number of reasons. No matter the social rank of the supplicant, the individual could pray to a saint to target anything from fertile fields and healthy farm animals to internal domestic and personal matters, including human illness, fertility, childbirth, marriage, and of course dying.

The relative homogeneity of liturgies in books of hours contrasts with the marked differences in devotion to particular saints. The honored saints were often determined locally—or even parochially. The preference for certain holy figures is reflected in the opening folios of a book of hours, where one encounters days of commemoration for local or regional saints in the calendar. In the suffrages (see Chapter 8), or short memorials to saints, invocation of select saints appears in a more dedicated format.[2] The Litany of the Saints stands conceptually in between these sections, at once catalogic and tailored. Together with calendars, Litanies (though not the suffrages) are used to "test" books of hours in order to localize and group them.[3] Localized geography and the customization one finds in books of hours could be thrown into disarray, however, if a book of hours changed hands and new saints were added.[4] In the pontificate of Pius V (r. 1566–72), there was some consolidation in the Litany aimed at standardization in the roster of saints and its accompanying music.[5] This chapter does not offer a close look at the long list of saints venerated in the Litany, since localization of books has been in the purview of other studies.[6] Rather, it is concerned with surveying the history, structure, musical territory, and performance cues in the Litanies from books of hours.

Set in an entrancing call-and-response musical style, the Litany must be counted as one of the most memorable and enduring of Christian traditions. Christians learned it at a young age in syllabaries with other central devotions like the Magnificat, *Salve regina,* and the Seven

DOI: 10.4324/9781003140511-10

Penitential Psalms.[7] As a section in books of hours, the pages enumerating the saints were evidently consumed heavily by users: some of the most worn-out, "dirtiest" folios of manuscript books of hours are found in the Litany.[8] Broadly speaking, a litany is simply a prayer cast in a repetitive structure. Its roots as an intercessory series of Christian devotions may date as early as the fifth century in the pontificate of Gelasius I (d. 496). Despite a "supplicatio litanie id est Kyrie eleison" ("invocation of the litany, which is the Kyrie eleison") specified in the Benedictine Rule and other types of early medieval litanical *preces*, the liturgy of Rome seems to have developed the practice of the invoking the saints in particular—and often in procession, a point to be addressed at the close of this chapter.[9] By the end of the twelfth century, this series of intercessions had gained so much popularity that litanies for individual saints including the Virgin Mary emerged and eventually needed to receive papal approval as they proliferated.[10] In the medieval liturgy, the Litany was reserved for some of the church's most important feasts. Amalarius of Metz divulged its use in the vigils for both Pentecost and Easter, for instance, performed in connection with the sacraments of baptism, confirmation, and ordination.[11]

In fifteenth-century books of hours, the Litany of the Saints immediately follows the Seven Penitential Psalms and precedes the Office of the Dead.[12] Of all sections in a book of hours, it is the least likely to be illustrated. Despite its name, the Litany of the Saints invokes general intercessions beyond the saints. The format of the Litany is characterized by a cantor-prompted "roll call" of holy personages, invocations, and supplications, which produces a musical response by a choir or community gathered. The full significance of the ritual materializes only when these two parts coordinate, the assembly answering the cantor's brief intention. Even in a private setting, a user of the *horae* can be imagined as "the people," hearing the invocation and compelled to participate in completion of the prayers, whether in the mind, murmured, or sung.

In its steady ebb and flow of sound, the Litany would be easier to execute practically than versicles and their varying responses. Even though no two Litanies are alike, the use of a single corporate response for long stretches of the Litany requires little thought from the participating respondent. BnF, n.a.l. 3117, may serve to demonstrate the general appearance of the Litany in books of hours (excerpts in Figures 7.1a–g). While the owner of this manuscript has not been identified, the illustrations have been linked to the workshop of Guillaume Lambert of Lyon in the last quarter of the fifteenth century.[13] The unfolding of the Litany (rubric: "letania") in this book of hours reveals some common characteristics one finds in this section. Some 60 saints are commemorated, plus more than 30 additional petitions. A methodical walk through the expected texts of the ceremony can illuminate the sections and kinds of pleas that make up the Litany.

A litanical formula with roots in the fourth century, the Kyrie eleison with congregational repetitions introduces the set of intercessions (Figure 7.1a).[14] Chanting the Kyrie alone was a basic exercise for the laity, especially among young people and women. The doubling of the cantors' invocation was standard in Roman practice since the time of Pope Gregory I and affirmed in later editions.[15] An enlarged decorated initial "K" of the Kyrie, often occupying multiple lines as in BnF, n.a.l. 3117, typically inaugurates the series. No miniature accompanies this Litany as expected. The ensuing formulations, consisting of a supplication and choral response, can be traced to traditions spanning the Mozarabic, Gallican, and Milanese liturgies.[16] After pleas to Christ to "hear us" ("audi/exaudi nos"), the cantor invokes God's various manifestations, as the assembly responds "miserere nobis" ("have mercy on us"), dutifully written out or abbreviated by the scribe.

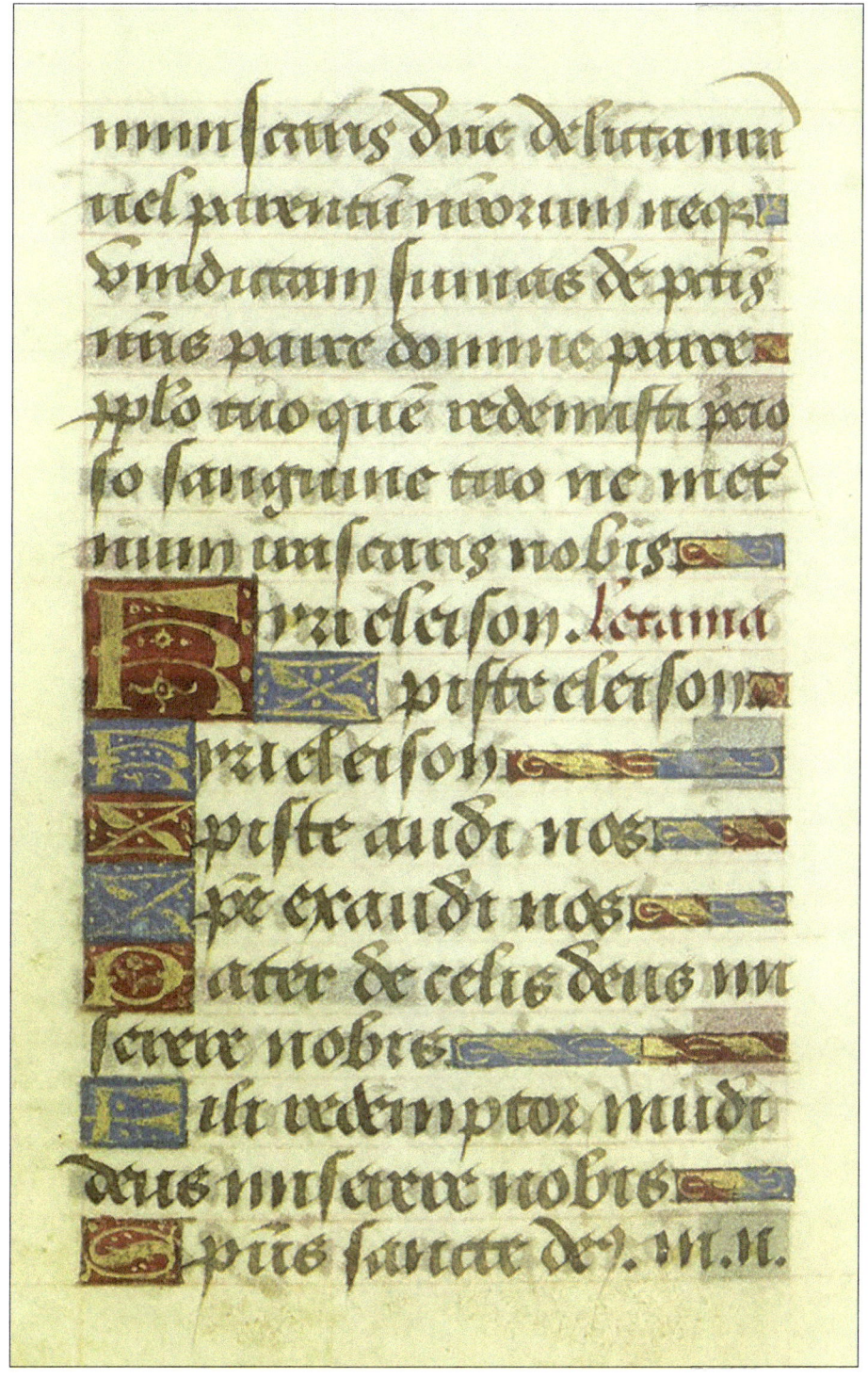

Figure 7.1a The Litany (excerpts). Paris, BnF, n.a.l. 3117, fols. 103v, 104r-v, 106r, 107r, 108r-v.

Figure 7.1b (Continued)

Figure 7.1c (Continued)

146 *Music beyond the Offices*

Figure 7.1d (Continued)

Figure 7.1e (Continued)

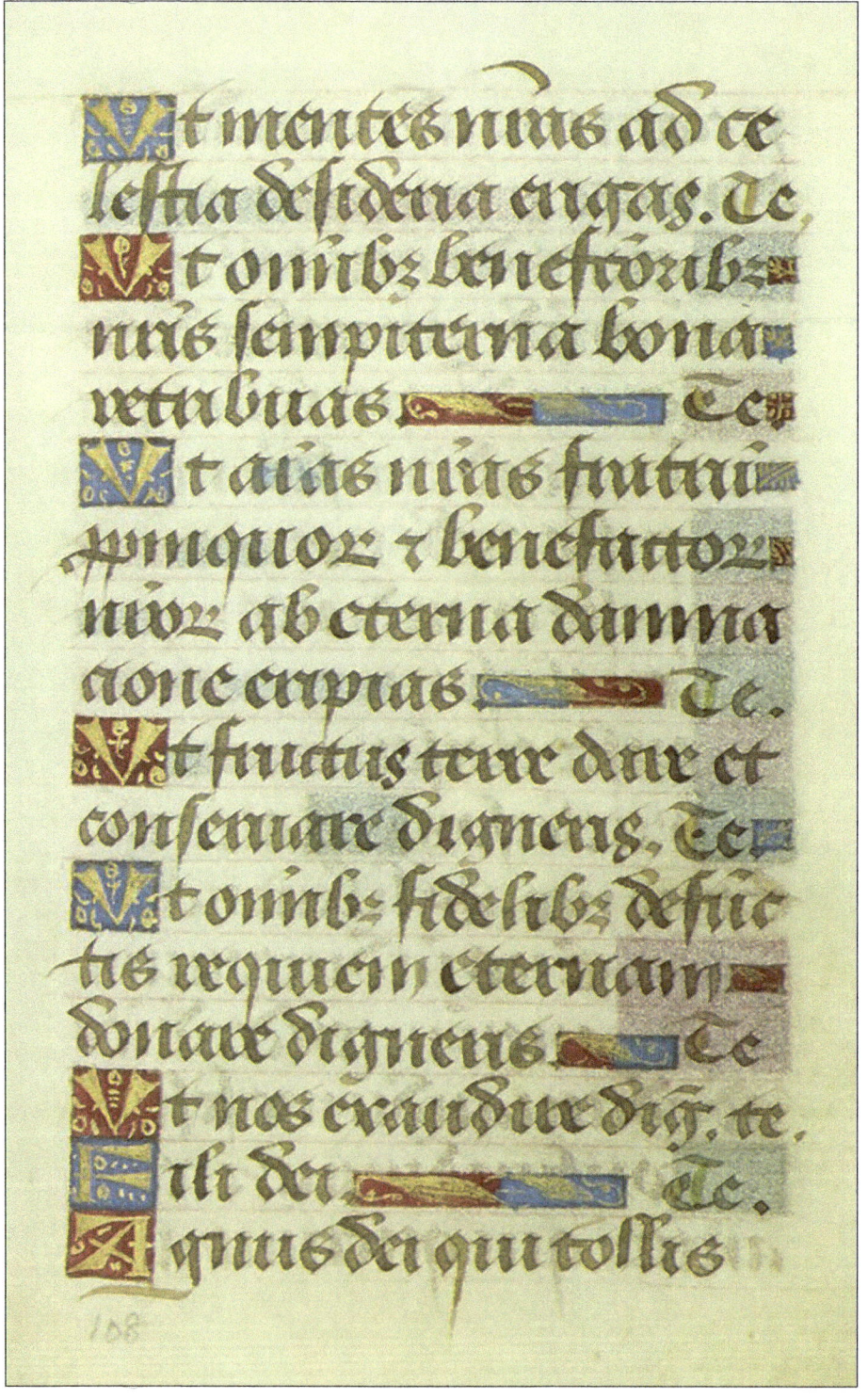

Figure 7.1f (Continued)

Figure 7.1g (Continued)

Invocation	Choral Response
Kyrie eleison.	Kyrie eleison.
Christe eleison.	Christe eleison.
[Kyrie eleison.]	[Kyrie eleison.]
Christe audi nos.	Christe audi nos.
Christe exaudi nos.	Christe exaudi nos.
Pater de celis deus.	Miserere nobis.
Fili redemptor mundi deus.	Miserere nobis.
Spiritus sancte deus.	Miserere nobis.
Sancta trinitas unus deus.	Miserere nobis.

The pecking order of saints follows in Figure 7.1b, beginning with a triad of calls to the Virgin Mary ("Sancta Maria"/"Sancta Dei genetrix"/"Sancta virgo virginum"). Each appeal is answered with a corporate reply, "ora pro nobis" ("pray for us"). The catalog of saints may be in the dozens, sometimes exceeding 100 in books of hours. Whatever the size of the roll call, compilers rigorously adhered to the sanctoral hierarchy after Mary: the order continued with angels, then apostles, martyrs, confessors, and finally virgin saints. Scribes observed this same hierarchy in the section of suffrages in the *horae* (Figures 7.1b–d). Appeals to classes of saints punctuate different series at the conclusion of a sanctoral rank. Examples from Figure 7.1b include "Omnes sancti angeli et archangeli," "Omnes sancti beatorum spirituum ordines," and "Omnes sancti patriarche et prophete" ("All holy angels and archangels," "All holy orders of blessed spirits," and "All holy Fathers and prophets," respectively). These plural forms dictated a corresponding "orate pro nobis" from the choir, often distinguished in books of hours with a superscript: "or^{te}."

As mentioned, the Litany contains more than a list of holy figures. While the valedictory bid "Omnes sancti et sancte [dei]" ("All holy men and women [of God]") ends the roll call, a user of the book of hours may be only halfway through the ritual. When the ranks have been exhausted, the pattern of responses breaks, and a new series of intercessions commences, often separated by the call "Propitius esto" and response "parce nobis Domine" ("Be merciful to us/spare us O Lord"), as in Figure 7.1d. A new sequence of petitions asks for deliverance from physical or moral catastrophes, each entreaty beginning with the preposition "ab" or "a" ("from"), using an ablative phrase to link syntactically with the choral response "libera nos Domine" ("deliver us, O Lord"). The Anglican Church would later call these appeals "deprecations."[17] Examples include:

Ab omni malo	"From all evil,"	libera nos Domine
Ab omni peccato,	"From all sin,"	libera nos Domine.
Ab ira tua,	"From your wrath,"	libera nos Domine
A subitanea et improvisa morte	"From sudden and unexpected death,"	libera nos Domine.

Another set of supplications ("obsecrations") maintains the choral response "libera nos Domine" but alters the form of the request, opening with another ablative construction beginning with the preposition "per." These petitions run through the life of Jesus from his conception, birth, and baptism to the resurrection, ascension, and the coming of the Holy Spirit. For instance:

Per adventum tuum	"Though your advent,"	libera nos Domine.
Per sanctam nativitatem tuam	"Through your holy nativity,"	libera nos Domine.
Per baptismum tuum	"Through your baptism,"	libera nos Domine.

Per passionem et sanctam crucem tuam	"Through your passion and holy cross,"	libera nos Domine.
Per mortem et sepulturam tuam	"Through your death and burial,"	libera nos Domine.

There is a final transition into a new set of repeated congregational responses following the "per" petitions.[18] The assembly will take up the answer "Te rogamus audi nos" ("we beseech you, hear us") nearly to the end of the Litany. Usually of greater length than the previous two sections, this concluding series of supplications (Anglican: "intercessions") presents a shift from the earlier sets. The cantorial prompts do not begin with an ablative phrase, but rather with the conjunction "Ut" ("That . . ."), which yields a subjunctive clause of purpose. Examples from Figures 7.1e–f include:

Ut nobis parcas	"That you might be merciful to us,"	te rogamus audi nos.
Ut mentes nostras ad celestia desideria erigas	"That you might raise our minds toward heavenly desires,"	te rogamus audi nos.
Ut omnibus benefactoribus nostris sempiterna bona retribuas.	"That you might render eternal blessings to all of our benefactors,"	te rogamus audi nos.
Ut fructus terre dare et conservare digneris.	"That you might vouchsafe to give and preserve the fruits of the earth,"	te rogamus audi nos.

The conclusion of the Litany is marked by a threefold *Agnus Dei*, somewhat similar to ones invoked in the Mass ("Agnus Dei, qui tollis peccata mundi" ["Lamb of God, you take away the sin of the world"]). These too are cast in a call-and-response format, but carry three different responses: "parce nobis Domine" ("spare us, O Lord"); "exaudi nos Domine" ("listen to us, O Lord"); and the familiar "miserere nobis" ("Have mercy on us, O Lord").[19] A handful of closing responses are echoed directly, the congregants repeating exactly what is intoned for them. The Kyrie that opened the Litany closes it as well, symmetrically encasing the series (Figure 7.1g).

Christe audi nos.	Christ, hear us.
Christe exaudi nos.	Christ, listen to us.
Kyrie eleison.	Lord, have mercy.
Christe eleison.	Christ, have mercy.
Kyrie eleison.	Lord, have mercy.

The patterns of enumeration and response in the Litany as a whole have been observed by liturgists and literary scholars alike. While there is some theoretical disagreement on the Litany's precise structure,[20] any participant in the ritual would recognize the recurring elements established for long stretches. In books of hours, the line-by-line petitions will of course vary, but a surprising degree of standardization may also be noticed on the whole. The steady congregational responses balanced the constant variance in the individual appeals, creating a dynamic and mesmerizing sound experience for those immersed in the practice.

Sounds of the Litany

While communal participation was generally not intended in most medieval liturgies, laypeople played a manifest role in the performance of the Litany. As the voice of the Church Universal, the assembly had executional responsibilities that a cantor could not assume in the ritual. The Litany's hypnotic refrains were no doubt seared into the medieval memory. The calls and responses form a kind of minimalist piece of music, producing a satisfying, mystical whole greater than the sum of its parts. Beholding the Litany of the Saints in a book of hours, the supplicant has the opportunity to relive not only the role of the choral respondent but also that of the clerical cantors charged with invoking the Litany's prompts. The cantor's formulaic musical cells were hardly different than the fixed replies users would have known.

Short phrases of limited musical shape dominate the Litany, allowing the gesture to stand out of the way of the text at hand. Recovering the musical notes applied to calls and responses is no easy task, however. As so often happens with melodies with wide circulation, few examples of the Litany have survived, and the ones that do present variant traditions. Stäblein has noticed three basic strands in the transmission of the Litany, each of them rooted in a tetrachordal frame for moderate stints: (1) a home of E with reciting note g; (2) a home of f with reciting note a; and (3) a home of a with reciting note c. Various transpositions are possible, so long as intervals are preserved; as always, the pitches do not indicate sound frequencies, only relationships between notes. Among these traditions for reciting the Litany, the Roman and related Franciscan versions are of interest here. These were sung with a as a reciting note and f as a lower boundary; the recitation however shifts to c as one progresses, breaking the confines of the initial tetrachord. A broad sense of the pervasive "Roman" sound of the Litany can be made with the aid of two surviving notated sources: (1) BnF, lat. 8886, an early fifteenth-century pontifical-missal from the circle of John, Duke of Berry; and (2) Washington, D.C., Library of Congress, Music Division, MS 36, a late fifteenth-century French processional belonging to Franciscan nuns.[21]

While launching on c, the Kyrie/Christe invocations settle on a as a destination, with the cantorial and choral response repeated in succession (Example 7.1).[22] The cantor reveals just two notes (c and a) tetrachord in the opening appeals. The ensuing summons to Christ ("hear us") takes the recitational a and accesses two steps beneath it (f and g). A set of appeals to the Trinity follows in the Litany and establishes the melodic formula that will dominate the rite through the roll call of saints, keeping the lower boundary of f and the continued reciting pitch of a. The cantor's bid begins on that written a and rises to b-flat on the accented syllable of "Deus" before skipping down to the g beneath the reciting tone. The responding choir then takes up that note g and answers the customary "ora pro nobis," dipping down to the boundary f before returning to a by step. The Franciscan source helpfully notates the b-flat to confirm that a tritone is not outlined in the call and response.[23]

The reading of the saints' names, beginning with appellations for the Virgin Mary, continues in this pattern with only slight adjustment. The cantor recites the saint or saints in the roll principally on a, consuming syllables until the final accented syllable arrives, which occasions a single b-flat. The cantor's excess syllables fall on g, duly notated in Example 7.1. The medial cadence, attentive to the accentuation of the finishing words, is known as a tonic cadence. As mentioned, multiple saints or collective ranks command the response "orate pro nobis." The syllable count of this reply precisely matches that of "miserere nobis" from the petitions to the Trinity preceding the register of saints, allowing for a fluid mapping

Example 7.1 Opening of the Litany. Transcribed from BnF, lat. 8886, fol. 53r.

of pitches (*g-g-f-g-a-a*). This formula does not however accommodate the assembly's text accentuation of "orate pro nobis": the lower neighbor tone *f* is the accented syllable of "miserere," whereas the same group of pitches applied to "orate" dictates that the strong syllable be assigned to the preceding *g*.

No melodic mode is assigned to the Litany in liturgical books or in literature on the practice, and rightly so. While the recitation under review revolves around *a*, the petitions that continue after the roll call of saints reveal new tonal territory. The formula emerges in the transition to the entreaties beginning "Ab" or "A", which continue with recitation on *c* (Example 7.2). As the cantor approaches the medial cadence, the final four syllables journey through the pitches *b-a-c-d*, a collection that transforms *b*-flat into *b*-natural.[24] The tonal territory expands in this invocation, an arrangement that is striking when performed vocally and when reaching the ear. With upward motion at the cadence (*a-c-d*), the soloist's petition defies the customary arch shape to a phrase of plainsong. The cantor's pitch sequence also

154 *Music beyond the Offices*

Example 7.2 Excerpts from the "Ab/A" and "Per" series in the Litany. Transcribed from BnF 8886, fol. 55r-v.

tends to accent the final syllable, as it is the highest note (*d*) of the phrase; yet, rarely is the accentuation on the final syllable in Latin. The variable accentuation of the litanical texts can cause strong syllables to fall differently with the four concluding notes, requiring extra concentration for execution. The chorus answers with a temporary retort in the transition ("parce nobis Domine") before settling on "libera nos Domine" for the entirety of the "Ab/A" series and into the cantor's next sequence beginning with "Per." Each corporate response carries seven syllables, making the assigned music a match (*c-c-a-g-a-g-f*) to the previous "parce" response with *f* as the common destination. The fresh point of rest for the assembly on *f* in the "Ab" and "Per" petitions stands in contrast to the suspended set of pitches intoned by the soloist for the same series.

A transition to the characteristically longer series of "Ut" petitions brings new alteration of the tonal space (Example 7.3). The cantorial supplications feature a slightly condensed cadence following the recitational *c*, departing the reciting pitch with three notes (*b-d-e*) instead of four of the previous group (*b-a-c-d*). In these "Ut" invocations, the soloist reaches the upper limit of the tonal space for the Litany (*e*), a step up from the ascending gesture of the "Ab/Per" series. While the cantor's cadence is marginally truncated, the individual "Ut" petitions themselves tend to be lengthier on average compared to the preceding sets of

Example 7.3 Select "Ut" petitions from the Litany. Transcribed from BnF, lat. 8886 fol. 56r.

prayers. A similar accentuation problem can be expected in both hearing and performing the *Ut* intonations, as unaccented final syllables will receive necessary stress by design from the relatively high ultimate pitch *e*. The choral response no longer relaxes down to its destination, but reverses upward within a tetrachord. The assembly's new answer—"Te rogamus audi nos"—presents a reverse arch shape, traversing down and up by step (*c-b-a-g-a-b-c*), counterbalancing the low *f* that was brought out for the previous "Ab/Per" group and establishing *c* as a musical terminus.

As the Litany winds down, the tonal space contracts to the span of a tetrachord as the call-and-response style continues into the trifold Agnus Dei (Example 7.4). Éamonn Ó Carragáin has written of the Agnus Dei that the melody was "as near as one could get, within a Latin liturgy, to a popular chant."[25] In the context of the Mass, the celebrant falls silent as he and his assistants participate in the fraction ceremony (the breaking of the bread), while other clergy and the assembly take responsibility for the invocations and simple musical rejoinders of the Agnus Dei. It is impossible to speak precisely about the music of the Agnus Dei in the Mass, since different melodies for this universal text were in circulation in the late Middle Ages.[26] However, an especially pervasive and presumably early Agnus Dei from the Mass XVIII ordinaries was routinely assigned to the litanies.[27] Indeed, the pontifical-missal BnF, lat. 8886 notates this Agnus Dei within its Litany.[28] The melody retains the local pitch *c* handed to the cantor from the latest choral response "Te rogamus audi nos," but lies in a newly configured tetrachord that presumably converts *b*-natural to *b*-flat again.[29] The effect produces the feeling of a transposed G mode with a whole step beneath the temporary final of *c* and two whole steps above it. After each of three identical phrases of the Agnus Dei is intoned, the gathered penitents supply three different answers in the Litany, as mentioned

156 *Music beyond the Offices*

Example 7.4 Concluding items from the Litany. Transcribed from BnF, lat. 8886, fols. 56v–57r.

earlier.[30] The responses are nearly identical in pitch content and text accent: the "exaudi nos Domine" response misses the opening trochaic pattern, while the "miserere nobis" lacks the final dactyl of the others.

The end of the Litany nears as its palindromic edges come into view with the continued calls to Christ to "hear" the forgoing petitions following the invocations of the Agnus Dei. The responses "Christe audi nos" and "Christe exaudi nos" are varied from the earlier iteration in Example 7.1; the shape is preserved but the cantor takes the recited *c* of the Agnus Dei as its point of departure, shifting the tonality yet again with the reintroduction of *b*-natural. The trifold Kyrie reemerges to frame the entire Litany both textually and musically. The assembly presumably repeats the first two statements, but a more elaborate conclusion for the last Kyrie is provided only by the cantor, whose melody comes to rest on a striking *E* final. As the Kyrie provides a proper and symmetrical conclusion to the Litany, a Pater noster is recited silently (*secreto*) by the celebrant.

Similar to any chant we have examined, the letter names of the notes in the Litany are by no means fixed pitch frequencies, as no such thing existed. Rather, the tones are locations in musical space that suggest an arrangement of whole and half steps, with the pedagogical gamut being a relatively comfortable range for singing. In the context of a layperson's experience with the book of hours, the reciting pitch—whether reimagined, murmured, or sung—could theoretically begin on any sounding frequency. But would any pitch suffice practically, even in the practice of audiation in the mind's ear? If the power of oral tradition reveals even a trace of rituals of the past, we could probably eliminate a spectrum of sound frequencies that would not contain the recitation pitch for a cantor and assembly. It is likely instead that the chosen recitation tone (at least at the outset—pitches tend to float in performative reality) was in the middle to high range of the cantor's voice. No pitch could be selected that is too low (say, lower than *C*), as the formula tends to encompass the lower tetrachord or pentachord. Nor could the reciting tone be too high (say, above *d*): this note had to be sustained and would quickly tax even the more seasoned cantorial voices charged with invoking an extensive list of holy figures and pleas. While the reciting tone is a centering mechanism throughout the votive ceremony and tetrachords may constrain tonal space for various time spans, pitch interrelationships are reorganized a few times in the Litany. As the Kyrie descends to its unexpected *E* final, it may leave the listener unsettled even after a long journey in resounding petitions.

Signs of engagement in the Litany

Could users of books of hours have a performative experience with the Litany? The *mise-en-page* in many *horae* seems to indicate so. Miniatures are universally absent in the Litany, so there is no time for gazing or distraction at the margins. But this should not be taken as lack of adornment, as visual markers in the Litany are among the most abundant and persistent one will encounter. The series has an unmistakable appearance, the roll call of saints in particular producing a distinct look. While psalm verses often consume multiple text lines, the invocation of an individual saint spans less than a single line, perhaps half of a given line depending on the book. The remainder of each line will usually carry a line-fill, creating a visual separation from the choral response (either "ora pro nobis" or "orate pro nobis"). The congregational answer is typically abbreviated "or," written in minuscule. That response sometimes manifests in superscript, with an even smaller "te" wedged in for saints in the plural, as has been said.

A saint's name could not be truncated since it was new material for the eye, but it is curious that the "ora" responses and those of other sections were conventionally provided each time. Surely, the user knew the response from years of witnessing the ritual from an early age. But the stubborn inclusion of these corporate replies offers a visual reminder of the importance of the sound exchange that is at the heart of the Litany. The invocations are simply incomplete on their own aurally, requiring the response each time. There are no short cuts in the ritual act in live performance; the same is true in an enacted or reimagined performance of the Litany in books of hours. Upon seeing or singing the name of the saint at the beginning of a line, the right-justified "or[a pro nobis]" or "l[ibera nos Domine]" triggers a differently textured sound in the voice or mind of the participant, who calls out or audiates the sonic remainder to fulfill the plea of the assembly.

In her study of significance of the materiality of the page, Bonnie Mak paid special attention to how the page layout affects interaction with it: "[T]he spaces between words, between lines, and around the text block can be understood as visual and cognitive breaks, employed by designers and readers as a way to moderate the pace of engagement with the page."[31] In a few books of hours, there is blank space between the invocation and the response in Litanies, pushing both to the margin of the writing block.[32] More often, however, illustrators present a decorative internal line-fill to occupy the void. Its variable length allows for the left justification of saints' names and the right justification of the assembly's response, line by line.[33] As it concerns the performance of the Litany, the line-fill also serves as a kind of notation. In many of the sources under consideration, the line-fills are drawn either as a solid color or as

158 *Music beyond the Offices*

a two-colored bar, with the colors evenly inhabiting the stripe, sometimes bisected with some kind of separator, as in an example from a book of hours from the east-central French town of Autun, once home to the Dukes of Burgundy (Figure 7.2).

Visually, the line-fill is not just separating text but also, as one can guess by now, articulating roles and sounds of the ritual. The sound of the solo intonation needs temporal space to release and be heard, providing that brief moment where the user or listener may call up an image of the saint. At the same time, the assembly must gather a corporate breath to chime in with the necessary reply. The decay of the cantor's call and the rise of the congregational response overlap in the profitable space afforded by the consistent line-fills. The switch of color too may illustrate the transition from the thin solo sound to the bellow of the large group. As the words of the cantor and congregation are isolated in this arrangement, the devotee may better hear the contrasting sonic textures they summon.

Figure 7.2 The Litany (excerpt). Paris, BnF, n.a.l. 3213, fol. 103v.

In the Litany, a capital letter begins each saint's name or petition on the left margin, decorated in the style of the capitals for verses of the psalms and hymns. From an experiential perspective, the soloist announces the next holy figure or petition at the capital letter, silencing the sound of the choir as it regathers for the response. Similar to the line-fill's position in the transition of sound textures, the same fading in and out of voices may take place when a book of hours user reaches the capital letter. In Figures 7.1 and 7.2 as in most books of hours, the decorative initial letters alternate colors, usually blue and red, either in the foreground or background. The checkered field prevents eyeskip as it regulates the sound.

Sometimes, in an effort to move the extensive Litany along, the solo singer may anticipate the intonation, allowing only a partial decay of sound (or no decay). One can picture a private experience with a book of hours, the ritual taking place outdoors where responses do not reverberate or indoors where sounds echo around a space. If singing or murmuring privately, users may take on the role of the congregation and audiate the invocation. Or, of course, the book of hours has also been an accessory for live processions, providing the substance of the ritual for lay attendees.

*

Studies of books of hours have long emphasized the private experience of devotion with these keepsake volumes. While honoring this mode of engagement, this study also acknowledges the role of public ritual in devotional practice, which likewise could have included use of the one's closely guarded book of hours. Although observations in this investigation have focused on sounds recalled internally or envoiced, exploration of the Litany reminds us that there is another somatic dimension to its execution. Namely, the Litany has always been bound up with the act of public procession. The Greek origins of the word ("lite" in particular but also "litaneuein" and "litaneia") specifically point to a procession that transpired outside the formal liturgy.[34] Remi Chiu has remarked that the word litany "stands in as a synecdoche for the term 'procession' itself."[35] Singing invocations to saints and other petitions in procession was a Gallican tradition that was adopted by the Roman church for its ritual.[36] And while books of hours and sacramentaries presented the Litany without notation, the prayers could be found notated in other kinds of service books, namely graduals, antiphoners, and processionals. The Litany's musical sound emerged in the performative act of the procession and no doubt in recollecting those events.

Here it is prudent to connect Litanies found in books of hours with those prescribed for public processions. While "lesser" Litanies known as Rogations were reserved for the three weekdays before the feast of the Ascension, the standard "major" Litany of Roman heritage took place on the feast of St. Mark (April 25), a point mentioned in Chapter 6.[37] There were numerous other occasions, however, for chanting the Litany: it could take place in times of natural disasters like drought or earthquakes. In France and England, the Litany was also included in funeral processions.[38] Opportunities for procession in song abounded. Amid the potential ambulatory context of the Litany, the question of a rhythm to regulate the movement arises. Although there is evidence of metrical versions of the Litany from as early as the ninth century, including by Carolingian scholar and poet Hrabanus Maurus (d. 856),[39] the format did not prevail in the late Middle Ages and does not appear in books of hours.[40] Nonetheless, a pattern attentive to words and accent can still emerge in the Litany, what Witold Sadowski calls a "litanic rhythm."[41] Always arising in the act of procession, such a recursive flow has implications for how the body—beyond the voice and the mind—may be activated in one's experience with the book of hours.

Notes

1 The literature on the saints is naturally enormous and wide-ranging in scope. Classic, foundational studies on the general role of the saints in early Christianity and medieval life include Brown, *The Cult of the Saints*; Head, *Medieval Hagiography*; Vauchez, *Sainthood in the Later Middle Ages*; Geary, *Living with the Dead*; and Wilson, *Saints and Their Cults*.
2 Delaisse, "The Importance of Books of Hours," 205.
3 Plummer, "'Use' and 'Beyond Use'," 149.
4 Rudy, *Piety in Pieces*, 331.
5 Huglo et al., "Litany," *NG* 14: 880.
6 Clark, "Beyond Saints," 213.
7 Van Orden, "Children's Voices," 209, 215, 236.
8 Rudy, "Dirty Books."
9 Huglo et al., "Litany," *NG* 14: 880. The Kyrie, an essential ingredient of the Litany, may have been known in the Latin West at a very early date. See Henry and Hadot, *Marii Victorini Opera 1*, 290-293. For more on the history of the Litany of the Saints, see Cabrol, "Litanies," in *DACL* 9(2): cols. 1540–1571; Lapidge, *Anglo-Saxon Litanies of the Saints*, 1–41; Jeffery, "Litany"; Stäblein, "Litanei"; Duchesne and McClure, *Christian Worship*, 58–63, 164–167 and *passim*; and Geldhof, "The Litany of the Saints."
10 The two most famous litanies are the Litany of Loreto and the Litany of Venice. On an early Marian litany in a thirteenth-century book of hours, see New York, Metropolitan Museum of Art, MS L.1990.38, fols. 173r–176r.
11 Hanssens, *Amalarii Episcopi Opera Liturgica Omnia*, 2: 183–184.
12 The consecutive arrangement of the Seven Penitential Psalms and the Litany can be found in *libelli precum*. See Coens, "Anciennes litanies des saints," 137.
13 Jacobs, "The Master of Getty Ms. 10," 55.
14 For the relationship between the Kyrie and the Litany of the Saints, see Jeffery, "The Meanings and Functions," 183–190.
15 *Ibid.*, 181–184.
16 Stäblein, "Litanei," 5: col. 1365.
17 Proctor and Frere, *A New History of the Book of Common Prayer*, 415.
18 The transition is often marked by the invocation "In die iudicii" ℟ "Libera nos Domine."
19 The order of the first two responses is sometimes reversed in the sources. "Miserere nobis" remains the final response.
20 Distinctions in the shape of the Litany are discussed in Sadowski, *European Litanic Verse*, 191–201.
21 BnF, lat. 8886, fols. 57r–64r; Washington, D.C., Library of Congress, Music Division, MS 36, fols. 71r–73v.
22 A trifold Kyrie, which can be expected in many versions of the Litany in books of hours, is not present in the notated sources under consideration.
23 Washington, D.C., Library of Congress, Music Division, MS 36, fol. 71r.
24 The Franciscan source unfortunately stops its notation of the Litany after the sanctoral roll call is initiated, so accidentals cannot be confirmed later in the ritual.
25 Ó Carragáin, *Ritual and the Rood*, 163.
26 Hiley, *Western Plainchant*, 165–168.
27 This melody is cataloged by Schildbach ("Das einstimmige Agnus Dei") as no. 101, long thought to be one of the oldest surviving Agnus Dei settings.
28 Fol. 63v.
29 BnF, lat. 8886 does not supply the *b*-flat, nor did it include that note in the roll call of saints. Modern chant books are split on that matter. *LU*, 776GG notates *b*-flat, and *GR*, 768 transposes the chant of Mass XVIII, essentially preserving what would be *b*-flat. The *Processionale monasticum* (71) however suggests a *b*-natural.
30 The ordering of the first two responses varies among the sources. BnF, lat. 8886 reverses the order of these responses seen in BnF, n.a.l. 3117, fols. 108r–v (Figure 7.1f–g). The former also erroneously includes "dona nobis pacem" (used at Mass) before correctly completing the response "miserere nobis" used in the Litany.
31 Mak, *How the Page Matters*, 17.
32 See, for example, BnF, n.a.l. 3234, fols. 72r–74v.

33 That the line-fill was secondary in the process of compiling the manuscript is demonstrated by books of hours where space is left for the line-fill but it was not completed. See, for example, the Litany in BnF, lat. 1414, fol. 156r–v.
34 Baldovin, *The Urban Character of Christian Worship*, 205–209; Jeffery, "Litany," 588.
35 Chiu, "Singing on the Street," 32.
36 Hiley, *Western Plainchant*, 554.
37 Although books of hours do not carry illuminations nor indications for procession in the Litany, the mid-sixteenth-century "Farnese Hours" provides a welcome exception. Its Litany depicts the Vatican's elaborate Corpus Christi procession winding its way into old St. Peter's Basilica in Rome. See New York, The Morgan Library & Museum, Medieval and Renaissance Manuscripts, MS M.69, fols 72v–73r.
38 Stäblein, "Litanei," 5: cols. 1365–1366.
39 Huglo et al., "Litany," *NG* 14: 880.
40 Sadowski, *European Litanic Verse*, 33–36. Examples of metrical litanies do abound in modern times, however. See, for example, Pollock, *The Litany Appendix*.
41 Sadowski, *European Litanic Verse*, 381–382.

8 Suffrages

*

For the owner of a book of hours, the section of suffrages captured the supplicant's personal attachment to a set of individual saints, celebrating them with a more deliberate devotion than could be achieved in the calendar or in the Litany where saints are merely acknowledged by name. Suffrages are grouped together toward the back of books of hours, usually following the Office of the Dead or occasionally preceding it. The number of suffrages to saints varies by manuscript, but generally represents a "short list" of favored saints. Because of the personal meaning of the selected saints in the suffrages, this section was customized for users and differed in arrangement from source to source. The list of holy figures could range from a handful to a dozen or more. An exceptional book of hours could honor 50 saints with individual commemorations.

Suffrages are effectively synonymous with memorials, which were minor liturgical observances that recognized a holy figure in some narrow, commemorative way.[1] Since the eleventh century, memorials took the form of brief votive offices appended to the services of Lauds and Vespers in the liturgical day and were offered by those gathered as special intentions.[2] The focus of the devotion was usually the Virgin Mary or a particular saint. Each suffrage to a saint consists of a short antiphon, a versicle-response pair, and a prayer called an oration (*oratio*).[3] The antiphon and oration in particular distill texts about the saint from scripture, apocrypha, or hagiographic texts, condensing them into a short tribute that could well have been memorized by owners of books of hours. Depending on the level of decoration in the hours, an inset miniature may accompany the text, illustrating a scene from the vita that further distinguishes the saint. As David Hiley has noted, the suffrage was a devotional item that could either be said or sung.[4]

There is some danger in overemphasizing the personal, "hand-picked" roster of saints included in the section of suffrages. While the exact names and number of saints will rarely be shared between any two books of hours, there is a surprisingly consistent core of venerated holy figures, which allows for study across the corpus of books of hours. Moreover, the ordering tends to observe the hierarchy found in the Litany. Thus, the unfolding of saints in the suffrages might prevent one's personal favorite patron saint from being elevated to the top of the list. If, for instance, a user held St. Katherine in especially high regard, the suffrage for the saint would not appear at the head of even a short series of memorials. The opening positions are normally reserved for the Trinity, St. Michael, John the Baptist, Peter and Paul, and so on, who also appear early in the Litany. To be sure, there were common favorites among the sanctoral ranks, particularly those who could protect against disease (St. Sebastian) and even toothaches (St. Apollonia).

As a section of books of hours, the suffrages have scarcely commanded attention. Though the assortment of saints they offer may help historians trace the local origins of various *horae*, the provenance of books of hours can be more quickly ascertained from calendars and Litanies. This chapter examines the individual components of the suffrage, bringing to light both norms and extraordinary features of these devotional texts and connecting them to familiar sounds within and outside the Divine Office. Two related phenomena that are best treated in this chapter are the role of the liturgical sequence in books of hours and the appearance of memorials and memorial-like devotions apart from the section of suffrages.

Suffrage antiphons

Of the three components of a conventional suffrage to a saint, music historians will be most attracted to the first liturgical item of the commemoration—the antiphon. One such historian, Frank Llewellyn Harrison, took special interest in the antiphons of the suffrages, noticing that, like processionals, they demonstrated how these exceptional melodies were extracted from the liturgy and performed without a psalm, making them "a separate item of ritual."[5] Antiphons are discernible not only by rubrics that identify the genre but also by the size of script, which is often reduced in appearance among the items of the suffrage, consistent with their appearance throughout books of hours. Unlike the dialogues and prayers in suffrages, most antiphons have clear musical referents. There has been no systematic study of even the most common antiphons found in the suffrages; therefore, this chapter serves in part to make some global observations about common selections.

In liturgical service books, a saint's feast day could include more than two dozen antiphons, but in the suffrages of the *horae*, only one will appear. This selected antiphon thus carries a certain burden for having to encapsulate most fully the holy figure. For the first commemorative item in the suffrage, compilers traditionally chose an antiphon that has a summarizing quality or perhaps one that occupies a prominent position in the Divine Office for the saint. The antiphon could also have represented a mantric text that was repeated at various times throughout the feast day or in procession. It was further possible to select an antiphon outside the office as well. The choice was not arbitrary, though, as antiphons tend not to vary widely from source to source. Across the corpus, only two or three different antiphons might be witnessed for a given saint. Table 8.1 highlights the most common antiphons for the saints customarily found in fifteenth-century French books of hours.

Table 8.1 Common antiphons in the suffrages

Honoree	Antiphon	CAO no.	Mode	Typical liturgical position
Trinity	Te invocamus, te adoramus	5119	4	MA4
St. Michael	Michael archangele paradisi	3754	4	Varies
John the Baptist	Inter natos mulierum	3370	3	Varies
St. John the Evangelist	Iohannes apostolus	3494	1	MA1
Sts. Peter and Paul	Petrus apostolus et Paulus doctor	4284	8	Varies
St. James	O lux et decus	—	—	

(Continued)

Table 8.1 (Continued)

Honoree	Antiphon	CAO no.	Mode	Typical liturgical position
St. Anthony	Vox de celo	205981*	5	Rare in liturgical sources
St. Christopher	Sancte Christofore martir	—	—	
St. Sebastian	O quam mira refulsit	—	—	
St. Nicholas	Amicus dei	1387	6	LA4
St. Katherine	Virgo sancta katherina	205274*	1	MA1
St. Anne	Celeste beneficium introivit	1832	1	Varies
St. Barbara	Gaude Barbara beata	—	—	
St. Margaret	Virgo gloriosa Margareta	—	—	
St. Mary Magdalene	Maria ergo unxit	3699	6	LAB
St. Apollonia	Beata Apollonia	—	—	

*Cataloged in the Cantus Index, not in CAO.

The table immediately exposes an obstacle in the study of antiphons for suffrages: several of these antiphons for saints do not stem from the office repertory. Of just the 15 antiphons shown here from books of hours, almost half cannot be traced reliably to known antiphons in service books. The stability of their appearance in the *horae* is therefore all the more remarkable. The liturgy was not anchoring some of these antiphons as one might expect, yet they remained consistent devotions in books of hours. We might then scrutinize use of the word "antiphon" as a label for the first item of a suffrage. Antiphons were not strictly office material belonging to that genre. This is not unlike the Marian "antiphons," which tended to lie outside of the office liturgy proper and also bore different stylistic features than typical antiphons. While Marian antiphons map to relatively stable melodies, the suffrage antiphons appear to be different. If they emerged in liturgies, they did not always have a uniform or prominent position, and some may not even have been associated with a melody at all. Despite the etymology of the word "antiphon" suggesting song, sound, or voice, antiphons evidently did not always refer to melodies and could have existed solely as texts. We caught a glimpse of this phenomenon in the hymn repertory of books of hours in Chapter 3, in which the condensed Hours of the Cross and Hours of the Holy Spirit revealed hymns that were not widely sung to melodies, but rather circulated primarily as rhythmical texts. We will revisit rhymed devotions in the context of suffrages shortly. For the moment, let us say a word about some antiphons with known connections to melodies from the office. These permit a sound experience for users that could accompany the popular antiphon texts.

The lone antiphon from Table 8.1 that is not connected to a saint is that for the Trinity, *Te invocamus, te adoramus*. While there are other suffrages for non-saints, the Trinity is the most common among them. The antiphon *Te invocamus, te adoramus* represents a mode 4 melody (CAO 5119), known from the earliest sources of the Trinity office. It falls with some regularity as the fourth antiphon of Matins, not a particularly notable position for antiphons in offices. The Trinity suffrage was highly portable, though, a point to be taken up later. Particularly widespread in suffrages is the mode 3 antiphon *Inter natos mulierum* for John the Baptist (CAO 3370). It had a variable liturgical position, not only dispatched for different feasts for the precursor saint, but sometimes slated more than once in the course of a single feast for the Baptist.[6] Cast in mode 8, *Petrus apostolus* (CAO 4284) likewise showed

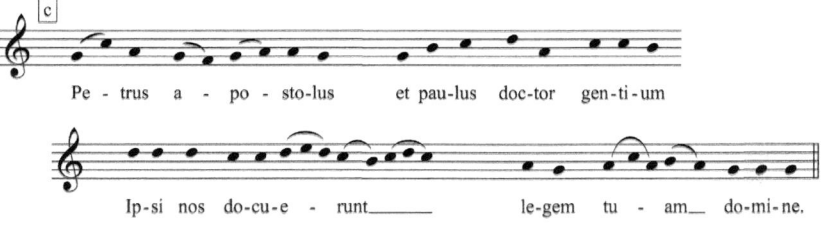

Example 8.1 Antiphons: (a) *Te invocamus, te adoramus* for the Trinity; (b) *Inter natos mulierum* for John the Baptist; (c) *Petrus apostolus* for Peter and Paul. Transcribed from BnF, lat. 15182 (fol. 91v); BnF, lat. 15181 (fol. 368r); and BnF, lat. 12044 (fol. 155v), respectively.

mobility across multiple Petrine and Pauline feasts. All three antiphons are succinct in their texts, contributing to their aphoristic character. They each feature relatively syllabic musical settings, most phonemes carrying one or two notes (Example 8.1). Though this feature is unremarkable for antiphons, the compressed melodic profile promotes ease of memorization and stable transmission.

Nonliturgical antiphons

The virgin martyr St. Apollonia is a curious case among the suffrages in books of hours. Although the saint was widely venerated, mass propers or offices for the February 9 feast day are virtually absent.[7] Details from her vita instead explain Apollonia's popularity. According to Jacobus de Voragine's mid-thirteenth-century *Legenda aurea* (or "Golden Legend," the popular encyclopedia of saints and feasts of its time), the virgin from Alexandria had her teeth shattered by anti-Christian tormentors when she refused to repeat their blasphemies. They lit a fire, threatening to hurl her alive into the raging flame if she would not yield. Apollonia instead threw herself into the pyre as her persecutors stood in awe.[8] The story of Apollonia's damaged teeth in particular was a powerful one for medieval Christians and offered relief for people at all levels of medieval society who suffered from dental problems and inadequate treatment for oral pain. Illustrated books of hours, such as Beinecke MS 435, from Lyon around the turn of the sixteenth century, depicts the saint with a forceps holding an extracted tooth (Figure 8.1).

166 *Music beyond the Offices*

Figure 8.1 Suffrage for St. Apollonia. New Haven, Yale University, Beinecke Rare Book and Manuscript Library, MS 435, fol. 107r. Photo credit: Beinecke Rare Book and Manuscript Library, Yale University.

The nonliturgical antiphon assigned to the saint, *Beata Apollonia*, is longer than the concise office antiphons that appear in the suffrages, but highlights in short space Apollonia's excruciating torment and her utility as a saint for tooth pain.

Beata Apolonia grave tormentum pro Domino sustinuit. Primo, tiranni extruerunt dentes eius cum multis afariis. Et cum esset in illo tormento oravit ad Dominum Iesum Christum ut quicumque nomen suum supra se portaret malum in dentibus non sentiret.	Blessed Apollonia suffered serious torture for the Lord: first, tormentors took out her teeth with iron hammers, and while she was in that torture she prayed to the Lord Jesus Christ that whosoever should devoutly call on her name should not feel pain in their teeth.

No known melody is associated with this "antiphon"; however, an anonymous choral motet with this text emerged in the early sixteenth-century Rusconi Codex.[9] As Howard Mayer Brown, Bonnie Blackburn, and others have shown, composers of polyphony had a penchant for setting texts from books of hours.[10] Being sanctoral mantras, the antiphon texts from the suffrages of books of hours were ripe candidates for motets honoring saints.

Antiphon texts much longer than the one for St. Apollonia emerge in the suffrages. At 130 words, *Sancte Christofore martir* for St. Christopher is by far the most extensive among the common antiphons in the memorials to saints.[11] Similar to the case of St. Apollonia, the prose text for St. Christopher cannot be traced to a melody associated with the saint's liturgy, nor would one be expected with its great length. Martyred in the third century while trying to convert pagans in Lycia, Christopher was the patron saint of travelers for many medieval Christians. The antiphon has no reference to journeying though; instead, Jacobus's *Legenda aurea* relays an episode that unlocks part of the suffrage antiphon for the saint.[12] The astonishing stability and prevalence of the unrhymed and nonrhythmical *Sancte Christofore martir* in books of hours testify to its centrality in devotional life. Its categorization as "antiphon" does, however, challenge a musicologist's traditional view of the genre: the sounding aspect of it was apparently in speech, not in song. The exceptional length of text for St. Christopher apparently disqualified it as a candidate for being set as a motet.

Another antiphon of unconventional length, *O desolatorum consolator*, honors St. Claudius of Besançon, a seventh-century bishop and abbot in eastern France.[13] (Suffrages for St. Claudius were by no means standard in French books of hours, hence are not shown in Table 8.1.) Similar to the other lengthy antiphon texts, this poem finds no match to a melody from the office repertory, a function of the dearth of surviving offices for St. Claudius. Invariably transmitted as the antiphon in suffrages for the saint, *O desolatorum consolator* presents a series of intercessory areas that Claudius offers, with playful assonance at the outset that must have been attractive to owners devoted to this popular French figure.[14]

O desolatorum consolator	O consoler of the desolate,
captivorum liberator	freer of captives,
resurrectio mortuorum	resurrection to the dead,
lumen caecorum	light to the blind,
auditus surdorum	hearing to the deaf,
mutorum eloquium	speech to the mute,
tutor naufragantium	teacher of sailors,
impotentium et languidorum sanator	healer of the weak and faint,
medicinae refugium	a refuge of the healing art,
via errantium	a road for those who go astray,
salus omnium in te sperantium.	and the deliverance of all who hope in thee,

Beate Claudi	O blessed Claudius,
benigne confessor Dei	kind confessor of God,
ora Deum pro nobis	pray for us to God,
qui te tot et tantis	who made you shine by so many
illustravit suffragiis.	and such great intercessions.
Nam pro tua sanctissimae vita,	Because of your most holy life,
quam tam pie et devote gessisti	which you have lived so piously and devoutly
in hac valle miseria;	in this vale of misery;
vana huius seculi	by spurning the vain things of this world
spernando et celestia sectando	and following heavenly things instead,
pro tuis meritis	in accord with your merits,
ad super polorum gaudia te	He has established you
ipsum collocavit innumeris.	among the joys of the heavens and countless wonders.
Beate Claudi,	Blessed Claudius,
gloriose confessor Dei:	glorious confessor of God,
implora apud Deum	make our appeal for help
pro nobis auxilium.	before God.

As witnessed in the antiphon for St. Apollonia, a popular text from books of hours may resist a monophonic form but still find its way directly into a polyphonic setting. *O desolatorum consolator* for St. Claudius is another such case. The text appears in motets by both Antonius Divitis and Jean Conseil, both talented musicians in distinguished roles. Divitis was a Netherlandish composer who served as chapel master for Anne of Brittany, the twice-crowned queen of France, beginning in 1510. Disseminated in a 1514 Petrucci print of 25 motets entitled *Motetti de la corona* (*Motets of the Crown*), Divitis's *O desolatorum consolator* was one of several motets to celebrate the French monarch in particular. The text honors the patron saint of Claude of France, the firstborn daughter of King Louis XII and Queen Anne.[15] Displaying no hint of an underlying plainchant, Divitis's motet traverses the text in duets and clarion homophonic declamation.[16] Also from the early sixteenth century, Conseil's *O desolatorum consolator* secures the importance of this text in the context of the French court. This setting of the text for St. Claudius was included in a manuscript copied around 1527 for use in the Sistine Chapel. A French singer sent by Louis XII to serve in the Sistine Chapel during the pontificates of both Leo X and Clement VII, Conseil composed O *desolatorum consolator* for six voices, no doubt easily handled by the pope's esteemed choir.[17] The motet appears as the penultimate work in the manuscript, which has seven masses and eight motets by composers with connections to the French crown, the pope's private chapel, or both.[18]

The examples for Apollonia, Christopher, and Claudius show the flexibility of the antiphon in the context of the suffrages. While the texts provided for antiphons often do refer to office melodies, some were simply prose texts honoring a saint. The genre of antiphon thus became a vessel for texts that were proper to the saint and might have even revealed poetic flair, as in the case of *O desolatorum consolator*. As we will see, the suffrage antiphons further provided a platform for rhythmical and rhymed texts for saints, primed for both recitation or musical articulation by lay users.

The sequence as antiphon

The antiphon most often encountered in suffrages for St. Barbara is *Gaude Barbara beata* (Table 8.1).[19] It is about half the length of the antiphon for St. Christopher, but the poetry—organized into tercets with a consistent 8.8.7 syllable count—is clearly identifiable as a sequence, one of the most discursive of liturgical genres. Sequences developed in the middle of the ninth century with Notker's *Liber ymnorum* and reached their zenith in the middle of the twelfth century with those of Adam of St. Victor. In that span of time, the sequence evolved from its "first epoch," in which a melody existed before text, to a new era that was dominated by versified forms, regularized accentuation within the line, and disyllabic end rhyme.[20] *Gaude Barbara beata* embraces the latter features.

St. Barbara is a curious figure in Christianity. While she was said to live in the time of the Roman emperor Maximian (d. 310), details of her life were not transmitted in early writings or martyrologies; her legend would develop only in the seventh century.[21] Jacobus's *Legenda aurea* may again be consulted for a popular understanding of the saint's vita.[22] The story begins with Barbara's father, a rich man and non-Christian, locking her in a tower to keep suitors away from her great beauty. Venturing out against her father's will, she took up brief residence near a cistern or fountain, which her father was building with the help of a team of workers. She instructed the workers to add a window to the tower in which she was kept, in clear disobedience to her father. Barbara was baptized at the reservoir by a holy man and continued to live there as an ascetic, consuming only locusts and honey, which, Jacobus notes, was in imitation of John the Baptist. When her father returned to see the new window, he was furious and brought her before a judge for her defiance, seeking grave punishment. In her vicious torment, Barbara confessed the Christian faith and was visited by Jesus, the Holy Spirit, and an angel, each of whom brought comfort and healing before her eventual martyrdom. Allusions to Barbara's diet and her brief restoration through an appearance by Christ emerge in the sequence found in books of hours. All but the final stanza notably begin with the exclamatory imperative "Gaude" ("Rejoice").

Gaude Barbara beata Summe pollens in doctrina Angeli mysterio.	Rejoice blessed Barbara most powerful in the mysterious doctrine of the angel.
Gaude virgo Deo grata Quae Baptistam imitata Es in vitae stadio.	Rejoice, Virgin, pleasing to God, you imitated the Baptist in the course of life.
Gaude cum te visitavit Christus vita et curavit Plagas actu proprio.	Rejoice, since Christ visited you in life, he healed your wounds by his own acts.
Gaude quia meruisti Impetrare quod petisti Dante Dei Filio.	Rejoice, for you deserved to obtain that which you sought, the son of God granting it.
Gaude namque elevata Es in coelo et velata Nobili martyrio.	Rejoice, for you have been raised to heaven and veiled with noble martyrdom.
Te laudantem familiam Trahe post te ad gloriam Finito exilio.	Your exile completed, draw the family praising you to glory after you.

There appears to be no discrete melody that could further fasten the poetry of *Gaude Barbara beata* in the minds of medieval owners of books of hours. The sequence text did occasion at least three settings in polyphony, however, one by French court composer Jean

170 *Music beyond the Offices*

Mouton and two by Sistine Chapel favorite Giovanni Pierluigi da Palestrina.[23] None of these works seems to contain an underlying plainsong melody. Despite the lack of a melodic anchor, we may still explore the performance implications of this popular sequence text, and perhaps musical possibilities, as we will see.

Many scribes recognized the poetic nature of *Gaude Barbara beata* and treated it differently than other texts in the context of the suffrages. In some cases, the sequence was not labeled as an antiphon, even though it always fell in that position.[24] In a book of hours owned at one point by the noble Comeau family of Créancey in the Burgundy region (BnF, n.a.l. 3197), we witness the special treatment of *Gaude Barbara beata* (Figure 8.2). The scribe

Figure 8.2 Suffrage for St. Barbara. Paris, BnF, n.a.l. 3197, fol. 122v.

avoided an indication of genre but did articulate the structure of the text with five decorative capitals across the six verses of the sequence. (The capital "G" of the second verse could have been made a capital mirroring the first "Gaude" but remained in regular script.) Illuminating the strophic organization, the scribe aligned each "Gaude" on the left margin, leaving space for a line-fill as needed after the third and fourth verses. The internal rhythm and rhyme in each stanza, however, were not isolated for the user.

Several performative possibilities can be imagined for executing *Gaude Barbara beata*, whether alone or in the company of other supplicants. Given that there is no direct melodic match to the sequence, one can first envision a rhythmical reading of the text—aloud, murmured, or internalized. The reading of the sequence was not implausible even liturgically, as a number of unnotated sequences in sequentiaries testify.[25] The voice (or "inner voice") settles in quickly to the syllable pattern, metrical stresses, and end rhyme characteristic of the genre. The customary trochaic meter dominates the sequence, each verse ending with a dactyl in the concluding seven-syllable line. F. J. E. Raby called this structure the "sequence measure."[26] As with hymns, the consistency and predictability of the stanzas in the "sequence measure" promoted easy absorption and recall, even in the absence of a melody to secure the text. Singsong texts need not be sung.

Alternatively, a musical world can be imagined for the execution of the sequence for St. Barbara. Some background is necessary for conceiving how envoicing the sequence would work without a traceable melody. Unlike hymns, sequence melodies do not repeat the same music as the text unfolds. Rather, they are arranged in musical pairs or double versicles, reciting the melody twice before advancing to another musical idea, sometimes in new tonal space. The sequences of Adam of St. Victor reveal widespread adoption across the Latin West, but most especially in France, where graduals from the twelfth century and onward indicate new melodies for sequences supplanting those of the "first epoch."[27] Importantly, the distinguished tradition of parody and contrafacture at the Abbey of St. Victor, a factory for the later sequence, has implications for musically rendering the sequence for St. Barbara in books of hours. As Margot Fassler has demonstrated, the flowering of poetic texts at the Parisian abbey produced examples that demonstrate how a single melody could serve any number of different texts. Alejandro Planchart has likewise observed that some of the newest poetry written in the "sequence measure" would be sung to pre-existing melodies. It seems to be the only way to explain "the inclusion in missals, well into the era of printing, of numerous 'sequences' for which we have not one source with music, but which could be sung easily by anyone who knew the 'timbre' for them."[28]

The Victorine sequences were highly subject to contrafacture and were still found widely around Paris in the fifteenth century. *Laudes crucis attolamus*—Adam's famous sequence for the Holy Cross known throughout Europe—was frequently retexted, the most famous cognate being *Lauda Sion salvatorem* for the feast of Corpus Christi.[29] For the sake of experiment, we can map the sequence for Barbara easily onto select verses of *Laudes crucis attolamus* (Example 8.2).[30] This imagined setting shows minimal melodic elaboration, reserved mainly for accented syllables; the hypothetical arrangement first reaches its melodic upper boundary (g') opportunely on the word *elevata*. While the Victorine model does feature expansion of the melody and meter in certain verses, only a few parts of the melody would need to be set in order to exhaust the poetry for St. Barbara. The consistent poetic rhythm through each versicle ensures that the text and music will come together seamlessly, no matter which melody or verse is chosen. Variants in melodies make no difference, as users could simply apply a melody of their choice when spotting a sequence text, especially with the help of scribal delineation of these poetic texts replacing the more modest antiphons in suffrages.

172 *Music beyond the Offices*

Example 8.2 Sequence, *Gaude Barbara beata*, set to select verses of *Laudes crucis attolamus* (1A, 2A, 4A). Melody drawn from BnF, lat. 14819, fol. 74r-v.

Barbara is not the only saint treated to a sequence in the suffrages of books of hours, but *Gaude Barbara beata* is the sequence most often encountered in this section. Examples of sequences for St. Katherine (*Gaude virgo Katherina*), St. Mary Magdalene (*Gaude pia Magdalena*), St. Margaret (*Gaude virgo Margareta*), and John the Baptist (*Gaude Iohannes baptista*) reveal that a "Gaude" model undergirds this complex of sequences.[31] The exemplar is no doubt the Marian sequence *Gaude virgo mater Christi*.[32] The origin of this text lies in thirteenth-century liturgies, but connections to the Mass loosen by the fifteenth century. The sequence would thereafter circulate widely as a stand-alone rhymed and rhythmical prayer in devotional books. While *Gaude virgo mater Christi* occasionally found a home in the accessory texts of some books of hours (apart from the suffrages), hundreds of sequences were written in imitation of it.[33] The command to "rejoice" at the beginning of the five stanzas could allude to the Five Joys of the Virgin. Another form of the word ("gaudio") concludes the sixth and final stanza, maintaining the parallelism of the sequence genre while preserving the odd number of joys.

Gaude, virgo mater Christi,	Rejoice, Virgin mother of Christ,
Quae per aurem concepisti	Who conceived through the ear
Gabriele nuntio.	By Gabriel's message.
Gaude, que a Deo plena,	Rejoice, you who, pregnant by God,
Peperisti sine poena	Bore without blame
Cum pudoris lilio.	With the lily of modesty.

Gaude, quia tui nati.	Rejoice, for the one born of you,
Quem dolebas mortem pati,	Whose death you sorrowed to experience,
Fulget resurrectio.	Shines in resurrection.
Gaude Christo ascendente	Rejoice in Christ who ascends,
Et in coelum te vidente	And who, seeing you in heaven,
Motu fertur proprio.	Is moved of his own accord.
Gaude, quod post ipsum scandis	Rejoice, you who ascend after him;
Et est honor tibi grandis	There is great honor for you
In caeli palatio.	In the palace of heaven.
Ubi fructus ventris tui	Where the fruit of your womb
Per te detur nobis frui	May be given to us through you
In perenni gaudio.	To delight in eternal rejoicing.

The sequence for St. Barbara echoes the "Gaude" salutations of the Marian prototype, opening all stanzas but the final one.[34] Other "Gaude" sequences for saints feature at least a handful of "Gaude" stanzas. Planchart located six different melodies for *Gaude virgo mater Christi*, none emerging with any special prominence.[35] Still, these rhymed prayers from books of hours and elsewhere, which never had a stable place in the liturgy, were good candidates for use in motets, as Howard Mayer Brown noticed.[36] And the "Gaude" sequences and other sequences were further susceptible to a monophonic recasting by their rhythmic nature. It is even tempting to see the assonance of the first word of *Laudes crucis attolamus* prompting a connection to the "Gaude" of a derivative sequence. Adam's sequence was just one widespread melody that could accommodate verses trumpeting Mary and the saints.

Excursus: Sequences beyond the suffrages

Apart from the suffrages, sequences like *Gaude virgo mater Christi* occasionally appear elsewhere in books of hours. A brief string of *Gaude* sequences, unusual in books of hours, surfaces in a source dating from the second quarter of the fifteenth century in southern France (BnF, n.a.l. 3196). Sadly, the manuscript is in too fragile a state to allow images to be reproduced; nonetheless, the texts it bears are significant. In this extraordinary book of hours from the small city of Rodez (northeast of Toulouse), the compiler provided three sequences after a Mass for the Virgin, itself a fairly uncommon liturgical accessory, as we will see in Chapter 9. The rubric "Sequ[u]ntur septem gaudia spiritualia beatissime virginis Marie" ("Here follows the seven spiritual joys of the most Blessed Virgin Mary") precedes the first Marian sequence of the group, *Gaude flore virginali*, at one time attributed to Thomas Becket, archbishop of Canterbury.[37] Its seven-stanza structure is organized into double versicles, rather than single strophes of 8.8.7, perhaps making it especially suitable for overlaying a monophonic sequence melody organized into verse pairs. The "joys" number seven in *Gaude flore virginali*, in contrast to the five of *Gaude virgo mater Christi*. Five joys were by no means a standard in Marian devotion; in the later Middle Ages, the number of the Virgin's joys ranged from 5 to 21. The seven joys of *Gaude flore virginali* were in fact the most common, a counterweight to the seven enumerated "sorrows" of Mary, which developed in the fourteenth and fifteenth centuries.[38] The joys in this sequence are not seven traditional events in the life of the Virgin, but rather reflections on Mary in heaven.[39]

The seven spiritual joys in BnF, n.a.l. 3196, are followed by a set of seven temporal joys of the Virgin with the familiar opening *Gaude virgo mater Christi*.[40] In comparison with the sequence of the same title given earlier, this version adds two rare verses to achieve its seven joys—"Gaude natum adorari" (for the Adoration of the Magi) and "Gaude sanctos informari" (for the descent of the Holy Spirit) in the third and sixth stanzas, respectively. The concluding non-"Gaude" stanza ("Ubi fructus ventris tui") matches the more popular version. That both of these "Gaude" sequences in BnF, n.a.l. 3196 are accompanied by a versicle, response, and at least one oration reveals an inclination to situate prayers of this kind within a suffrage-like context, while substituting the rhymed prayer for the customary antiphon.

The "Gaude" sequences persist in BnF, n.a.l. 3196. After a series of prayers, including an extraordinary rhymed and rhythmical litany of saints attributed to St. Peter of Luxembourg,[41] the compiler reprises the seven spiritual and temporal joys in full before presenting another five joys (rubricated simply as "gaudia") titled *Gaude virgo gloriosa*, a prayer that breaks with the sequence meter.[42] Several prayers intervene, most in unrhymed prose, before two related rhymed poems round out this substantial section of accessory prayers. Both stem from the popular *Stabat mater dolorosa*, the sequence focused on Mary's own agony as she stood weeping for Jesus at the foot of the cross.[43] Once attributed to the Franciscan Jacopone da Todi (d.1306?), the *Stabat mater* was a rhymed prayer of 20 stanzas, each of which assumed the "sequence measure" of 8.8.7. In the poem, the supplicant begs the Virgin to experience her grief and to suffer Christ's pain at the crucifixion. The *Stabat mater* was widely known as a spoken prayer through at least the sixteenth century and had circulation in books of hours, if not copiously in French sources of the fifteenth century. The text occasioned several settings in polyphony of the fifteenth and sixteenth centuries, including by Josquin des Prez and Palestrina, and it has proved an attractive text for composers into the modern era.[44] Affective poetry on Mary's sorrows could be found in various genres, from hymns and sermons to passion plays and laments (*planctus*).[45] The Dominicans—mainly in Germany—appear to have been the early stewards of a broader Marian "compassion" movement, thanks in no small part to mystic Henry Suso, whose *Horologium sapientiae* from the mid-1330s relays vivid reflections on the Virgin's anguish.[46]

The *Stabat mater* itself emerges first with slight variants, including its opening word, "Salve."[47] Otherwise, the sequence mirrors that found in many books of hours as a standard accessory prayer located outside of the offices. A planctus invoking some of the language of the *Stabat mater* follows *Salve mater dolorosa* in BnF, n.a.l. 3196, separated by a versicle, response, and prayer. Labeled "alia oratio," the rhymed prayer *Ante crucem mater stabat* is next in the series of prayers in the manuscript, but its appearance looks nothing like typical orations in books of hours. Unfolded in quatrains of eight-syllable lines resembling a hymn, it was in fact a Latin planctus, another lament of the Virgin at the scene of the cross, which survived in numerous manuscripts.[48]

Despite its more characteristic status as a spoken prayer with rhythm and rhyme, the *Stabat mater* did take musical shape in the late Middle Ages, though the melodic assignment is inconsistent. Cesarino Ruini recently discovered a notated version of the Marian sequence in a thirteenth-century Dominican gradual, by far the earliest identified setting.[49] The text had been set again to music in the late fifteenth century and was included as the sequence in the liturgy for the Compassion of the Virgin, a new feast rooted in the devotion of the Seven Sorrows.[50] Both sequences have *f* finals, though the former was the rarer setting.[51] On the latter *Stabat mater*, Nancy van Deusen noted the broad concordance patterns among a large network of more than 50 sequences across Europe, of which that popular sequence was a part. The group she identified, which also includes *Laudes crucis attolamus* and other well-known sequences, could be found in sequentiaries throughout the continent. Her remarks on the cultural awareness of sequences among the general populace are pertinent here: "Together all of the sequences . . . indicate what even an ordinary person without special training in music or even a general education, from the late eleventh to the end of the sixteenth century, would have recognized as a sequence."[52]

Among the more performance-oriented occurrences of the *Stabat mater* in French books of hours is that found in BnF, lat. 1181 (Figure 8.3). The sequence is preceded by an exquisite miniature of Mary holding her lifeless son, surrounded by three women at the scene of the Crucifixion.[53] The prayer beneath the scene begins with a large capital "S" spanning the initial tercet. Periods separate each line of eight syllables, with a capital letter and *pied-de-mouche* beginning each subsequent line to regulate oral or internal recitation. The appearance of the verses on the verso establishes a clear pattern for user engagement. Each stanza begins with a capital set against alternating red and blue backgrounds. The first two lines of each stanza consist of the requisite four trochees; the next line never encroaches on it. When one of these eight-syllable lines falls short (as in the lines "Fuit illa benedicta" and "Et dolebat cum iudebat"), a two-toned line-fill is added to propel the user to the next line. The final seven-syllable line of each strophe is always filled with the colored bar. Line-fills occupy no small part of the text block and subsequent folios not shown of the sequence.

Were a medieval user to rehearse the *Stabat mater* to music, the sequence meter itself would open up further possibilities for private or public envoicing. Adam of St. Victor's *Laudes crucis attolamus* was known throughout France, England, and the Rhineland, and was not infrequently applied to the text of the *Stabat mater*, similar to the experiment with the sequence for St. Barbara.[54] Fassler reminds us that it did not matter whether these mix-and-match rhymed sequence texts were sung or read aloud: they offered great rewards for any kind of poetic performance, bordering on a playful game, for those who knew Latin.[55] We must recall that some owners of books of hours could not read Latin but used the prayers therein to cultivate an understanding of the language that they had heard. Slotted prominently in the position of the antiphon in a suffrage or elsewhere in books of hours, sequences could act as a mini-primer to remember the Latin through its structured flow. The fluidity of the language in the sequences stands in contrast to the more cumbersome and less predictable prose of the book's gospel readings, antiphons, and orations. Rhymed and rhythmical poetry continues to act as a tool for those learning the rudiments of a language but also for those in search of vivid imagery in the context of prayer.

With regard to the "Gaude" complex of rhymed sequences highlighted here, it is significant to note that nuns in particular observed the Mary's joys with fervent devotion. The earliest extant evidence of *Gaude virgo mater Christi* in fact has ties to an English convent. This early example of the prayer in turn was used in connection with the antiphon *Gaude dei genetrix* (CAO 2920), itself filled with a handful of "Gaude" exclamations and deployed on various Marian feasts.[56] Though BnF, n.a.l. 3196 reveals an exceptional case of the "Gaude" sequences and further opens a window into the famous *Stabat mater* in an emergent stage, these rhymed texts were surprisingly not fixtures in French books of hours. As we transition away from the antiphons in the suffrages, we encounter the more modest genre of the versicle with response, familiar from Chapter 5, but situated in a dedicated position in the suffrages.

Suffrage dialogues

A versicle and its attendant response occupy the middle part of a suffrage. True to its function as a connective device, the dialogue here links the antiphon to the typically lengthy oration. Similar to those found throughout books of hours, the versicle in a suffrage is a short

Figure 8.3 Sequence, *Stabat mater*. Paris, BnF, lat. 1181, fol. 175r-v.

Figure 8.3 (Continued)

supplicatory text, followed by a collective choral rejoinder. Dominated by memorials to individual saints, the suffrages commonly presented a simple versicle to the saint by name: "Ora pro nobis beate/beata [N.]" ("Pray for us blessed/St. [N.]"). The formulation combines the request and the name of the saint into a single entreaty, unlike in the Litany where the two parts are separated ("St. [N.]"/"Pray for us"). In the suffrages, the customary response to this appeal is always "Ut digni efficiamur promissionibus Christi" ("that we may be made worthy of the promises of Christ."), a clause of purpose in the subjunctive mood. Although the corporate response following the prompt was well known and automatic, it was often written out in full in the suffrages each time it occurred, echoing the diligence witnessed elsewhere in books of hours.[57] The appearance of the versicle-response pair has two notable features. The script typically remains small, matching the preceding antiphon in the suffrage. More crucially for imagining or performing the voices of the suffrage, the scribe will often rubricate the versicle and response with ℣ and ℟, respectively. The change of subgenre cues the fuller choral interjection as an answer to the intoned entreaty.

The single interior dialogue of the suffrages bears a level of musical simplicity similar to that found throughout books of hours. Amounting to a little less than half of all versicle-responses, the conventional "Ora/Ut digni" grouping (CAO 8164) was the most prevalent pairing in the suffrages, though it was reserved generally for saints of lower rank or of local interest. Table 8.2 summarizes the chief versicles and responses for the common saints of the suffrages in fifteenth-century books of hours. Seven of the 15 dedicatees represented were usually assigned the generic "Ora/Ut digni" dialogue, beginning with St. James ("Iacobus") and continuing down the hierarchy. This versicle and response were subject to other textual variation. While the name of the saint was necessarily altered in the opening intonation, the classification of that saint sometimes ventured beyond "beate" or "beata" for male and female saints, respectively. A versicle for St. Apollonia, for example, could add that she was a virgin, a martyr, or both.[58] The response for St. Sebastian veers from the model not in its versicle but in the customary answer, offering an extra plea against the threat of plague for which the saint was known: "Ut mereamur pestem epidimie illesi transire et promissionem Christi obtinere" ("That we may deserve to pass unscathed from pestilence and obtain the promise of Christ").[59]

For the suffrage versicles that do not draw on the "Ora/Ut digni" pair, French books of hours do reveal some consistency in the assignments, though a single versicle did not always emerge as dominant for some saints. While some texts are attached to saints with regularity, they may not always mention the appointed holy figure by name. For instance, some pairings could be extracts from the Psalter, which were ready-made in two parts to suit the genre of the dialogue. Suffrages for St. Katherine and St. Anne feature a versicle that traces to Psalm 44:3 ("Diffusa est gratia"), a verse used for various female saints, though primarily for virgin saints.

Table 8.2 Common versicle-response pairings in the suffrages

Honoree	Versicle	Response	CAO no.
Trinity	Sit nomen Domini benedictum	Ex hoc nunc et usque in saeculum	8199.1
St. Michael	In conspectu angelorum psallam tibi deus meus.	Adorabo ad templum sanctum tuum et confitebor nomini tuo.	8092
John the Baptist	Fuit homo missus a deo	Cui nomen erat Iohannes	8075
St. John the Evangelist	Valde honorandus	Qui supra pectus	8230

Honoree	Versicle	Response	CAO no.
Sts. Peter and Paul	In omnem terram exivit sonus eorum	Et in fines orbi terre verba eorum.	8097
St. James	Ora pro nobis beate Iacobe	Ut digni efficiamur promissionibus Christi	8164
St. Anthony	Ora pro nobis beate Anthoni	Ut digni . . .	8164
St. Christopher	Ora pro nobis beate Christofore	Ut digni . . .	8164
St. Sebastian	Ora pro nobis beate Sebastiane	Ut mereamur pestem . . .	8164
St. Nicholas	Ora pro nobis beate Nicolae	Ut digni . . .	8164
St. Katherine	Diffusa est gratia in labiis tuis	Propterea benedixit te deus in eternum.	8014
St. Anne	Diffusa est gratia in labiis tuis	Propterea benedixit te deus in eternum.	8014
St. Barbara	Ora pro nobis beata Barbara	Ut digni . . .	8164
St. Margaret	Specie tua et pulchritudine tua	Intende prospere procede et regna.	8201
St. Mary Magdalene	Dimissa sunt ei peccata multa	Quoniam dilexit multum.	800106*
St. Apollonia	Ora pro nobis beata Apollonia	Ut digni . . .	8164

*Cataloged in the Cantus Index, not in CAO.

Liturgical service books prescribed the "Ora/Ut digni" dialogue at different points in the Divine Office, spanning all of the services on various saints' feasts. As one can guess from the broader discussion of versicles and responses in Chapter 5, the versicle-response pair will be formulaic, the response echoing the pitches of the versicle custom fit to its text. The melodic shape of the "Ora/Ut digni" pairing did not take one form but rather different forms, which makes classification as a single entity CAO 8164 misleading.[60] The variance, of course, would not be obvious from books of hours, since they lack notation. Further, it was rare for scribes of most liturgical sources to indicate the melody, especially with all the times the versicle and response might be employed. A few sources, fortunately, provide notation for CAO 8164, allowing a glimpse of the different musical possibilities.[61]

A late twelfth-century antiphoner from Marseille reveals pitch content for the "Ora pro nobis" intonation amid a liturgy for St. Martin. This was a saint sometimes celebrated in suffrages, but surprisingly not as a staple in French books of hours. A recitation tone is immediately evident, scrupulously repeated on f above each syllable, before peeling off into a cadential flourish (Example 8.3). Because the remnant of the staff lines etched by the rostrum is visible, a secure retrieval of the nine pitches for the versicle's termination is possible (E-f-E-D-C-D-f-E-D), presumably assigned to the final syllable. The missing "Ut digni" response would likewise follow this formula, taking the cadential cursus with a final destination of D. This recitation and termination highly resembles the versicle "Diffusa est gratia" for St. Katherine and St. Anne (CAO 8014) provided in Example 5.1.

This concordance is encouraging: we can now point to a formula that applies to versicles in both the office and the suffrages for different saints. Further, since the suffrages for

Example 8.3 Versicle for St. Martin. Transcribed from BnF, lat. 1090, fol. 228r.

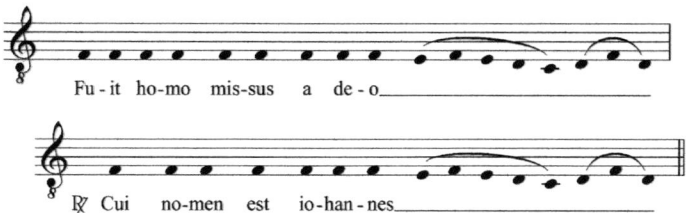

Example 8.4 Versicle and response for John the Baptist. Transcribed from BnF, n.a.l. 1412, fol. 62r.

St. Katherine and St. Anne prescribed CAO 8014 from the Common of a Virgin or Virgins, there lies the potential—from the scant evidence we have—to connect this melody to the dominant versicle (CAO 8164) typically encountered in the suffrages. It is tempting to project the common intonation on a larger scale, but again CAO 8164 had other melodic manifestations.

Other versicles in the suffrages may also co-opt the tone that we have seen for CAO 8164 and 8014. A mantric verse for John the Baptist from the Gospel of John 1:6, "Fuit homo missus" (CAO 8075), was perhaps the most consistently assigned of all versicle-responses in the suffrage corpus. A notated incipit to this text is given twice in the late twelfth-century antiphoner from Marseille, indicating an unwavering recitation on *f*, but with an unknown termination.[62] A Cistercian antiphoner from northern Italy in the same period reveals those same notes but continues to unveil the full extent of the versicle and response, to wit the prevailing termination formula, albeit with a minor variant (Example 8.4). Similarly, the dialogue "Specie tua," often seen in the suffrages for St. Margaret and drawn from Psalm 44:5, is recoverable in notated form from the Marseille antiphoner with the intonation reflecting the "Ora/Ut digni" formulation.[63]

Absent a larger set of notated sources of versicles and responses, there is still some confidence that the tone chosen in the middle part of a suffrage could both accommodate the various texts required and also retain some melodic consistency. Though it should never be understood as a proxy for medieval sources, the *Liber usualis* recommends this same tone for versicles and responses for different parts of the liturgy, providing additional comfort in the widespread nature of this tone.[64] While no universal musical experience can be realistically posited in execution of CAO 8164 and its relatives, users of books of hours might have had access to a simple and flexible option to hear specific sounds linking antiphon to the oration.

Orations

The orations (*orationes*) are the longest of the texts provided in a given suffrage; they are prose prayers characteristically presented in a script size noticeably larger than the antiphon, versicle, and response. Their length was exceeded only by the occasional sequence text that stood in for the suffrage antiphon. The oration as a genre highly resembles the Collect of the Mass (*collecta, collectio*), a proper supplication found at the end of the introductory rite.[65] The presence of the Collect can be traced to the fifth century. It is usually found without notation in books called sacramentaries, which also contained the Preface and the Canon of the Mass. In books of hours and in liturgies, the oration will sometimes be preceded by a call to corporate prayer "oremus" ("let us pray"), delivered on a single pitch by a celebrant or deacon. Musically, the prose of the oration, like the Collect at Mass, was chanted to the simplest of musical formulas, similar to—and likely simpler than—the prior versicle and response. Placed mainly on a single comfortable (or slightly elevated) pitch, the oration's musical course took on the character of liturgical recitative associated with readings. Individual lines could include a flex tone, and full stops would carry a formulaic cadence or even a single note of contrasting distinction, perhaps a half step or minor third below the reciting tone. Despite the musical plainness, the possibilities were still many for how the intonation was to be executed.

In the spirit of the Collect, most orations in books of hours consist of at least two or three sentences (often more) and are always specific to the saint in question. There is a conventional three-part structure behind these prayers, made up of a *protasis*, *apodosis*, and concluding doxology (or "simple pleading"). The protasis is an invocation calling upon God or the saint who is being commemorated. This opening part of the prayer usually contains a "relative predicate" or ascription of praise or statement of truth in a relative clause, which leads to the apodosis—the petition itself.[66] The final pleading, usually abbreviated in books of hours, is "Per Christum Dominum nostrum" ("through Christ our Lord"), which is followed by an "Amen." In the concluding "Amen," a user of a book of hours would recognize another brief dialogue at that moment, as the voice of the assembly is summoned. The call and response is one with musical potential, executed with textural distinction, moving from the extended monotonous recitation of a single voice to a sonorous retort of a large group for the collective "Amen." As prose, orations lack performative cues outside of punctuation. Occasionally, there will be two orations to close a saint's suffrage, usually signaled by the rubric "alia oratio" or similar.[67]

We may briefly note the extraordinary case of a book of hours—BnF, n.a.l. 3209—prepared in the mid-fifteenth century for Hugues of Cluny, a member of an elite Burgundian family that produced dignitaries of church and state. The collection of nine saints in the suffrages is mostly unremarkable, though Lazarus is a rare inclusion.[68] Most notable are the large decorative initials, which fall precisely at the oration, not with the opening antiphon as was customary. Four of the initials further were illuminated, highly atypical in that position. For both kinds of adornment, Hugues might have been lured away from the antiphons, versicles, and responses, which remain in smaller script. In the opening suffrage for St. Michael (Figure 8.4), the prescribed antiphon *Dum sacrum mysterium* presents the text of a widely circulated eighth-mode Magnificat antiphon (CAO 2469) for the feast of the archangel, though it did not surface as often as *Michael archangele paradisi* in books of hours (Table 8.1).[69] The imposing illuminated capital "D" is placed at the beginning of the oration, pulling the user away from the other parts of this suffrage.[70] The illuminator, identified as Antoine de Lonhy, depicts the protector saint, cloaked in red around his armor.[71] With his sword drawn and his hand clasping a human-like serpent, St. Michael is ready to slay the enemy. The text of the suffrage for St. Michael, beginning "Deus qui miro ordine" does not mention the saint by name, but rather speaks of the angels at large who both serve God in heaven and protect the faithful on earth: "O God, who in a marvelous order established the ministries of angels and of men, | mercifully grant that as your attendants serve you in heaven, so also may our life on earth be defended through them. | Through Christ our Lord. Amen." In its three constituent parts, this oration is of typical length and ends with the anticipated change of voice from the soloist's prose to the choral "Amen."

Figure 8.4 Suffrage for St. Michael. Paris, BnF, n.a.l. 3209, fol. 75v.

This oration for St. Michael was widely found in connection with suffrages of the saint in books of hours. Despite the variable nature of prose prayers in general and even across books of hours, certain orations tend to recur with particular saints. Among other relatively consistent orations across books of hours were those for John the Baptist ("Presta quesumus omnipotens"), John the Evangelist ("Ecclesiam tuam quesumus"), St. James ("Esto Domine plebis tue"), St. Margaret ("Deus qui beatam Margaretam"), and St. Mary Magdalene ("Largire nobis"). The stability of these orations suggests that these prayers bore patterns of transmission similar to the antiphons, versicles, and responses associated with fifteenth-century suffrages. While it is natural to think of prose prayers as highly mutable, we are reminded that even these lengthier texts resisted deviation across generations of usage in books of hours.

Memorials outside the suffrages

In the earlier discussion of "Gaude"-inspired sequences, it was noted that a few of these were followed by a dialogue and oration, effectively structured as suffrages in an accessory section of a book of hours. This phenomenon exists elsewhere in books of hours, most visibly in the short commemoration for All Saints, found outside the suffrages in more than half of extant sources. Invariably slated without a miniature, the All Saints memorial was an appendage to each of the hours in the Office of the Virgin, except for the first service of Matins. In its shadowing of a principal office celebration, the observance of All Saints across the hours mirrors the original function of the Office of the Virgin itself, affixed to the primary round of daily liturgical services at the Cathedral of Notre Dame in Paris as early as the thirteenth century. The appended sanctoral commemoration might be rubricated "De omnibus sanctis," "Pro sanctis," or similar. In its suffrage format, the memorial for All Saints offered a consistent antiphon, versicle, and response. The designated antiphon was always *Sancti dei omnes* (CAO 4726), a melody assigned to various hours on the feast of All Saints and in suffrages to the heavenly throng found in liturgical sources.[72] The dialogue *Laetamini in Domino/Et gloriamini omnes* (CAO 8120) was likewise a standard text allocated to the memorial. However, the orations usually changed across the liturgical hours.

One of the most richly illuminated books of hours in all of European history—the Hours of Louis de Laval (BnF, lat. 920)—can reveal the parts of the All Saints memorial *in situ*. Louis de Laval (1411–1489) was a French nobleman of many titles (Lord of Châtillon, for one) and counselor to King Louis XI; he must be counted as one of the great bibliophiles of the fifteenth century. Jean Colombe illuminated for Louis this lavish *horae*, which was initiated around 1470 but not completed until the last years of the lord's life. The massive book of some 342 folios is flooded with artistic images—more than 1,200 in all; 157 of them are full-page miniatures. The illuminations operate on two levels: Old Testament scenes intermingle with more conventional devotional images, typically juxtaposed on a single leaf. The traditional imagery of Mary and Jesus may have some connection to the principal text of each folio, while the Old Testament depictions unfold stories independently, with no obvious link to the content of the hours.

At the end of Lauds in the Office of the Virgin of BnF, lat. 920, the All Saints memorial appears with two orations (Figure 8.5), not uncommon for this suffrage across the corpus. The memorial text is surrounded on all sides by differing adornments. The vernacular prose in both upper panels describes the episode from Genesis 39 between Joseph and the wife of the Egyptian official Potiphar, while the lower panels depict these same Old Testament scenes. On the bottom of the verso, Joseph is leaving while the woman holds his cloak, ready

Figure 8.5 Memorial for All Saints. Paris, BnF, lat. 920, fols. 92v–93r.

Figure 8.5 (Continued)

Figure 8.6 Memorial for the Trinity. LBL, Yates Thompson MS 3 ("The Dunois Hours"), fols. 14v–15r. © The British Library Board.

Figure 8.6 (Continued)

to accuse him of sexual transgressions. On the lower recto, he is held by guards while she relays her fabricated story to Potiphar. A depiction of Jesus as "Salvator mundi" holding a cross-bearing orb occupies the leftmost panel of the opening, while the opposite side shows Christ washing the apostles' feet. Colombe's lateral images were by no means arbitrary, usually inspired by a text in the interior. The suffrage in the middle of the page is conventional, and the genres are clearly marked for the noble user. The antiphon *Sancti dei omnes* is rubricated with the proper genre but bears no indications of articulation. In the remaining parts of the memorial, only the first oration does not offer a clue to envoicing. The second oration beginning on the recto (only partially shown) features a yellow *pied-de-mouche* and colon to regulate delivery, while the response uses the same color at the change of texture on the preceding verso. The text of the first oration ("Protege Dominum populum tuum") is one of four used in the All Saints memorial; these orations rotated through the hours from Lauds to Compline.[73] The artist's "Salvator mundi" image seems to have been prompted the text of this oration.[74]

Beyond the All Saints commemoration, it is possible, though rarer, to find suffrages to individual saints outside of the dedicated section of suffrages in books of hours. The Trinity memorial is occasionally found apart from the suffrages, for instance. This suffrage to the triune God is commonly found in a section of books of hours that has scarcely received mention in this study—the readings of the four evangelists. The gospel excerpts—John 1: 1–14, Luke 1: 25–38, Matthew 2: 2–12, and Mark 16: 14–20—customarily fall after the opening calendar in books of hours, carrying importance in both their position and textual invariance. The simplest textural distinctions of sound may be deciphered in the evangelical texts and the congregational "Deo gratias," which concludes each reading. It may also be noted that the celebrant's text "In illo tempore," occasionally preceding the reading of the synoptic gospels in books of hours, signals a liturgical performance and listening experience, rather than a plain biblical text.[75] This text served no function except to introduce the passage generically as a kind of envoiced alert. Additional layers of sound were introduced when the Trinity memorial appears following the gospel lessons.

The antiphon for the Trinity, assigned to this new "evangelical" position as well as in the suffrages, is the mode 4 melody *Te invocamus, te adoramus* (CAO 5119) shown earlier in Example 8.1. Reminiscent of part of the Gloria from the Mass Ordinary, this antiphon unfolds in a series of short sentences in the first-person plural: "We call on you, we adore you, we praise you, O blessed Trinity."[76] Although transmission of the antiphon text in notated liturgical sources is stable, books of hours show more unevenness with *Te invocamus, te adoramus*. Appearing to conflate the text with the Gloria, some books of hours will insert "te glorificamus" into the text.[77] Examples of the extraneous text reveal that it could be placed anywhere in the series, not necessarily after the "te adoramus," if one is truly confusing it with the series from the Mass Ordinary. Following the reading from John's Gospel in the "Dunois Hours" from the 1440s, the Trinity antiphon shows the "te glorificamus" as second in the series (Figure 8.6). Erroneously or not, the scribe also copied the added modifier "sancta" to the concluding "O beata trinitas." Typical for this antiphon, scribes punctuated the series, here with a dot of separation.

The remainder of the Trinity suffrage is unremarkable. The versicle and response draw from Psalm 112:2: *Sit nomen Domini benedictum* ("Blessed be the name of the Lord") pairs with the consequent *Ex hoc nunc et usque in seculum* (From henceforth now and forever"). The suffrage is prolonged in its interior by an additional versicle and response, the ubiquitous *Domine exaudi/Et clamor* (CAO 8025). The dialogues lead to the intoned "Oremus," which prepares the common oration for the Trinity suffrage "Protector in te sperantium Deus"

("God, protector of all who trust in you"), a prayer that doubled as a Collect for the third Sunday after Pentecost.

*

The structure of the suffrages—antiphon, versicle, response, and oration—is essential to recognize in the study of books of hours, as this ceremonial unit may be found well outside the suffrages, whether amid the offices, as is the case with the pervasive All Saints memorial, or in different pockets of prayer apart from the formal liturgies. All items had sonic potentiality for those who recognized it. Suffrage-type arrangements may supplant the antiphon with a sequence as seen earlier or with other types of texts, even well-known pieces of music. Two of the three freestanding devotions that open BnF, lat. 1181, for example, assumed the memorial configuration. The first is rubricated "orison de nostre damme" [sic], but it is the familiar antiphon *Salve regina*, followed by an appropriate Marian versicle, response, and oration. The second grouping, designated "orison du saint espirit himne," conflates two genres (prayer and hymn) in its description of *Veni creator spiritus*, of which seven stanzas are given before reaching the remaining parts of the memorial to the Holy Spirit.[78] Unlike the pervasive suffrages, the final topic we explore in this sound journey through the book of hours—the Mass for the Virgin Mary—is something of a rare gem. Its texts are unmistakable, though, and refer to some of the most sumptuous melodies one could include for devotion.

Notes

1 The word *suffragium* has broader significance than *memoria*; it signals an intercessory purpose above simple commemoration. See Bennett, "Commemoration of the Saints in Suffrages," 56–62.
2 Leroquais, *Les livres d'heures manuscrits*, 1: xxi.
3 For background on the suffrages in books of hours, particularly in the early sources, see Bennett, "Commemoration of the Saints in Suffrages," 54–78.
4 Hiley, *Western Plainchant*, 29.
5 Harrison, *Music in Medieval Britain*, 76–77.
6 In BnF, lat. 12044, for example, *Inter natos mulierum* can be found as an antiphon in both Vespers (fol. 143r) and Lauds (fol. 145v) for the Baptist's June 24 feast, but it is also prescribed in the second nocturn of Matins (fol. 179v) for the Decollation of the Baptist (August 29).
7 The gradual Spišská Kapitula, Knižnica Spišskej Kapituly, Nr. 1 contains five proper chants for the mass (fol. 221r), none matching the title of the prevalent antiphon from the suffrages.
8 Jacobus, *The Golden Legend of Jacobus de Voragine*, 164.
9 Bologna, Museo Internazionale e Biblioteca della Musica, MS Q.19, fols. 202v–203r, dated to ca. 1518.
10 Brown, "The Mirror of Man's Salvation"; Blackburn, "The Virgin in the Sun"; Cumming, " Petrucci's Publics"; and Macey, "Galeazzo Maria Sforza," for example.
11 See the full text, for example, in Bethlehem, Lehigh University, Special Collections, Codex 18, fol. 130r–131r.
12 Jacobus, *The Golden Legend of Jacobus de Voragine*, 377–382.
13 On Claudius's life, see Goyau, "Saint-Claude," in *CE* 13: 341–342.
14 Occasionally, the concluding appeal, "Beate Claudi, gloriose confessor . . . ," is omitted in books of hours.
15 On the motet, see Heartz, *Pierre Attaingnant*, 39–40.
16 For an edition, see *Divitis: Collected Works*, 221–230.
17 Vatican City, Biblioteca Apostolica Vaticana, Cappella Sistina MS 55, fols. 133v–136r. For an edition of Conseil's motet, see Brauner, "Jean du Conseil," 124–132.
18 Despite the utility of this text for the French monarch by one of its prized singer-composers, Jeffrey Dean reminds us that Cappella Sistina MS 55 was mainly copied by Claudius Bouchet and Claudius Gellandi, who had every reason to include a motet honoring their shared namesake.

19 *AH* 29: 97. Minor variants can be found in the texts of books of hours.
20 Kruckenberg, "Sequence," 1: 300–356; Bower, "From Alleluia to Sequence."
21 J.P. Kirsch, "Barbara, Saint, Virgin and Martyr," in *CE* 2: 284–285.
22 Jacobus, *The Golden Legend or Lives of the Saints*, 6: 198–205. This is a later edition of the *Legenda*.
23 Editions of Morales's mass and Mouton's motet may both be found in Morales, *Opera Omnia*, 6:34–66, 133–41. Palestrina has motet settings for four and five voices (*Werke*, 7: 70–72; 2: 59–67, respectively), the former cast in homophony, the latter mostly in imitative polyphony and in two *partes*. For an edition of Adrian Willaert's *Missa Gaude Barbara*, see Willaert, *Opera omnia*, 9: 108–143.
24 The scribes of BnF, lat. 923 (fol. 96r) and BnF, Ars. 1188 (fol. 89r) omit a genre designation before the Barbara suffrage, though other suffrages in those manuscripts are labeled as antiphons.
25 Sometimes sequences are entered without notation in otherwise notated service books. See Van Deusen, "The Use and Significance of the Sequence," 23.
26 Raby, *A History of Christian-Latin Poetry*, 348.
27 Clemens Blume, "Prose or Sequence," in *CE* 12: 482–484.
28 Planchart, "What's in a Name?" 171–172.
29 Fassler, *Gothic Song*, 64–78 and *passim*. *Laudes crucis attollamus* (*AH* 54:188) and *Lauda Sion salvatorem* (*AH* 50:584) essentially draw on the same melody. The former begins with a single versicle for the first verse, while the first verse of *Lauda Sion salvatorem* begins with a double versicle. Other texts to the melody (all containing melodic variants) include *Zema vetus* (*AH* 54:227); *Templum cordis* (*AH* 54:307); *Laus erumpat* (*AH* 55:288); *Gaude Sion et laetare* (*AH* 55:28); and *Dies ista celebretur* (*AH* 54:180).
30 The unpaired opening verse of *Laudes crucis attollamus* (1A) is repeated in this experimental setting, echoing the structure of *Lauda Sion salvatorem*. Verse 3 of *Laudes crucis attollamus* is also bypassed in this example because it doubles in length (8.8.7. 8.8.7 for the versicle) and would consume the sequence text for Barbara before reaching its parallel statement. For a complete transcription of *Laudes crucis attollamus*, see Fassler, *Gothic Song*, 416–418.
31 For examples of these sequences, see LBL, Add. MS 38126 (fol. 144r) for Katherine; BnF, lat. 1171 (fol. 84v) for Mary Magdalene; and BnF, n.a.l. 3214 (fol. 176r and 158v) for Margaret and John the Baptist, respectively.
32 *AH* 24: 57.
33 Wieck, *Time Sanctified*, 103.
34 For a discussion of the sequence *Gaude virgo mater Christi*, see Nosow, "Du Fay and the Cultures of Renaissance Florence," 106–107, 112.
35 Planchart, "What's in a Name?" 171.
36 Brown, "The Mirror of Man's Salvation," 751–753.
37 BnF, n.a.l. 3196, fols. 143v–145r. The sequence text is cataloged as *AH* 31:198–99. The chronology would militate against the attribution to Thomas, if *Gaude virgo mater Christi* were its model.
38 Schuler, "The Seven Sorrows of the Virgin," 16. On the development of the Joys of Mary, see also Winston-Allen, *Stories of the Rose*, 34–46.
39 The seven joyful events vary, but usually include the Annunciation, Visitation, Nativity, Adoration of the Magi, Finding in the Temple, Resurrection, and Coronation of the Virgin.
40 BnF, n.a.l. 3196, fols. 145v–146r. For an example of a prayer book with *Gaude virgo mater Christi* following *Gaude flore virginali*, see New York, The Morgan Library & Museum, Medieval and Renaissance Manuscripts, MS H.3 (fol. 147r–148v), a Parisian prayer book from 1490 belonging to the De la Roche family.
41 *AH* 15: 167–169.
42 BnF, n.a.l. 3196, fol. 161v. The poetry corresponds to *AH* 29: 31.
43 For the sequence, see *AH* 54: 312–313. On the desire to understand Mary's suffering in the late Middle Ages, see Bestul, *Texts of the Passion*, 122–132; Fulton, *From Judgment to Passion*, 405–470.
44 Settings by three different composers are found in a single fifteenth-century manuscript, the Eton Choirbook (Eton College Library, MS 178). For an edition of Josquin's *Stabat mater/Comme femme desconfortée*, see the *New Josquin Edition* 25.9. Palestrina composed one *Stabat mater* for eight voices, another for 12. For editions, see Palestrina, *Werke*, 6: 96–108, 7: 130–150. Bitter (*Eine Studie zum Stabat Mater*) noted more than 100 *Stabat mater* settings between 1700 and 1883.

45 For studies on the planctus and compassion traditions, see, for example, Sticca, *The Planctus Mariae*; Schuler, "The Seven Sorrows of the Virgin"; Schuler, "The Sword of Compassion," 20–117.
46 Künzle, *Heinrich Seuses Horologium sapientiae*, 513–514 (Bk. 1, ch. 16).
47 BnF, n.a.l. 3196, fols. 167v–169r. Clues to its performance are in evidence, as the *mise-en-page* shifts to a format reminiscent of psalms and hymn verses. Decorated capital letters adorn the start of each verse throughout the *Salve mater dolorosa* while punctuation—whether the colon or the dot—articulates the interior verses of each tercet. Line-fills also occur at the end of each stanza.
48 BnF, n.a.l. 3196, fols. 169v–170v. The text with variants can be found in *AH* 15: 76.
49 Ruini, "Un antico versione dello *Stabat Mater*," esp. 225–227.
50 Thelen, "The Feast of the Seven Sorrows," 277–278.
51 For a setting of the latter *Stabat mater*, see Vienna, Österreichische Nationalbibliothek, Cod. Palatin. Vindobonensis MS 3787, fols. 95v–96v.
52 Van Deusen, "Sequence Repertories," 109–111.
53 The canonical Gospels disagree on the number of women present at the crucifixion and their names. It was Mary Magdalene plus some other women.
54 For an example of the *Stabat mater* set twice to Adam's *Lauda Sion salvatorem* at the turn of the sixteenth century in south Germany (Neresheim), see Regensburg, Fürst Thurn und Taxis Hofbibliothek, F.K. mus. 7/11, fols. 72v, 74v.
55 Fassler, "Women and Their Sequences," 627–628.
56 The antiphon *Gaude Dei genetrix* was known in Italy in the eleventh century. Peter Damian recommended its recitation at the Abbey of Monte Cassino. See Damian, *Opusculum 34: De variis miraculosis narrationibus*, in *PL* 145: col. 588.
57 See, for example, the omitted response *Ut digni efficiamur* in a suffrage for St. Barbara in BnF, Ars. 290, fol. 199v.
58 For St. Apollonia described as both virgin and martyr in the versicle of a suffrage, see BnF, Ars. 426, fol. 22r.
59 See this variant response, for example, in BnF, Ars. 1191, fol. 84v.
60 For highly variant settings of the *Ora/Ut digni* text, see Klosterneuburg, Augustiner-Chorherrenstift Bibliothek, MS 1012, fol. 90v and LBL, Add. MS 23935, fol. 113v.
61 The Cantus Index does not identify a mode or notes the letter "r" in the category of mode for ID 008164 "to represent any of the simple formulas to which short responsories and versicles are sung."
62 BnF, lat. 1090, fols. 167r and 169r.
63 BnF, lat. 1090, fol. 275r. Liturgically, the versicle and response was prescribed for virgin saints and feasts of the Virgin Mary.
64 *LU*, 118.
65 For orations labeled *collecta*, see, for example, BnF, n.a.l. 3214, fol. 66r, 71r in the customary memorial for All Saints accompanying the Office of the Virgin.
66 Parkes, *Pause and Effect*, 76.
67 See, for example, two orations for St. Maurus (abbot and disciple of St. Benedict) in LBL, Add. MS 27697, fols. 99v–100r.
68 There are suffrages for St. Michael, John the Baptist, St. John the Evangelist, St. Lazarus, St. Sebastian, St. Christopher, St. George, St. Katherine, and All Saints (fols. 75v–79v). Three suffrages to female saints (St. Margaret, St. Barbara, and St. Anne) were added in a later hand after the formal end of the suffrages (fol. 80r-v). Miniatures are included for St. Michael, St. Lazarus, St. Sebastian, and St. Christopher.
69 The following versicle, *Michael prepositus paradisi*, bears resemblance to the antiphon just mentioned and does not match what would be expected in suffrages for the archangel (*In conspectu*, CAO 8092; see Table 8.2). The absence of the rubric for a response to the versicle was not uncommon, but the fact that this text was not known as a dialogue in extant liturgical sources suggests that it is either rare or a mistake.
70 A similar build to the oration can be found in the suffrages of New York, The Morgan Library & Museum, Medieval and Renaissance Manuscripts, MS M.12, fols. 67r ff.
71 Given the artist's activity after 1460, this book of hours from 1440 to 1450 must be counted as one of his earlier artistic projects.
72 There appear to be distinct versions of *Sancti dei omnes*, each with *g* finals. The antiphon's scarce notation makes a more prevalent version difficult to discern. For a Parisian source bearing one

version, see BnF, lat. 15182, fol. 118r. For the other setting of the text in a central European source, see Klosterneuburg, Augustiner-Chorherrenstift Bibliothek, MS 589, fol. 102r.
73 The second oration "Omnes sancti tui," often rubricated *alia oratio*, generally stayed constant when there were two prayers provided, but it could be used alone as well. The remaining orations were "Protege Domine populum," "Exaudi nos Deus," and "Presta quesumus."
74 My thanks to Roger Wieck for his insight into the artist.
75 See, for example, "In illo tempore" preceding the reading from Mark in LBL, Yates Thompson MS 3, fol. 20v.
76 Compare with this segment of the Gloria: "Laudamus te, benedicimus te, adoramus te, glorificamus te . . ."
77 See, for example, BnF, lat. 1160, fol. 2r-v.
78 BnF, lat. 1181, fols. 2v–4v.

9 Mass for the Virgin

*

The celebration of Mass was the main event of any liturgical day. If the medieval laity were lucky enough to experience the liturgy in daily life, it was more likely to be the Mass than the Office. It may come as some surprise then that a widespread devotional book emulating liturgical practice would only sometimes reveal texts for the Mass and instead would place consistent emphasis on key commemorative offices. When a Mass does appear in a book of hours, it will almost certainly be the Mass in honor of the Virgin Mary. This mass was votive in nature, not assigned to a specific feast but rather woven into the activities of an institution. Liturgical manuscripts reveal that votive masses were designated for certain days of the week. Sundays, for example, were often reserved for a special Mass for the Trinity (Thursdays for Corpus Christi, Fridays for the Holy Cross). The Mass for the Virgin Mary, one of the most popular votive masses, was widely commemorated on Saturdays throughout Europe.[1] These masses took place not at a church's main altar but at side chapels, which were frequently endowed with specific ceremonies to honor bequests of local patrons.

The "Lady Mass" in particular had major consequences in music history. The Mass for the Virgin Mary alone seemed to spur the development of polyphonic music in the fourteenth and fifteenth centuries, accounting for some of the earliest settings of the Mass Ordinary. At Reims Cathedral, Guillaume de Machaut's iconic *Messe de Nostre Dame* graced the celebration of the Saturday Mass for the Virgin each week with polyphony for more than a century.[2] That the Christian laity also clung dearly to the Lady Mass is evidenced by the frequency with which they specified its performance in their funeral arrangements instead of the conventional Requiem Mass.[3] Books of hours reflect this preference, being far more likely to bear a Mass for the Virgin than a Mass for the Dead.

Three possibilities for Mass Propers can emerge for the Mass for the Virgin in the liturgical sources. The seasons determine the appropriate Mass for use. Two sets are assigned to just a short part of the year—one for Advent with the Introit *Rorate celi desuper*, the other for Christmas until the feast of the Purification (February 2) with the Introit *Vultum tuum*. The Lady Mass with the Introit *Salve sancta parens* consumed the majority of the year, cycling from Purification to the beginning of Advent. In books of hours that contain the Mass for the Virgin, most sources offer only the Mass that would be heard most often during the year, although a few books offer more than one, with the seasonal designations specified. This chapter reviews the proper musical contents of the dominant Mass for the Virgin (Introit: *Salve sancta parens*). It further illuminates examples that suggest cues to its performance and concludes with an exceptional source offering an unexpected treasury of masses.

DOI: 10.4324/9781003140511-12

194 *Music beyond the Offices*

Lady Mass Propers

The Propers of the principal Mass for the Virgin are well known, if little studied as a group. Books of hours assemble these texts, occasionally in conjunction with those of the Mass Ordinary, which would have been heard at any celebration of the Mass. The Marian Propers are an amalgam of texts from different sources, not all of which directly mention the Virgin. The fifth-century poet Sedulius penned the text of the Introit *Salve sancta parens*, which constitutes two lines from a eulogy for the Virgin in his lengthy poem *Carmen paschale*.[4] Though not as pervasive as the Marian antiphon *Salve regina*, this "Salve" Introit was nonetheless a popular song. In a Middle English analog of Chaucer's *Prioress's Tale* from ca. 1380, a little boy, restored to life miraculously, sings *Salve sancta parens*.[5] James McKinnon located a number of sources of *Salve sancta parens* from the eleventh and twelfth centuries and observed, as have others, that the Marian Introit was modeled on an older Introit, *Ecce advenit*, for Epiphany.[6] The music of the mode 2 *Salve sancta parens* is solemn, rising from the lowest modal register available before reaching a comfortable vocal range, never touching the octave above the lower boundary (Example 9.1). The formulaic verse paired with the Introit in the *horae* ("Sentiant omnes") was not drawn from the Psalter as was customary for the opening Mass Proper, but rather from the end of Fulbert's "Sancta Maria succurre nobis" from around the turn of the eleventh century.[7] In a few books of hours, a different verse, "Virgo dei genitrix," was assigned to the Introit.[8] This same text was always assigned, however, as the verse of the Gradual, the next Proper in the Mass for the Virgin.

Benedicta et venerabilis es is invariably the Gradual provided for the Lady Mass in the *horae*. The Gradual and adjacent Alleluia were responsorial style chants with melismatic passages and verses reserved for soloists. If a book of hours contained a Mass for the Virgin, the Gradual and Alleluia texts situated before the reading of the Gospel represented the height of musical splendor signaled in the prayer book. Specified as the Gradual for various festal masses beyond the votive Mass for the Virgin, *Benedicta et venerabilis es* addresses Mary directly, emphasizing not only her purity but her exceptionality as the vessel for the Savior, whom "the whole world could not contain."[9] Not atypical of Graduals, this mode 4 melody has different points of rest outside of its *E* final and introduces *b*-flat as an upper neighbor to the mode's expected prominent pitch *a* (Example 9.2). The music then soars at the first mention of the name "Maria." Outside of the final melisma on the word "homo,"

Translation: Hail holy Mother, child-bearer who brought forth the king who rules heaven and earth for all ages.

Example 9.1 Introit, *Salve sancta parens*. Transcribed from *GR*, 403 without Paschaltide Alleluias and verse.

the most extensive melodic flourish is reserved for the salutatory "Virgo" at the outset of the verse. In contrast to the responsories witnessed in the Divine Office, the Gradual does not engage in a repetition of all or part of its opening section. Rather, the ritual presses on with the declamation of the Alleluia.

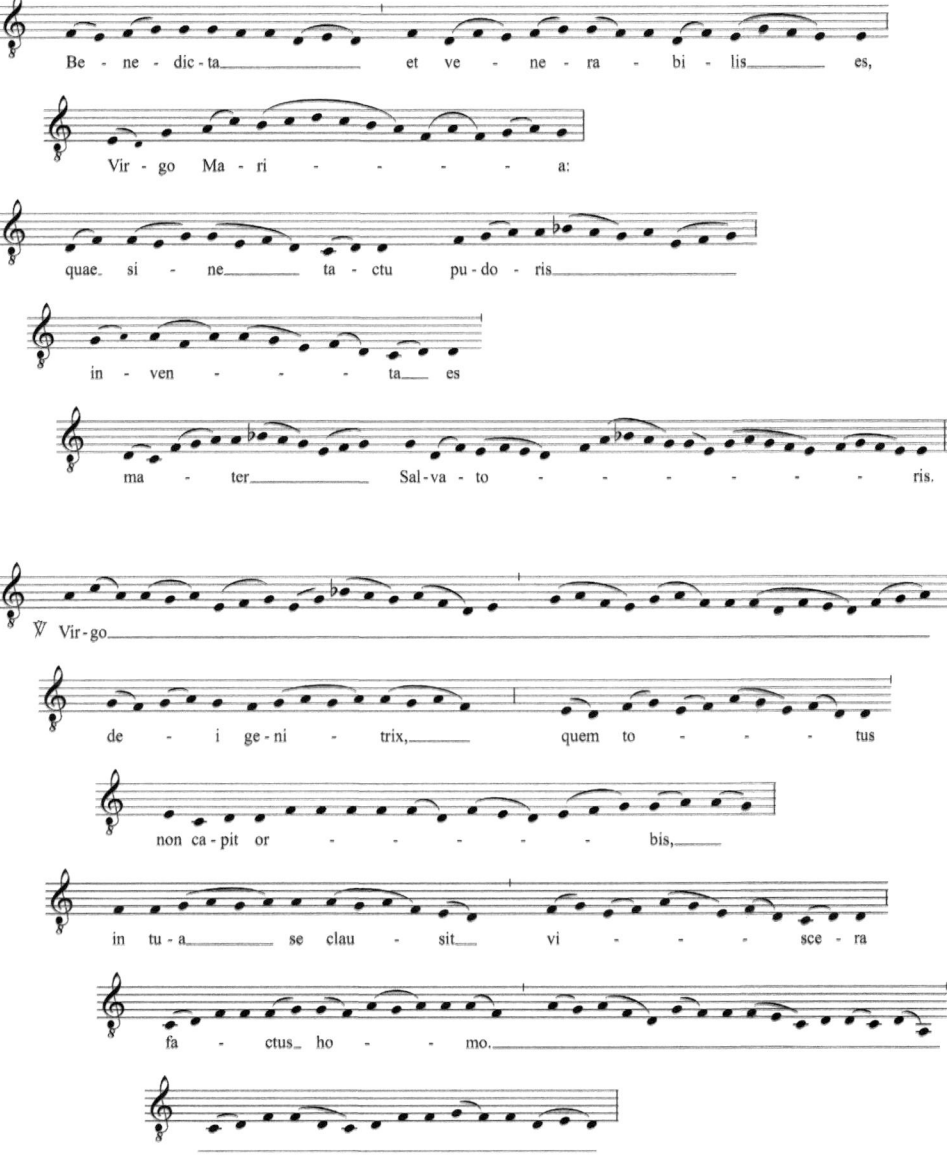

Translation: You are blessed and venerable, Virgin Mary; you were found to be the Mother of the Savior without stain. ℣ O Virgin Mother of God, He whom the whole world could not contain enclosed himself in your womb being made man.

Example 9.2 Gradual, *Benedicta et venerabilis*. Transcribed from *GR*, 407–408.

With its single word acclamation, the Alleluia of the Mass poured forth the purest melismatic melody of any liturgical genre. Books of hours reveal two possible Alleluias in the Mass for the Virgin, deployed about evenly in sources. One carries the verse "Virga iesse floruit," the other "Post partum virgo."[10]

Alleluia. ℣ Virga iesse floruit, virgo Deum et hominem genuit, pacem Deus reddidit, in se reconcilians ima summis.	Alleluia. The branch of Jesse blooms, a Virgin brings forth God and man: God restores peace, reconciling in Himself the lowest with the highest.
Alleluia. ℣ Post partum virgo inviolata permansisti: dei genitrix intercede pro nobis.	Alleluia. After childbirth, you, O Virgin, remained inviolate: Mother of God, intercede for us.

In some cases, a scribe will provide both verses of the Alleluia, as in the Hours of Louis of Savoy (Figure 9.1). In the opening shown, the word "versus" (or ℣) appears six times as a rubric, the first to indicate the verse of the Gradual and the next two for verses in association with the Alleluia. The presentation of the Alleluia may strike some as discreet in the *horae*. It is common for no rubric to mark the Alleluia, since the initial word doubles as the genre itself. A decorated capital adorns its beginning on the verso in Louis's book of hours. The separate capitals further make it clear that the two Alleluias cannot be combined in practice. Their incompatibility can also be surmised by the melodic modes of each. *Alleluia ℣ Virga iesse* is a mode 8 melody, both its Alleluia and verse ending on a *g* final. *Alleluia ℣ Post partum virgo*, on the other hand, is cast in mode 4, its two main sections both ending on *E*.[11] As a responsorial plainchant, the Alleluia would normally return to its opening at the conclusion of the verse, but this example does not provide that. Books of hours are split on notating the repeat. The remaining three rubricated "versus" on the recto of Figure 9.1 apply to the tract *Audi filia*, a rare inclusion in the Mass for the Virgin Mary, designed to replace the Alleluia in a penitential season.

The Offertory and Communion of the Mass for the Virgin round out the Propers of the Mass. The Offertory text *Felix namque es* had some liturgical currency, set as an office antiphon for the Nativity of Mary (CAO 2861) and a widespread responsory (CAO 6725), notably the third and final responsory in the Office of the Virgin (Example 4.3). As an Offertory, *Felix namque es* does not survive among the earliest layer of manuscripts for the Mass, but has been located in sources from Aquitaine, Benevento, and northern Italy. It is a rare case of an extraneous piece entering the Roman repertory after its transmission to the Franks. The melody is cast in mode 1 (Example 9.3) and spans only a sixth in its range (*C-a*). Like many early Offertories, *Felix namque es* had verses, which were dropped in the later Middle Ages and thus in the heyday of books of hours.[12]

Like *Felix namque es*, the Communion antiphon *Beata viscera* was assigned to mode 1 (Example 9.4). Its text was half of the length—textually and melodically—of the Offertory, not unexpected for the genre of the Communion. Although *Beata viscera* was more succinct than *Felix namque es*, its range was surprisingly greater than the Offertory, spanning the octave *C-c* and unveiling a *b*-flat along the way as was characteristic in emphasizing the mode's reciting tone of *a*.

Historians of European music are well acquainted with the Mass for the Virgin Mary and its importance in the late Middle Ages. However, their knowledge has come chiefly through

Translation: Blessed are you, O holy Virgin Mary, and most worthy of all praise: for out of you rose the sun of justice, Christ our God.

Example 9.3 Offertory, *Felix namque es*. Transcribed from *GR*, 422.

Translation: Blessed is the womb of the Virgin Mary that bore the Son of the Eternal Father.

Example 9.4 Communion, *Beata viscera*. Transcribed from *GR*, 423 without Paschaltide Alleluias.

the lens of polyphony, as choral settings not infrequently were specified for Marian votive rituals. While the nobility and some layfolk might have had access to hear the polyphonic splendor brought to the Lady Mass, these multivoice adornments scarcely attracted the multitudes. The wider audience of users of books of hours was more likely to have encountered the conventional chants themselves (both the Propers above and select Ordinaries), perhaps hearing them in connection with special institutional or memorial ceremonies. Their handheld guides to devotion even reveal traces of the actions and sounds behind the ritual of the Lady Mass.

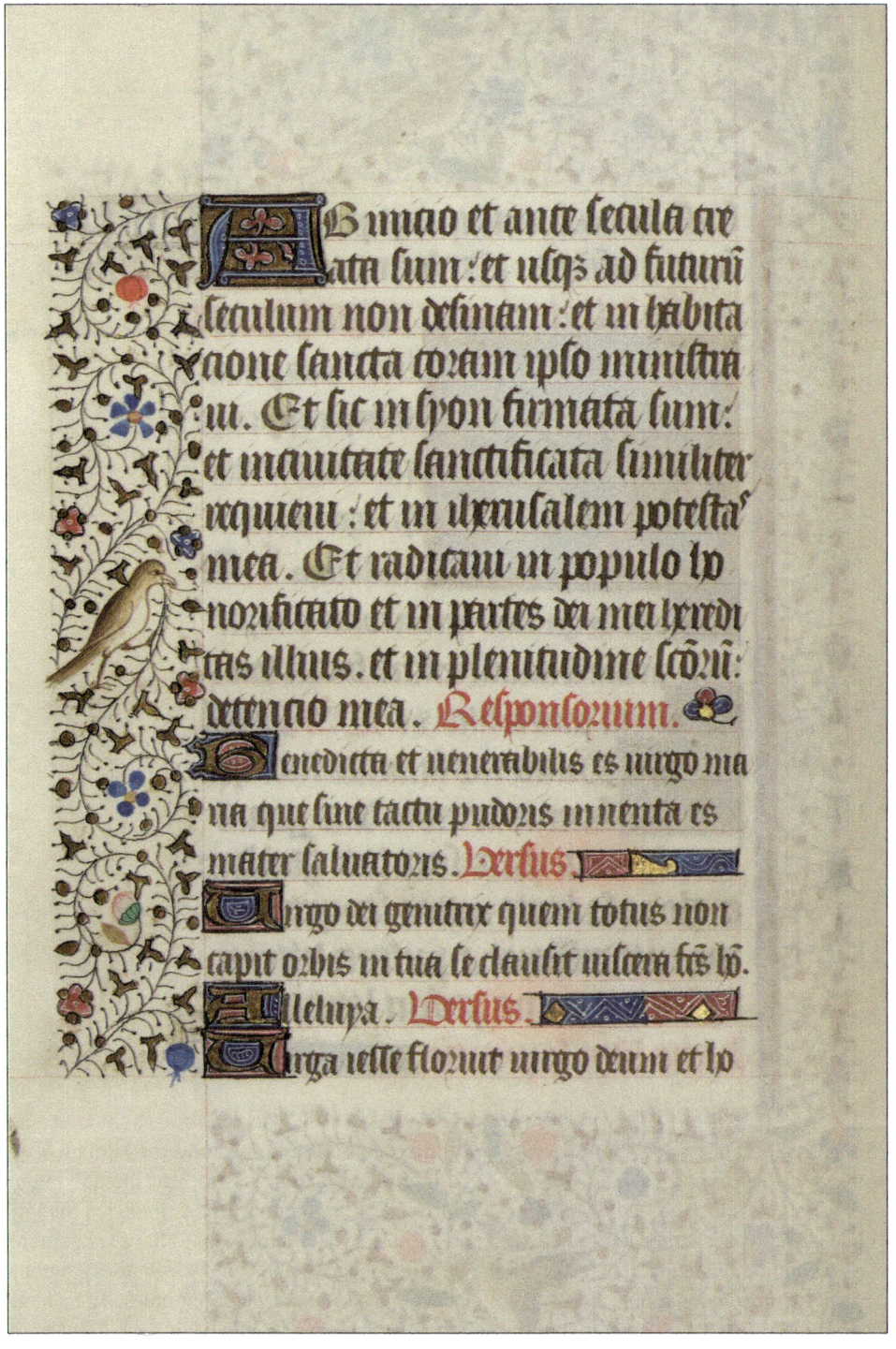

Figure 9.1 Two Alleluias, Mass for the Virgin. Paris, BnF, lat. 9473, fols. 160v–161r.

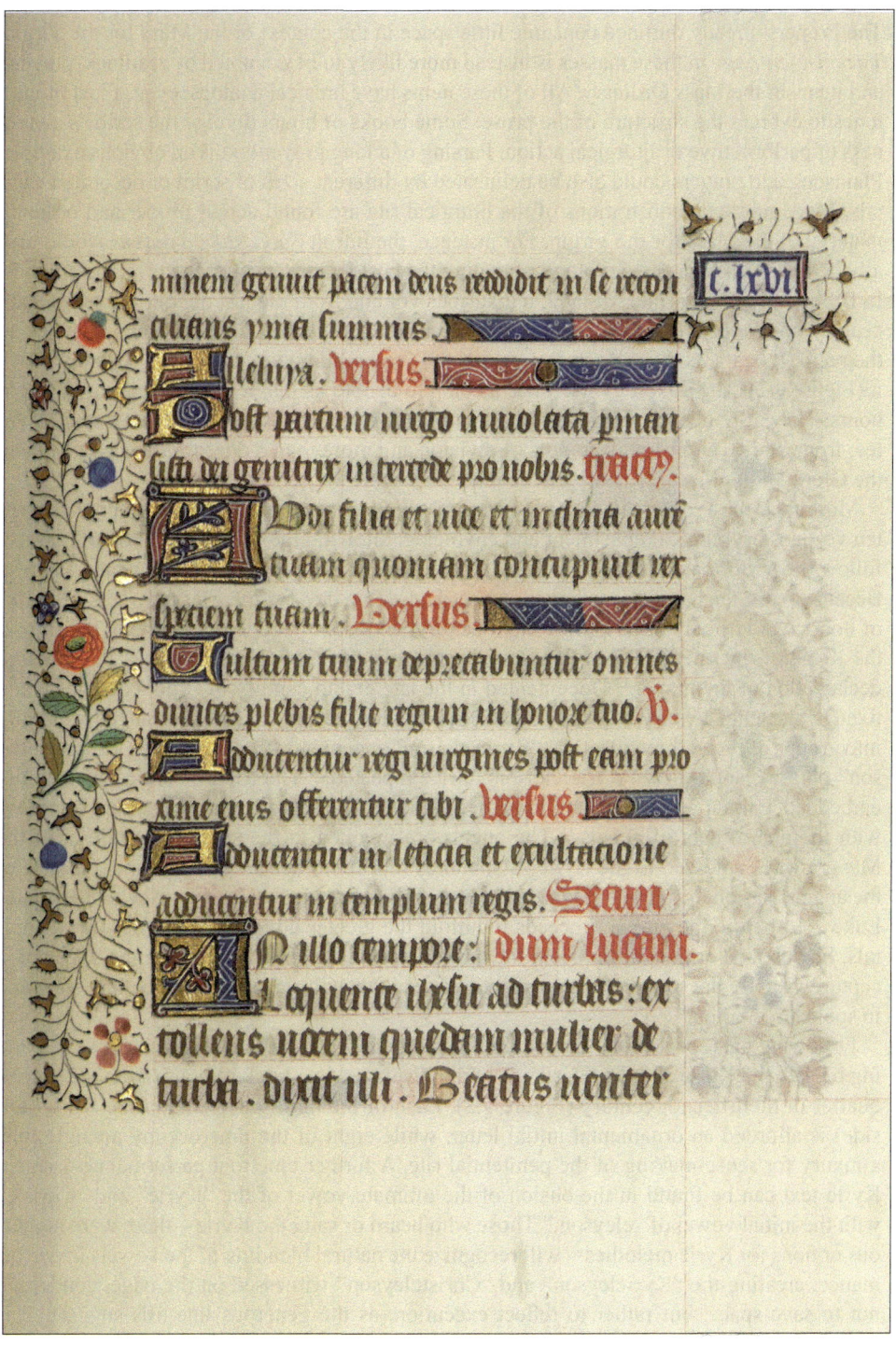

Figure 9.1 (Continued)

Hearing the Mass for the Virgin

The Propers already outlined consume little space in the context of the Mass for the Virgin. The *mise-en-page* in these masses is instead more likely to be occupied by readings, prayers, and items of the Mass Ordinary. All of these items have musical analogs, even if just modest tones to express the structure of the prose. Some books of hours divulge the scribe's awareness of performative or liturgical action. Parsing of a long prayer text is an obvious example. Plainsong and prayers could also be delineated by different sizes of script or decorated capitals. More subtle demonstrations of the liturgical rite are found across proper and ordinary material of the Mass for the Virgin. For instance, the Introit *Salve sancta parens* would usually be rewritten after the doxology, signaling the customary repeat of the principal melody. In Bibliothèque Mazarine, MS 502, a luxurious volume from the last quarter of the fifteenth century, a full repeat of the entire Introit is provided after the doxology, spanning the verso to the recto. It bears its own decorative capital "S", resembling the "G" of the "Gloria" above it (Figure 9.2). The doxology itself has a colon to denote its major caesura, rare in books of hours. The entire opening is further filled with performance markers for the unknown devotee, from rubrics and capitals to dots of division and more than a dozen *pieds-de-mouche* in the Gloria of the Mass Ordinary on the recto.

More than the Propers, items of the Mass Ordinary indeed more readily emerge as written vestiges of liturgical enactment and envoicing, allowing the user of the book of hours to follow the performative flow of the ritual more than an unmarked text alone would suggest. Because these unchanging texts were prescribed every day for the Mass, owners of books of hours would likely have known them better than a set of Propers. Following the Introit, the Kyrie of the opening rite often unveils a familiar performance tradition—the ninefold declamation of the prayer.[13] Documented in the late eighth century in Ordo Romanus 4 and fixed by the tenth century, probably by the Franks, the nine petitions were arranged musically into groups of three: three identical "Kyrie eleison" statements, three matching "Christe eleison" phrases, and a new "Kyrie eleison" thrice repeated.[14] The tripartite division naturally embedded Trinitarian symbolism, though Guillaume Durand associated the nine iterations with the nine orders of angels.[15] The angels are invoked in the succeeding Gloria of the Mass, always adjoined to the Kyrie. Sometimes rubricated as "laus angelorum" ("praise of the angels") as on the recto of Figure 9.2, the angelic salutation "Gloria in excelsis deo" cites Luke 2:14 before the prayer proceeds to unfold the greater doxology. With decorated capitals, line breaks, or dots of division, the appearance of the angelic hymn on the page could capture visually the sound of the succinct phrases in the Gloria, articulated both in song and in spoken recitation.

Following the repeat of the Introit *Salve sancta parens* (rubricated "reiteratur"), the parsing of both the Kyrie and the Gloria is vividly displayed in a book of hours from the second quarter of the fifteenth century (Figure 9.3). Each of the nine statements of the Kyrie (left side) is afforded an ornamental initial letter, while eight of the nine occupy a single line, a luxury for sense-making of the penitential rite. A further clue to a performance-oriented Kyrie text can be found in the elision of the ultimate vowel of the "Kyrie" and "Christe" with the initial vowel of "eleyson." Those who heard or sang the Kyrie—there were numerous options for Kyrie melodies—will recognize the natural blending of the vowels in performance, creating the "Kyrieleyson" and "Christeleyson" witnessed on the page, condensed not to save space, but rather to reflect execution, as the generous line-fills suggest. It is uncommon, but edifying, to see the Gloria (right side) likewise deconstructed for the user to grasp its uneven flow.

Continuing with the Mass Ordinary, we may note that the Credo will necessarily consume a great deal of space in the Mass for the Virgin on account of its length. The three acclamations of the Sanctus and three statements of the Agnus Dei, which appear consecutively in the Mass, merit special comment as they have analogs elsewhere in the book of hours. The appearance of these tripartite items will usually mimic their presence in the Te Deum and the Litany, respectively. The texts do not perfectly match in each case, but they begin in the same way. In the Te Deum, when the angels proclaim the heavenly song, scribes will often plan for decorative capitals to adorn each of the three "Sanctus" iterations. The ornamental letters may all be placed in a single line or may be broken into three lines, visibly separated by line-fills. A user could expect the same look in the Sanctus of the Mass. Enhancement of the sound world in the mind's ear may occur when we consider that the Sanctus was often accompanied by bells, amplifying the moment of consecration. While the three Agnus Dei statements at the end of the Litany occasion three different responses, the Agnus Dei of the Mass has two identical consequents ("miserere nobis") before the concluding "dona nobis pacem." The parallel structure was not lost on scribes who communicated that arrangement in books of hours.

In most masses for the Virgin in French *horae*, one finds a differentiation in script size among the various texts, a phenomenon to which we have become accustomed. The appearance of the handwriting follows the convention witnessed in the offices and elsewhere in the prayer books: lessons and prayers tend to command a larger script, while smaller lettering was supplied for proper musical items. In a mid-fifteenth-century book of hours from Avignon (BnF, n.a.l. 3229), the distinction in size of handwriting is clear between vocal textures of songs and readings (Figure 9.4). In this condensed presentation of the Mass, the Offertory *Felix namque es* and Communion *Beata viscera* appear consecutively on the recto, noticeably minuscule compared to the lection preceding them and the Postcommunion that follows. This scribe has confused the musical genres of these items, however, labeling the Offertory as a responsory (℟) and the Communion apparently as its verse (℣).[16] The chant at the top of the preceding verso is another exceptional occurrence of the tract, in this case the mode 2 *Gaude Maria virgo*, which was assigned to the feast of the Purification in its earliest instantiations.[17] In a liturgical context, the verses of the tract are performed *in directum*, that is, successively, without return to the opening musical statement. The scribe misses the indication for the first verse ("Que Gabrielis"), but has marked the others, though not uniformly (℣ for "versus" is the norm, not ℟ for response).

With melismas up to 30 notes per syllable, the elaborate tract *Gaude Maria virgo* stands in stark contrast to the vocally monochromatic reading from Luke's Gospel (11:27–28) beneath it. The two brief verses from the evangelist are consistent across books of hours. In the short span, three distinct voices emerge in this evocative excerpt:

In illo tempore loquente Iesu ad turbas extollens vocem quedam mulier de turba dixit illi:	At that time, as Jesus was speaking to the crowd, a woman from the crowd, lifting up her voice, said to him:
"Beatus venter qui te portavit et ubera que suxisti"	"Blessed is the womb which carried you and the breasts that you sucked."
"Quinimo beati qui audiunt verbum Dei et custodiunt illud."	"Blessed are they who hear the word of God and keep it."

Figure 9.2 Introit, Kyrie, and Gloria from the Mass for the Virgin. Paris, Bibliothèque Mazarine, MS 502, fols. 24v–25r.

Figure 9.2 (Continued)

Figure 9.3 Kyrie and Gloria from the Mass for the Virgin. Paris, BnF, n.a.l. 3111, fol. 27r-v.

Figure 9.3 (Continued)

Figure 9.4 Mass for the Virgin Mary (excerpt). Paris, BnF, n.a.l. 3229, fols. 73v–74r.

Figure 9.4 (Continued)

The passage begins with Luke contextualizing the event, as Jesus preaches to the throng. A woman from the crowd then speaks, and Jesus answers in return. Contrary to some renderings of this passage, no indication is made of the dialogic transition between the woman and Jesus; users of books of hours must have been aware of Christ's commanding retort. Though scribal marks are often used to delineate longer passages of prose, Figure 9.4 (verso) indicates the exchange of voices in the gospel passage with three capital letters and yellowish *pieds-de-mouche*. A celebrant of the Mass would have punctuated the gospel tone just before these capitals, enhancing the feeling of dialogue through application of a melodic formula and consequent pause. An alternative reading from John (19:25–27) succeeds the sentences from Luke's Gospel. As the rubric indicates, the lection is to be read between Easter and the feast of Pentecost. The scene involves Mary, the mother of Jesus, standing at the foot of the cross, accompanied by Mary Magdalene, another Mary (the wife of Cleophas), and an unnamed disciple. Jesus says to his mother, "Woman, behold thy Son" (the third of the "seven last words" of Christ) and to his disciple, "Here is your mother."[18] The voice of Jesus in this second gospel reading is marked at his first utterance ("Mulier") with a capital letter, embellished with a *pied-de-mouche*. The sonic textures throughout just this single opening of a Mass for the Virgin are elucidated, not only in the size of handwriting that distinguishes florid melody from recitation, but also fortuitously, in scribal marks showing the exchange of speaking voices in the brief sentences from Luke's Gospel.

Mass quantities

BnF, n.a.l. 3229 is remarkable among books of hours for more than its Mass for the Virgin, already a nonstandard occurrence. The manuscript in fact unveils additional masses, an exceedingly rare phenomenon for the genre. Perhaps least surprising is the Mass for the Dead (Requiem Mass), forming a symmetrical arrangement—one office and one mass each for the Virgin and for the Dead. The Requiem, earning its name from the solemn mode 6 Introit *Requiem aeternam*, is rubricated "Missa pro omnibus fidelibus defunctis" ("Mass for all of the faithful departed"). In liturgical sources, the Mass for the Dead was as stable as the Office of the Dead in the *horae*. Spanning just three folios in BnF, n.a.l. 3229, the mass does not attempt to capture all of the texts of the funeral ceremony. The entire Requiem consists of little more than the Introit, Gradual, Tract, Offertory, and readings from 2 Maccabees and John the Evangelist (11:21–27). Still, the mere inclusion of the Mass for the Dead is highly distinctive.[19]

BnF, n.a.l. 3229 provided its user with yet more liturgies, further heightening its exceptionality as a book of hours. Just as the Office of the Virgin often included liturgical prescriptions for use in Advent, alternatives for seasonal use follow the Mass for the Virgin in BnF, n.a.l. 3229.[20] Beginning with the Introit *Rorate caeli*, the Mass Propers and readings for Advent enrich the experience of the hours with texts and melodies dispatched in anticipation of Christ's nativity. The user was further treated to a set of texts for the Lady Mass to be used between Christmas and the feast of the Purification.[21] Like all of the extra masses, the items are limited. The key replacements are the Introit (*Vultum tuum*, mode 2) and readings from Titus (3:4–5) and Luke's Gospel (2:15b–20).

Other masses appear in BnF, n.a.l. 3229, paired with familiar offices. A Mass for the Holy Spirit, featuring the Introit *Spiritus Domini replevit* and the popular sequence *Veni sancte spiritus* for the feast of Pentecost, flows directly from the standard Hours of the Holy Spirit in the manuscript.[22] The transition from the Office to the Mass of the Spirit is marked by full recitation of *Veni creator spiritus*, the well-known hymn that occasionally follows the

Hours of the Cross and in at least one other manuscript supplants the traditional hymn *Patris sapientia* threaded through that office.[23] A bit further in the manuscript, a Mass for the Holy Cross supplements the Hours of the Cross, led by the Introit for Holy Thursday, *Nos autem gloriari oportet*.[24] Three extraordinary Office-Mass pairs complete the liturgies of BnF, n.a.l. 3229. Hours for the Trinity, All Saints, and Corpus Christi are each coupled with a mass, headed by the esteemed introits *Benedicta sit sancta trinitas*, *Gaudeamus omnes in Domino*, and *Cibavit eos*, respectively.[25]

Mention must be made of another book of hours that trounces the number of supplemental masses found in BnF, n.a.l. 3229. BnF, Ars. 616 (referenced in Chapter 2) is a Breton source compiled around 1420. Despite a variant liturgical usage of Rennes, the book of hours proceeds as one might expect. Situated between the Office of the Dead and the closing prayer, however, is an astonishing chain of 25 masses spanning 46 folios. Toward the end of the manuscript, two masses detached from the series (a Requiem Mass and a Mass for the Nativity of the Virgin), plus provisions for the Canon of the Mass and Prefaces for select high feasts, bring the total content for the ritual of the mass to more than one-third of the material in this book of hours.[26] Although the mass texts are relatively stable and well known from liturgical sources, their presence to this extent in a book of hours is exceptional for the genre. Each mass in BnF, Ars. 616 reveals Propers and lections for the respective commemorations, and all but one of them is adorned with a miniature consuming at least half of a page.[27] Space does not afford a full description of the individual items—especially the dozens of venerable melodies of the Church—unfolded in the masses of this stunning book of hours. Table 9.1 shows the assortment of the consecutive masses and their introits. Some brief observations may still be made about the masses both individually and collectively.

Table 9.1 Masses in Paris, BnF, Ars. Ms-616 réserve, with their Introits

"Temporale"		"Sanctorale"	
Commemorative Mass (fols.)	Introit	Commemorative Mass (fols.)	Introit
Nativity of the Lord (73r–75v)	Puer natus est nobis	Mass for the Virgin (102r–103r)	Salve sancta parens
Epiphany (75v–77r)	Ecce advenit Dominator	Michael (103v–104v)	Benedicite Dominum
Purification (78r–80r)	Suscepimus deus	Common of an Apostle (105r–106v)	Michi autem
Advent (80r–81v)	Rorate celi desuper	Common of Apostles (107r–108v)	Michi autem
Resurrection of the Lord (82r–83r)	Resurrexi et adhuc tecum sum	Common of Doctors (108v–110r)	In medio ecclesie
Ascension (83v–85r)	Viri galilei	Common of a Martyr (110v–111v)	Letabitur iustus
John the Baptist (85v–87r)	De ventre matris mee	Common of Martyrs (112r–113v)	Intret in conspectus tuo
Chair of St. Peter (87r–88v)	Statuit ei	Common of Confessor Bishop (113v–115r)	Statuit ei
Corpus Christi (89r–92r)	Cibatvit eos	Common of a Confessor, not a Pope (115v–116v)	Os iusti

(Continued)

Table 9.1 (Continued)

"Temporale"		"Sanctorale"	
Commemorative Mass (fols.)	Introit	Commemorative Mass (fols.)	Introit
Peter and Paul (92v–94r)	Nunc scio vere	Common of Pope and Confessor (117r-v)	Sacerdotes tui
All Saints (94v–96r)	Gaudeamus omnes in Domino	Common of Pope and Martyr (118r-v)	Os iusti
Assumption (97r–98r)	Gaudeamus omnes in Domino		
Pentecost (98v–100r)	Spiritus Domini		
Holy Thursday/Holy Cross (100v–101v)	Nos autem gloriari oportet		

The consecutive masses in BnF, Ars. 616 are loosely organized into a kind of temporale and sanctorale arrangement. The temporale is not strictly a slate of movable feasts but rather events in the life of Christ, plus key figures of the faith, namely the feasts of John the Baptist (June 24) and Ss. Peter and Paul (June 29). It begins with a mass for Christ's Nativity and its iconic Introit *Puer natus est nobis* (Figure 9.5), decorated with an image of the angel of the Lord appearing to the shepherds in the field to announce the birth of the Messiah, a realization of Luke 2:8–15. The temporale subsection concludes with a mass for the movable feast of Holy Thursday, the items of which are equivalent to the Propers for the Mass for the Holy Cross in BnF, n.a.l. 3229, beginning with the Introit *Nos autem gloriari oportet*. The solemnities are not all ordered temporally, the feast of All Saints preceding the Assumption, for example.

The "sanctorale" of BnF, Ars. 616 demonstrates a smoother progression, beginning with a Mass for the Virgin and its traditional Introit *Salve sancta parens*. While this series includes only one additional named saint (St. Michael), the remaining nine masses celebrate different ranks of saints, ordered systematically from a common Mass for an Apostle through a Mass for a Pope and Martyr. The most visually and musically striking item among the masses is the presence of the distinguished sequence for Corpus Christi, *Lauda Sion salvatorem* (Figure 9.6). Rubricated "pr[o]s[a]" in the manuscript, the sequence bears the text penned by Thomas Aquinas, which was set as a contrafact to a melody composed by Adam of St. Victor. Line-fills organize the 24 verses, paired melodically in liturgical practice; the shift in the *mise-en-page* roughly doubles the length of this mass compared to the other 26 masses, none of which contains a sequence.

*

The extraordinary outpouring of masses in BnF, Ars. 616 and BnF, n.a.l. 3229 is another reminder of the difficulty in studying manuscript books of hours on the whole. Each manuscript source constitutes a precious idiosyncratic object, cut from a conventional ceremonial mold for a user with particular devotional needs. The exceptional nature of each book of hours encourages individual microstudies that account for peculiarities and noteworthy

Figure 9.5 Mass for Christmas Day (opening). Paris, BnF, Ars. Ms-616 réserve, fol. 73r.

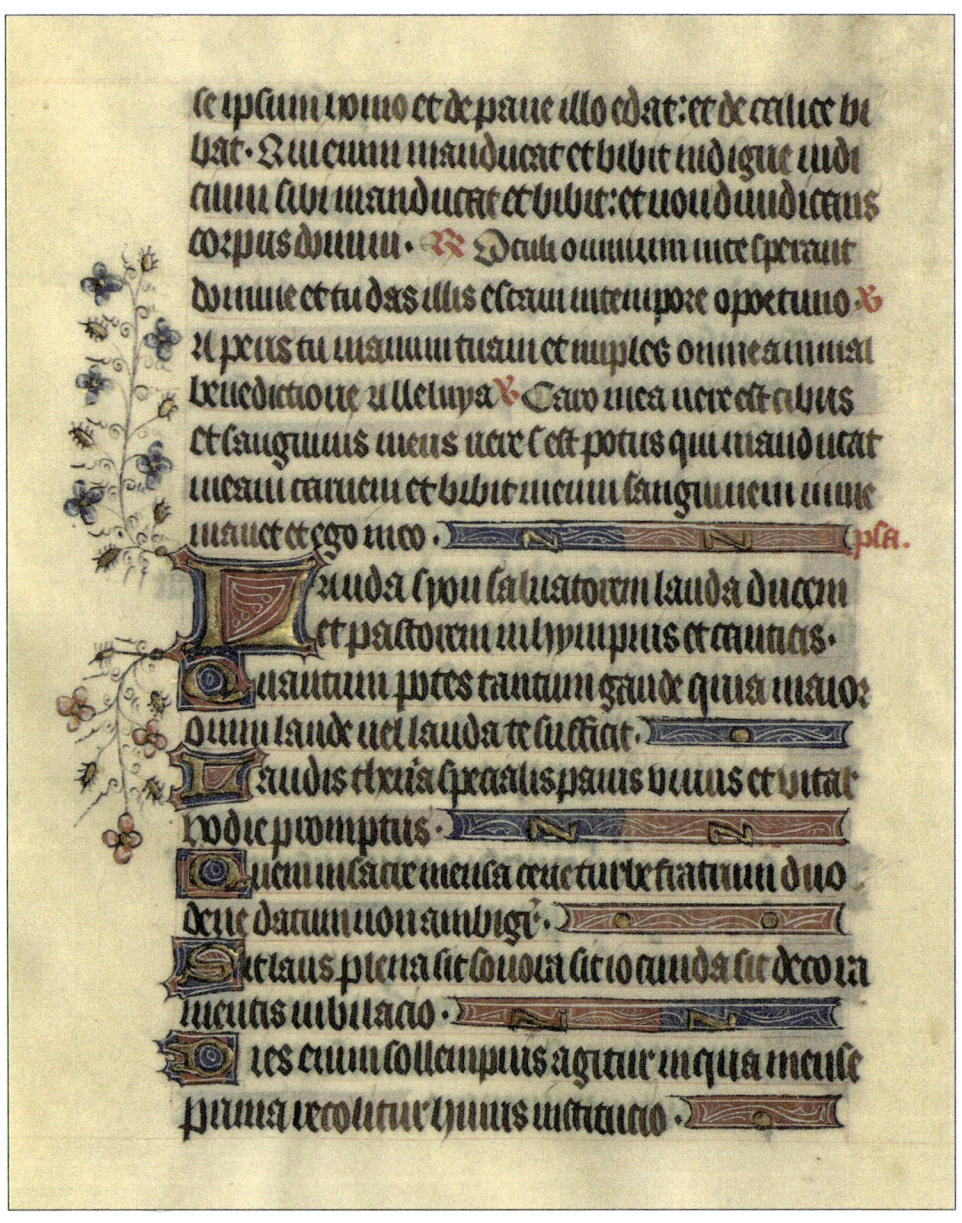

Figure 9.6 Sequence, *Lauda Sion salvatorem* (beginning). Paris, BnF, Ars. Ms-616 réserve, fol. 90r.

features rare for the genre, such as the unusual series of masses. The field of study has mostly followed in this direction, publishing close readings of "one-hit wonders." Yet single-source studies can succeed only if stable general studies are available against which to index the uniqueness of individual manuscripts. The proportion of general studies of books of hours to individual studies remains more lopsided than one would like; perhaps this is understandable, given the unwieldy nature of the corpus. But the digitization of manuscripts by libraries worldwide has changed the nature of the work. Manuscripts may now be quickly ascertained on a mobile phone, without a researcher's credentials being examined or the prospect of a reading room closing for an extended holiday. More wide-ranging studies of the *horae* could be reasonably expected from the changing landscape of work with primary sources.

What few broad investigations of books of hours are available stood in the court of art historians for decades. Studies in the past ten years have wrested the genre from them to some extent, allowing for perspectives on these valuable books from the realm of ethnography, prayer, and now sound. Music historians are no strangers to books of hours, but have been reticent to study the sonic potential of the genre. Many opportunities await the music historian or a historian attentive to sound and performance in the study of books of hours in areas relatively untrod by colleagues in art history. As we have seen here, the individual sources and select topics will still continue to command attention, exceeding the limits of an overview of this type. It is my hope that this effort to unlock a multitextured sound world of plainchant in books of hours will inspire more people to hear the sounds that a user might have heard or even sung in the pages of this most treasured personal possession of Christians in the late Middle Ages.

Notes

1 Haggh, "Votive ritual," *NG* 26: 902–903; Hughes, *Medieval Manuscripts*, 157.
2 Robertson, *Guillaume de Machaut and Reims*, 257–275.
3 Haggh, "Votive ritual," *NG* 26: 902.
4 Sedulius, *The Paschal Song and Hymns*, 48–49. Sedulius borrowed the opening three words from Virgil's *Aeneid* (5.80).
5 Putter, "Prudentius and the Late Classical Biblical Epics," 361.
6 McKinnon, "Introit," *NG* 12: 510. The shared melody has been noticed by Gajard, *The Rhythm of Plainsong*, 64 and others.
7 Fulbert's text is also captured in an antiphon, CAO 4703 (*Sancta Maria succurre miseris*), assigned to various Marian feasts.
8 See, for example, BnF, n.a.l. 3229, fols. 71v–72r.
9 Except for its opening greeting to the Virgin, the verse draws on the words of St. Bonaventure. See Bonaventure, *Opera omnia*, 14: 245a.
10 The verse *Virga iesse floruit* borrows imagery from Numbers 17:8.
11 For editions, see *GR*, 416–17, for *Alleluia ℣ Virga iesse* and *GR*, 414–15, *Alleluia ℣ Post partum virgo*.
12 See Maloy, *Inside the Offertory*, 85.
13 The ninefold shape is not in evidence in Figure 9.2, only the tripartite form, which still could have signaled the expanded form.
14 Jeffery, "Litany," 593; Crocker, "Kyrie eleison," *NG* 14: 73.
15 Durand, *Rationale divinorum officiorum*, 1: 296 (Bk. IV, ch. xii, 2).
16 It is likewise unusual to see a truncation of text in the Offertory or any of the Propers. About half of the Offertory text is missing and replaced with an *ut supra* indication. *Felix namque es* is a responsory in the Office of the Virgin (MR3) with the text and melodic mode identical to that of the Offertory, but with a distinct melody. This responsory is located some 40 folios earlier (fol. 31r).
17 Hornby, *Medieval Liturgical Chant and Patristic Exegesis*, 155. For a modern edition of this tract, see *GR*, 418.

18 The mysterious identity of the wife of Cleophas, called a "sister" of the Virgin Mary by the evangelist, gave rise to the notion of the "Three Marys," which in turn drove a popular belief in the three marriages of St. Anne, the apocryphal mother of the Virgin Mary and her two "sisters." See Anderson, *St. Anne in Renaissance Music*, 5–9.
19 BnF, n.a.l. 3229, fols. 145r–147v.
20 *Ibid.*, fols. 74v–75v.
21 *Ibid.*, fols. 75v–77v.
22 *Ibid.*, fols. 148r–150v (Hours), 151v–153v (Mass). The liturgies are separated by the hymn *Veni creator spiritus* (fol. 150v–151r).
23 See BnF, Ars. 424, fols. 74r–87v.
24 BnF, n.a.l. 3229, fols. 170r–173r (Hours), 173r–174v (Mass).
25 *Ibid.*, fols. 92r–93v (Mass for the Trinity), fols. 156v–159v (Mass for All Saints), and fols. 162v–164v (Mass for Corpus Christi).
26 The consecutive masses in BnF, Ars. 616 span fols. 73r–118v. The Mass for the Dead is found on fols. 127r–128v; the Mass for the Nativity on fols. 145r–147r.
27 Some masses are incomplete, leaving out an Alleluia, Communion, or Postcommunion, for example. Some parts of masses are displaced as well. The Mass for the Assumption conspicuously lacks a miniature.

Sources and bibliography

Select manuscript books of hours consulted

Baltimore, Walters Art Museum, MSS W. 281, 289, 291, 445, 447
Bethlehem, Lehigh University, Special Collections, Codices 17, 18, 20
Clermont-Ferrand, Bibliothèque du Patrimoine, Overnia, MSS 76, 83, 1508
London, British Library, Add. MSS 27697, 35214, 38126
London, British Library, Yates Thompson MS 3
Montpellier, Bibliothèque numérique patrimoniale, MS 332
New Haven, Yale University, Beinecke Rare Book and Manuscript Library, MSS 108, 287, 411, 435
New York, Metropolitan Museum of Art, MS L.1990.38
New York, The Morgan Library & Museum, Medieval and Renaissance Manuscripts, MSS M.7, M.12, M.282, M.359
Paris, Bibliothèque Mazarine, MS 502
Paris, BnF, Bibliothèque de l'Arsenal, MSS 290, 424, 428, 434, 562, 575, 616, 637, 638, 641, 644, 645, 649, 651, 652, 655, 1191, 1194 (all *réserve*)
Paris, BnF, Département Arsenal, 4-T-934
Paris, BnF, Département des manuscrits, latin 920, 923, 1156B, 1157, 1160, 1165, 1170, 1171, 1181, 1184, 1187, 1188, 1192, 1194, 1355, 1363, 1369, 1374, 1375, 1377, 1386, 1399, 1404, 1408, 1414, 9471, 9472, 9473, 9474, 10527, 10544, 13289, 13308, 18015
Paris, BnF, Département des manuscrits, n.a.l. 215, 3107, 3110, 3111, 3114, 3116, 3117, 3120, 3181, 3187, 3188, 3196, 3197, 3204, 3209, 3210, 3213, 3214, 3229, 3234, 3258
Paris, BnF, Département Réserve des livres rares, VELINS-918
Philadelphia, Free Library of Philadelphia, Lewis E 109, 110, 111, 113, 212, 214
Philadelphia, Philadelphia Art Museum, Department of Prints, Drawings, and Photographs, MSS 1945-65-8, 1945-65-11, 1945-65-13, 1945-65-15
Toulouse, Bibliothèque municipale de Toulouse, MSS 2881 and 2882.

Other manuscript sources cited

Bologna, Museo Internazionale e Biblioteca della Musica di Bologna, MS Q 19
Brussels, Bibliothèque royale de Belgique, MS 9848.
Eton, Eton College Library, MS 178
Karlsruhe, Badische Landesbibliothek—Musikabteilung, Aug. LX
Klosterneuburg, Augustiner-Chorherrenstift Bibliothek, MSS 589 and 1012
Leipzig, Universitätsbibliothek, MS 1494
New Haven, Yale University, Beinecke Rare Book and Manuscript Library, MS 205
New York, The Morgan Library & Museum, Medieval and Renaissance Manuscripts, MSS H.3, M.69
Oxford, Bodleian Libraries, MS Bodl. 416
Paris, Bibliothèque Sainte-Geneviève. Ms. 113

Paris, BnF, Bibliothèque de l'Arsenal. Ms-279
Paris, BnF, Département des manuscrits, fr. 146
Paris, BnF, Département des manuscrits, lat. 1235, 8886, 12044, 14819, 15181, 15182, 17315
Paris, BnF, Département des manuscrits, n.a.l. 1412
Regensburg, Fürst Thurn und Taxis Hofbibliothek, F.K. mus. 7/11
Spišská Kapitula, Knižnica Spišskej Kapituly, Nr. 1
Trent, Biblioteca Capitolare/Museo Diocesano di Trento, MSS BL and 1377
Vienna, Österreichische Nationalbibliothek, Cod. Palatin. Vindobonensis MS 3787
Washington, D.C., Library of Congress, Music Division, MS 36
Wroclaw, Biblioteka Uniwersytecka (University Library), I F 401

Primary texts and musical editions

Agricola, Alexander. *Opera omnia*. 5 vols. Ed. Edward R. Lerner. Corpus mensurabilis musicae 22. Rome, 1961–70.
Albertus Magnus. "Biblia Mariana." In *B. Alberti Magni Ratisbonensis episcopi, ordinis Prædicatorum, Opera omnia*. 38 vols. Ed. Auguste and Émile Borgnet. Paris, 1898. Pp. 365–443.
Augustine. *Confessions*. Ed. Michael P. Foley. Trans. F. J. Sheed. 2nd ed. Indianapolis, 2006.
Bede. *Beda Venerabilis opera Didascalica*. Ed. C. W. Jones et al. Corpus Christianorum Series Latina 123A. Turnhout, 1975.
Beleth, Johannes. *Summa de ecclesiasticis officiis*. Ed. Heriberto Douteil. Corpus Christianorum Continuatio Medievalis 41A. Turnhout, 1976.
Bonaventure. *Opera omnia Sancti Bonaventuræ*. 15 vols. Ed. Adolphe C. Peltier. Paris, 1864–1871.
Cassian, John. *Collationes, XXIIII*. Ed. Michael Petschenig. Supplemented by Gottfried Kreuz. Corpus Scriptorum Ecclesiasticorum Latinorum. 13 vols. 2nd ed. Vienna, 2004.
———. *The Conferences*. Trans. Boniface Ramsey. New York, 1997.
Cassiodorus. *Expositio psalmorum*. 2 vols. Ed. Marc Adriaen. Corpus Christianorum Series Latina 97–98. Turnhout, 1958.
Catholic Church. *The Little Office of the Blessed Virgin Mary in Latin and English: In Conformity with the 1961*. Editio Typica of the Roman Breviary Being That Permitted by Summorum Pontificum. London, 2007.
Conrad of Saxony. *Speculum seu salutatio beatae Mariae virginis ac sermones mariani*. Ed. Pedrode Alcántara Martínez. Biblioteca Franciscana Ascetica Medii Aevi II. Rome, 1975.
de Pizan, Christine. *The Treasure of the City of Ladies or the Book of the Three Virtues*. Trans. Sarah Lawson. Harmondsworth, 1985.
Divitis, Antonius. *Collected Works*. Ed. Bill Allen Nugent. Recent Researches in the Music of the Renaissance 94. Madison, 1993.
Durand, Guillaume. *Rationale divinorum officiorum*. 2 vols. Ed. Anselme Davril and Timothy M. Thibodeau. Corpus Christianorum Continuatio Medievalis 140 and 140A. Turnhout, 1995–1998.
Elders, Willem, ed. *New Josquin Edition*. 30 vols. Utrecht, 1987.
Fabri, Felix. *The Wanderings of Felix Fabri*. 4 vols. Trans. Aubrey Stewart. Palestine Pilgrims' Text Society 7–10. New York, 1971.
Fremantle, W. H., and E. G. Martley, trans. *Jerome: Letters and Select Works*. 14 vols. Ed. Phillip Schaff and Henry Wace. VI vol. of Nicene and Post-Nicene Fathers, Series II. Edinburgh, 1989.
Gerber, Rudolf, Ludwig Finscher, and Wolfgang Dömling, eds. *Der Mensuralkodex des Nikolaus Apel*. 3 vols. Das Erbe deutscher Musik 32–34. Kassel, 1956–75.
Götz, Georgius Polycarpus, ed. *Liber quare*. Corpus Christianorum Continuatio Mediaevalis 60. Turnhout, 1983.
Graduale Romanum. Venice, 1575.
Hanssens, Jean Michel, ed. *Amalarii Episcopi Opera Liturgica Omnia*. 3 vols. Vatican City, 1948–50.
Hull, Dame Eleanor. *The Seven Psalms: A Commentary on the Penitential Psalms*. Ed. Alexandra Barratt. Early English Text Society. Oxford, 1995.

Isidore of Seville. *The Etymologies of Isidore of Seville*. Ed. Stephen A. Barney, W. J. Lewis, J. A. Beach, and Oliver Berghof. Cambridge, 2006.

Jacobus de Voragine. *The Golden Legend of Jacobus de Voragine*. Trans. William Granger Ryan and Helmut Ripperger. New York, 1969.

———. *The Golden Legend or Lives of the Saints*. 7 vols. Ed. F. S. Ellis. New York, 1973.

John of Salisbury, *Metalogicon*. Ed. John Barrie Hall and K. S. B. Keats-Rohan. Corpus Christianorum Continuatio Mediaevalis 98. Turnholt, 1991.

Künzle, Pius, ed. *Heinrich Seuses Horologium sapientiae*. Freiburg, 1977.

Lassus, Orlando de. *Psalmi Davidis poenitentiales, modis musicis redditi . . . His accessit psalmus Laudate Dominum de coelis, 5vv*. Munich, 1584.

Le Grand, Léon. *Statuts d'hotels-Dieu et de léproseries. Recueil de textes du XIIe au XIVe siècle*. Paris, 1901.

Limbourg, Pol de, and Jean Colombe. *The Très riches heures of Jean, Duke of Berry: Musée Condé, Chantilly*. New York, 1969.

Mauburnus, Ioannis (Jan Mombaer). *Rosetum exercitatorium spiritualium et sacrarum meditationum*. Milan, 1603.

Meurier, Hubert. *Traicté de l'institution et vray usage des processions tant ordinaires, qu'extraordinaires, qui se font en l'Eglise Catholique, contenant ample discours de ce qui s'est passé pour ce regarde en la Province de Champaigne, depuis le 22. de Juillet jusques au 25. d'Octobre, 1583*. Reims, 1584.

Morales, Cristóbal de. *Opera omnia*. 9 vols. Ed. Higini Anglès. Monumentos de la música española. Rome, 1952.

Ockeghem, Johannes. *Collected Works*. 3 vols. Ed. Dragan Plamenac and Richard Wexler. New York, 1947–1992.

Palestrina, Giovanni Pierluigi da. *Pierluigi da Palestrina's Werke: Erste kritisch durchgesehene Gesammtausgabe*. 33 vols. Ed. F. X. Haberl et al. Leipzig, 1862–1907.

Possidius. *Sancti Augustini vita scripta a Possidio episcopo*. Ed. Herbert T. Weiskotten. Princeton, 1919.

Processionale monasticum ad usum Congregationis Gallicae Ordinis Sancti Benedicti. Solesmis, 1888.

Quintilian. *The Institutio oratoria*. Ed. and trans. H. E. Butler. New York, 1921–1922.

Sarbak, Gábor, and Lorenz Weinrich, eds. *Sicardi Cremonensis episcopi Mitralis de officiis*. Corpus Christianorum Continuatio Mediaevalis 228. Turnhout, 2008.

Sedulius. *The Paschal Song and Hymns*. Ed. and trans. Carl P. E. Springer. Atlanta, 2013.

Vicentino, Nicola. *Ancient Music Adapted to Modern Practice*. Ed. Claude V. Palisca. Trans. Maria Rika Maniates. New Haven, 1996.

Willaert, Adrian. *Opera omnia*. 14 vols. Ed. Hermann Zenck et al. Corpus Mensurabilis Musicae 3. Rome, 1950.

Secondary literature

Alexopoulos, Cassandra, Katherine Grasso, and Nicholas A. Palomares. "Social Cognition." In *The Sage Encyclopedia of Communication Research Methods*. 4 vols. Ed. Mike Allen. Thousand Oaks, CA, 2017. Pp. 1618–1623.

Anderson, Michael Alan. "Enhancing the Ave Maria in the *Ars Antiqua*." *Plainsong and Medieval Music* 19 (2010): 35–65.

———. "Magnificat—Christianity—Medieval Times and Reformation Era." In *The Encyclopedia of the Bible and Its Reception*. 30 vols. Ed. Constance M. Furey et al. Berlin, 2019. Pp. 511–513.

———. *St. Anne in Renaissance Music: Devotion and Politics*. Cambridge, 2014.

Avril, François, Louisa Dunlop, and Brunsdon Yapp, eds. *Les petites heures de Jean, duc de Berry (ms. lat. 18014 de la Bibliothèque Nationale, Paris)*. 2 vols. Lucerne, 1988–1989.

Baldovin, John F. *The Urban Character of Christian Worship: The Origins, Development, and Meaning of Stational Liturgy*. Orientalia Christiana Analecta 228. Rome, 1987.

Baltzer, Rebecca A. "The Little Office of the Virgin and Mary's Role at Paris." In *The Divine Office in the Latin Middle Ages: Methodology and Source Studies, Regional Developments, Hagiography*. Ed. Rebecca A. Baltzer and Margot E. Fassler. New York, 2000. Pp. 463–484.

Baroffio, Giacomo. "Testo e musica nei libri d'ore." *Rivista Italiana di Musicologia* 46 (2011): 19–77.

Bazinet, Geneviève. "Singing the King's Music: Attaingnant's Motet Series, Royal Hegemony and the Function of the Motet in Sixteenth-Century France." *Early Music History* 39 (2018): 45–89.

Bell, Susan Groag. "Medieval Women Book Owners: Arbiters of Lay Piety and Ambassadors of Culture." *Signs* 7 (1982): 742–768.

Bennett, Adelaide. "Commemoration of the Saints in Suffrages: From Public Liturgy to Private Devotion." In *Objects, Images, and the Word: Art in the Service of the Liturgy*. Ed. Colum Hourihane. Index of Christian Art Occasional Paper 6. Princeton, 2003. Pp. 54–78.

———. "A Thirteenth-Century French Book of Hours for Marie." *The Journal of the Walters Art Gallery* 54 (1996): 21–50.

Bestul, Thomas H. *Texts of the Passion: Latin Devotional Literature and Medieval Society*. Philadelphia, 1996.

Bitter, Karl Hermann. *Eine Studie zum Stabat Mater*. Leipzig, 1883.

Blackburn, Bonnie J. "Messages in Miniature: Pictorial Programme and Theological Implications in the Alamire Choirbooks." In *The Burgundian-Habsburg Court Complex of Music Manuscripts (1500–1535) and the Workshop of Petrus Alamire*. Ed. Bruno Bouckaert and Eugeen Schreurs. Leuven, 2003. Pp. 161–184.

———. "Te Matrem Dei laudamus: A Study in the Musical Veneration of Mary." *The Musical Quarterly* 53 (1967): 53–76.

———. "The Virgin in the Sun: Music and Image for a Prayer Attributed to Sixtus IV." *Journal of the Royal Musical Association* 124 (1999): 157–195.

Booton, Diane E. *Manuscripts, Market and the Transition to Print in Late Medieval Brittany*. Burlington, VT, 2010.

Bower, Calvin M. "From Alleluia to Sequence: Some Definitions of Relations." In *Western Plainchant in the First Millennium*. Ed. Sean Gallagher, James Haar, John Nádas, and Timothy Striplin. Burlington, VT, 2003. Pp. 351–398.

———. *The Liber ymnorum of Notker Balbulus*. 2 vols. London, 2016.

Bowles, Edmund A. "A Checklist of Musical Instruments in Fifteenth Century Illuminated Manuscripts at the Bibliothèque Nationale." *Notes* 30 (1974): 474–491.

———. "A Checklist of Musical Instruments in Fifteenth Century Illuminated Manuscripts at the British Museum." *Notes* 29 (1973): 694–703.

———. "A Checklist of Musical Instruments in Fifteenth-Century Illuminated Manuscripts at the Pierpont Morgan Library." *Notes* 30 (1974): 759–765.

———. "A Checklist of Musical Instruments in Fifteenth-Century Illuminated Manuscripts at the Walters Art Gallery." *Notes* 32 (1976): 719–726.

Boynton, Susan. "From Book to Song: Texts Accompanying the Man of Sorrows in the Fourteenth and Fifteenth Centuries." In *New Perspectives on the Man of Sorrows*. Ed. Catherine R. Puglisi and William L. Barcham. Kalamazoo, 2013. Pp. 117–146.

———. "Glossed Hymns in Eleventh-Century Continental Hymnaries." Ph.D. diss. Brandeis University, 1997.

———. "Orality, Literacy, and the Early Notation of the Office Hymns." *Journal of the American Musicological Society* 56 (2003): 99–168.

———. "*Prayer as Liturgical Performance in Eleventh- and Twelfth-Century Monastic Psalter.*" Speculum 82 (2007): 896–931.

Bramley, Henry Ramsden, ed. *The Psalter or Psalms of David and Certain Canticles with a Translation and Exposition in English by Richard Rolle of Hampole*. Oxford, 1884.

Brauner, Mitchell. "Jean du Conseil (Johannes Consilium): His Life and Motets." M. F. A. thesis. Brandeis University, 1978.

Brown, George. "The Psalms as the Foundation of Anglo-Saxon Learning." In *The Place of the Psalms in the Intellectual Culture of the Middle Ages*. Ed. Nancy van Deusen. Albany, 1999. Pp. 1–24.

Brown, Howard Mayer. "The Mirror of Man's Salvation: Music in Devotional Life About 1500." *Renaissance Quarterly* 43 (1990): 744–773.

Brown, Peter. *The Cult of the Saints: Its Rise and Function in Latin Christianity*. Chicago, 1981.

Buckland, Rosina. "Sounds of the Psalter: Orality and Musical Symbolism in the Luttrell Psalter." *Music in Art* 28 (2003): 71–97.

Burkholder, J. Peter, Donald J. Grout, and Claude V. Palisca. *A History of Western Music*. 10th ed. New York, 2019.

Burn, A. E. *The Hymn 'Te Deum' and Its Author*. London, 1926.

Busse Berger, Anna Maria. *Medieval Music and the Art of Memory*. Berkeley, 2005.

Caldwell, Mary Channen. "A Medieval Patchwork Song: Poetry, Prayer and Music in a Thirteenth-Century Conductus." *Plainsong and Medieval Music* 29 (2016): 139–165.

Canal, José. *Salve regina misericordiae: historia y leyendas en torno a esta antífona*. Rome, 1963.

Carruthers, Mary. *The Book of Memory: A Study of Memory in Medieval Culture*. 2nd ed. Cambridge, 2008.

Chevalier, Ulysse, ed. *Repertorium hymnologicum: Catalogue des chants, hymnes, proses, séquences, tropes en usage dans l'église latine depuis les origines jusqu'à nos jours*. 6 vols. Leuven and Brussels, 1892–1912.

Chiu, Remi. "Singing on the Street and in the Home in Times of Pestilence: Lessons from the 1576–78 Plague of Milan." In *Domestic Devotions in Early Modern Italy*. Ed. Maya Corry, Marco Faini, and Alessia Meneghin. Leiden, 2018. Pp. 27–44.

Clanchy, Michael T. *From Memory to Written Record: England 1066–1307*, 3rd ed. Chichester, 2013.

Clark, Gregory T. "Beyond Saints: Variant Litany Readings and the Localization of Late Medieval Manuscript Books of Hours, the Case of the d'Orges Hours." In *Books of Hours Reconsidered*. Ed. Sandra Hindman and James H. Marrow. Studies in Medieval and Early Renaissance Art History. London, 2013. Pp. 213–233.

Coens, Maurice. "Anciennes litanies des saints." In *Recueil d' études bollandiennes*. Ed. Maurice Coens. Brussels, 1963. Pp. 137–322.

Cohen, Thomas V., and Lesley K. Twomey, eds. *Spoken Word and Social Practice: Orality in Europe (1400–1700)*. Leiden, 2015.

Colette, Marie Noelle. *Le Répertoire des Rogations d'après un Processional de Poitiers (XVIe siècle)*. Paris, 1976.

Constant, John. "A Book of Hours for Pope Leo X." In *Music from the Middle Ages Through the Twentieth Century: Essays in Honor of Gwynn S. McPeek*. Ed. Carmelo P. Comberiati and Matthew C. Steel. New York, 1988. Pp. 314–334.

Costley [King'oo], Clare. "David, Bathsheba, and the Penitential Psalms." *Renaissance Quarterly* 57 (2004): 1235–1277.

———. *Miserere Mei: The Penitential Psalms in Late Medieval and Early Modern England*. Notre Dame, IN, 2012.

Crocker, Richard. "Thoughts on Responsories." In *Essays on Medieval Music: In Honor of David G. Hughes*. Ed. Graham M. Boone. Cambridge, MA, 1995. Pp. 77–85.

Crook, David. "The Exegetical Motet." *Journal of the American Musicological Society* 68 (2015): 255–316.

Cumming, Julie. "Petrucci's Publics for the First Motet Prints." In *Making Publics: People, Things, and Forms of Knowledge*. Ed. Paul Yachnin and Bronwen Wilson. New York and London, 2010. Pp. 96–122.

Delaisse, L. M. J. "The Importance of Books of Hours for the History of the Medieval Book." In *Gatherings in Honor of Dorothy E. Miner*. Ed. Ursula E. McCracken, Lilian M. C. Randall, and Richard H. Randall Jr. Baltimore, 1974. Pp. 203–226.

Deuffic, Jean-Luc, and Diane E. Booton. *Le livre d'heures enluminé en Bretagne: Car sans heures ne puys Dieu prier*. Turnhout, 2019.

Dillon, Emma. *The Sense of Sound: Musical Meaning in France, 1260–1330*. New York, 2012.

———. "Unwriting Medieval Song." *New Literary History* 46 (2015): 595–622.

Dobszay, László. "The Responsory: Type and Modulation." *Studia Musicologica* 49 (2008): 3–33.

Driscoll, Michael S. "The Seven Penitential Psalms: Their Designation and Usages from the Middle Ages Onwards." *Ecclesia Orans* 17 (2000): 153–201.

Driver, Martha W. "Mirrors of a Collective Past: Re-Considering Images of Medieval Women." In *Women and the Book: Assessing the Visual Evidence*. Ed. Lesley Smith and Jane H. M. Taylor. London, 1997. Pp. 209–229.

Duchesne, Louis, and M. L. McClure. *Christian Worship: Its Origin and Evolution. A Study of the Latin Liturgy up to the Time of Charlemagne*. Rev. ed. London, 1904.

Duffy, Eamon. *Marking the Hours: English People and Their Prayers, 1240–1570*. New Haven and London, 2006.

———. *The Stripping of the Altars: Traditional Religion in England, c. 1400–c. 1580*. New Haven, 1992.

Dumitrescu, Theodor. "Reconstructing and Repositioning Regis's *Ave Maria . . . virgo serena*." *Early Music* 37 (2009): 73–88.

Dyer, Joseph. "The Psalms in Monastic Prayer." In *The Place of the Psalms in the Intellectual Culture of the Middle Ages*. Ed. Nancy van Deusen. Albany, 1999. Pp. 59–89.

———. "Roman Processions of the Major Litany (*litaniae maiores*) from the Sixth to the Twelfth Century." In *Roma Felix: Formation and Reflections of Medieval Rome*. Ed. Éamonn Ó Carragáin and Carol L. Neuman de Vegvar. Aldershot, 2007. Pp. 113–138.

———. "The Singing of Psalms in the Early-Medieval Office." *Speculum* 64 (1989): 535–578.

Eastman, John R. "Die Werke des Aegidius Romanus." *Augustiniana* 44 (1994): 209–231.

Edwards, Owain T. "Dynamic Qualities in the Medieval Office." In *Liturgy and the Arts in the Middle Ages: Studies in Honour of C. Clifford Flanigan*. Ed. C. Clifford Flanigan, Eva Louise Lillie, and Nils Holger Petersen. Copenhagen, 1996. Pp. 36–63.

———. *Matins, Lauds, and Vespers for St. David's Day: The Medieval Office of the Welsh Patron Saint in National Library of Wales MS 20541 E*. Suffolk, 1990.

Elsig, Frédéric. *Antoine de Lonhy*. Milan, 2018.

Falassi, Alessandro. "Le Contrade." In *Storia di Siena II: dal granducato all'unità*. Ed. Roberto Barzanti, Giuliano Catoni, and Mario De Gregorio. Siena, 1996. Pp. 95–108.

Fassler, Margot. *Gothic Song: Victorine Sequences and Augustinian Reform in Twelfth-Century Paris*. Cambridge, 1993.

———. "Women and Their Sequences: An Overview and a Case Study." *Speculum* 94 (2019): 625–673.

Foley, Edward. "The Song of the Assembly in Medieval Eucharist." In *Medieval Liturgy: A Book of Essays*. Ed. Lizette Larson-Miller. New York, 1997. Pp. 203–234.

Forney, Kristine K. "Music, Ritual, and Patronage at the Church of Our Lady, Antwerp." *Early Music History* 7 (1987): 1–57.

Frandsen, Mary. "*Salve regina/Salve rex christe*: Lutheran Engagement with the Marian Antiphons in the Age of Orthodoxy and Piety." *Musica Disciplina* 55 (2010): 129–218.

Fulton [Brown], Rachel. *From Judgment to Passion: Devotion to Christ and the Virgin Mary, 800–1200*. New York, 2002.

———. *Mary and the Art of Prayer: The Hours of the Virgin in Medieval Christian Life and Thought*. New York, 2018.

———. "Praying with Anselm at Admont: A Meditation on Practice." *Speculum* 81 (2006): 700–733.

Fulton [Brown], Rachel, and Bruce Holsinger, eds. *History in the Comic Mode: Medieval Communities and the Matter of Person*. New York, 2007.

Gajard, Joseph. *The Rhythm of Plainsong According to the Solesmes School*. New York, 1945.

Gardet, Clément. *Les Heures d'Aimée de Saluces, Vicomtesse de Polignac, et Catherine d'Urfé*. Annecy, 1985.

Geary, Patrick. *Living with the Dead in the Middle Ages*. Ithaca, 1994.

Geldhof, Joris. "The Litany of the Saints of the Easter Vigil in the Roman Rite." In *The Litany in Arts and Cultures*. Ed. Witold Sadowski and Francesco Marsciani. Turnhout, 2020. Pp. 175–195.

Gevaert, François. *La mélopée antique dans le chant de l'Église latine*. Gand, 1895.

Gittings, Clare. *Death, Burial, and the Individual in Early Modern England*. London, 1984.

Goody, Jack. *The Interface Between the Written and the Oral*. Cambridge, 1987.
Grant, George. *The Last Crusader: The Untold Stry of Christopher Columbus*. Wheaton, 1992.
Gunkel, Hermann. *Die Psalmen*. Göttigen, 1926.
Haggh, Barbara. "The Meeting of Sacred Ritual and Secular Piety: Endowments for Music." In *Companion to Medieval and Renaissance Music*. Ed. Tess Knighton and David Fallows. London, 1992. Pp. 60–68.
Hale, Edward E. *The Life of Christopher Columbus from His Own Letters and Journals*. Chicago, 1891.
Harrison, Frank L. L. "Faburden in Practice." *Musica Disciplina* 16 (1962): 11–34.
———. *Music in Medieval Britain*. 2nd ed. London, 1963.
Harthan, John. *Books of Hours and Their Owners*. London, 1977.
Head, Thomas, ed. *Medieval Hagiography: An Anthology*. New York, 2001.
Heartz, Daniel. *Pierre Attaingnant: Royal Printer of Music; A Historical Study and Bibliographical Catalogue*. Berkeley, 1969.
Henry, Paul, and Pierre Hadot, eds. *Marii Victorini Opera 1*. Corpus Scriptorum Ecclesiasticorum Latinorum 83. Vienna, 1971.
Hiley, David. *Western Plainchant: A Handbook*. Oxford, 1993.
Hindman, Sandra. "Books of Hours: State of the Research." In *Books of Hours Reconsidered*. Ed. Sandra Hindman and James H. Marrow. Studies in Medieval and Early Renaissance Art History. London, 2013. Pp. 5–16.
———. "Review of 'Die illuminierten Handschriften und Inkunabeln der Österreichischen Nationalbibliothek, Französische Schule, II by Otto Pächt and Dagmar Thoss'." *The Art Bulletin* 62 (1980): 654–658.
Hindman, Sandra, and James H. Marrow, eds. *Books of Hours Reconsidered*. Studies in Medieval and Early Renaissance Art History. London, 2013.
Hornby, Emma. *Medieval Liturgical Chant and Patristic Exegesis: Words and Music in the Second-mode Tracts*. Woodbridge, 2009.
———. "Preliminary Thoughts About Silence in Early Western Chant." In *Silence, Music, Silent Music*. Ed. Nicky Losseff and Jennifer R. Doctor. Aldershot, 2007. Pp. 141–154.
Hucke, Helmut. "Musikalische Formen der Offiziumsantiphonen." *Kirchenmusikalisches Jahrbuch* 37 (1953): 7–33.
———. "Untersuchungen zum Begriff 'Antiphon' und zur Melodik der Offiziumsantiphonen." Ph.D. diss. University of Freiburg, 1951.
Hughes, Andrew. *Late Medieval Liturgical Offices: Sources and Chants*. Toronto, 1996.
———. *Medieval Manuscripts for Mass and Office: A Guide to Their Organization and Terminology*. Toronto, 1982.
———. "Modal Order and Disorder in the Rhymed Office." *Musica Disciplina* 37 (1983): 29–51.
Hunt, Noreen. *Cluny Under St. Hugh, 1049–1109*. Notre Dame, IN, 1967.
Jacobs, Lynn F. "The Master of Getty Ms. 10 and Fifteenth-Century Manuscript Illumination in Lyons." *The J. Paul Getty Museum Journal* 21 (1993): 55–83.
Jeffery, Peter. "Litany." In *Dictionary of the Middle Ages*. 13 vols. Ed. J. R. Strayer, New York, 1986. Pp. 588–594.
———. "The Meanings and Functions of *Kyrie eleison*." In *The Place of Christ in Liturgical Prayer: Trinity, Christology, and Liturgical Theology*. Ed. Bryan D. Spinks. Collegeville, 2008. Pp. 127–194.
König, Eberhard. *Französische Buchmalerei um 1450: Der Jouvenel-Maler, der Maler des Genfer Boccaccio, und die Anfänge Jean Fouquets*. Berlin, 1982.
Kruckenberg, Lori. "Sequence." In *Cambridge History of Medieval Music*. 2 vols. Ed. Mark Everist and Thomas Forrest Kelly. Cambridge, 2018. Pp. 300–356.
Kugel, James L. *The Idea of Biblical Poetry: Parallelism and Its History*. New Haven, 1981.
Labarre, Albert. *Le livre dans la vie amiénoise du seizième siècle: L'enseignement des inventaires après décès (1503–1576)*. Paris, 1971.
Lapidge, Michael, ed. *Anglo-Saxon Litanies of the Saints*. London, 1991.

Leesti, Elizabeth. "A Late Fifteenth-Century Parisian Book of Hours in a Canadian Collection." *RACAR: Revue d'art canadienne* 22 (1995): 40–52.

Leneghan, Francis. "Making the Psalter Sing: The Old English *Metrical Psalms*, Rhythm and *Ruminatio*." In *The Psalms and Medieval English Literature: From the Conversion to the Reformation*. Ed. Tamara Atkin and Francis Leneghan. Cambridge, 2017. Pp. 173–197.

Leroquais, Victor. *Les livres d'heures manuscrits de la Bibliothèque Nationale*. 3 vols. and supplement. Paris and Mâcon, 1927–43.

Levy, Kenneth. "The Trisagion in Byzantium and the West." In *Report of the Eleventh Congress Copenhagen 1972*. 2 vols. Ed. Henrik Glahn et al. International Musicological Society. Copenhagen, 1974. Pp. 761–765.

Loades, David M. "Rites of Passage and the Prayer Books of 1549 and 1552." In *Prophecy and Eschatology*. Ed. Michael Wilks. Studies in Church History 10. Oxford, 1994. Pp. 205–215.

Lord, Albert B. *The Singer of Tales*. Cambridge, MA, 1960.

Macey, Patrick. "Galeazzo Maria Sforza and Musical Patronage in Milan: Compère, Weerbeke and Josquin." *Early Music History* 15 (1996): 147–212.

———. "Josquin, Good King René, and O bone et dulcissime Jesu." In *Hearing the Motet: Essays on the Motet of the Middle Ages and Renaissance*. Ed. Dolores Pesce. New York, 1998. Pp. 213–242.

Mahrt, William P. *The Musical Shape of the Liturgy*. Richmond, 2012.

Maier, Johannes. *Studien zur Geschichte der Marienantiphon Salve Regina*. Regensburg, 1939.

Mak, Bonnie. *How the Page Matters*. Toronto, 2011.

Maloy, Rebecca. *Inside the Offertory: Aspects of Chronology and Transmission*. New York, 2010.

Mansfield, Mary C. *The Humiliation of Sinners: Public Penance in Thirteenth-Century France*. Ithaca, 1995.

Margolin, Jean-Claude. "L'apprentissage des éléments et l'education de la petite enfance d'après quelques manuels scolaires du XVIe siècle." In *L'Enfance et les ouvrages d'education*. 3 vols. Ed. Paul Pénigault-Duhet. Nantes, 1983–86. Pp. 73–104.

Marsolek, C. J. "What Is Priming and Why?" In *Rethinking Implicit Memory*. Ed. J. S. Bowers and C. J. Marsolek. New York, 2003. Pp. 41–64.

Maschke, Eva M. "*Deus in adiutorium intende* Revisited: Sources and Contexts." In *The Montpellier Codex, The Final Fascicle: Contents, Contexts, Chronologies*. Ed. Catherine A. Bradley and Karen Desmond. Rochester, 2018. Pp. 100–120.

McIlvenna, Una. "The Power of Music: the Significance of Contrafactum in Execution Ballads." *Past & Present* 229 (2015): 47–89.

Meiss, Millard, Sharon Off Dunlap, and Elizabeth H. Beatson. *French Painting in the Time of Jean de Berry: The Limbourgs and Their Contemporaries*. New York, 1974.

Mone, F. J., ed. *Lateinische Hymnen des Mittelalters*. 3 vols. Aalen, 1964.

Morgan, Emerson. "Chant and Urban Procession in Rouen 1150–1450." Ph.D. diss. Harvard University, 2018.

Morgan, Nigel. "English Books of Hours c. 1240–c. 1480." In *Books of Hours Reconsidered*. Ed. Sandra Hindman and James H. Marrow. Studies in Medieval and Early Renaissance Art History. London, 2013. Pp. 65–95.

Morin, Germain. "Nouvelles recherches sur l'auteur du Te deum." *Revue bénédictine* 11 (1894): 49–77.

Neale, John Mason, and Richard Frederick Littledale. *A Commentary on the Psalms: From Primitive and Mediaeval Writers and from the Various Office-Books and Hymns of the Roman, Mozarabic, Ambrosian, Gallican, Greek, Coptic, Armenian, and Syriac Rites*. 4 vols. London, 1869–1883.

Nosow, Robert. "Du Fay and the Cultures of Renaissance Florence." In *Hearing the Motet: Essays on the Motet of the Middle Ages and Renaissance*. Ed. Dolores Pesce. New York, 1998. Pp. 104–121.

Nowacki, Edward. "The Latin Antiphon and the Question of Frequency of Interpolation." *Plainsong and Medieval Music* 21 (2012): 23–39.

Ó Carragáin, Éamonn. *Ritual and the Rood: Liturgical Images and the Old English Poems of the Dream of the Rood Tradition*. London, 2005.

Ong, Walter J. *Orality and Literacy: The Technologizing of the Word*. 2nd ed. New York, 2002.

Orme, Nicholas. *Medieval Schools: From Roman Britain to Renaissance England*. New Haven, 2006.
Ottosen, Knud. *The Responsories and Versicles of the Latin Office of the Dead*. Aarhus, 1993.
Owens, Margareth. "Musical Subjects in the Illumination of Books of Hours from Fifteenth-Century France and Flanders." Ph.D. diss. University of Chicago, 1987.
Palisca, Claude V. "Mode Ethos in the Renaissance." In *Essays in Musicology: A Tribute to Alvin Johnson*. Ed. Lewis Lockwood and Edward Roesner. Philadelphia, 1990. Pp. 126–139.
Palti, Kathleen. "Singing Women: Lullabies and Carols in Medieval England." *The Journal of English and Germanic Philology* 110 (2011): 359–382.
Parkes, M. B. *Pause and Effect: An Introduction to the History of Punctuation in the West*. Berkeley, 1993.
Parry, Milman. *The Making of Homeric Verse: The Collected Papers of Milman Parry*. Ed. Adam Parry. Oxford, 1971.
Parsons, Gerald. *Perspectives on Civil Religion*. London, 2017.
Penketh, Sandra. "Women and Books of Hours." In *Women and the Book: Assessing the Visual Evidence*. Ed. Lesley Smith and Jane H. M. Taylor. London, 1997. Pp. 266–281.
Pezzini, Domenico. "Le 'Ore della Croce' nelle liriche inglesi tardo-medievali." *Aevum* 83 (2009): 669–710.
Planchart, Alejandro. "What's in a Name? Reflections on Some Works of Guillaume Du Fay." *Early Music* 16 (1988): 165–175.
Plotzek, Joachim. *Andachtsbücher des Mittelalters aus Privatbesitz*. Cologne, 1987.
Plummer, John. "'Use' and 'Beyond Use'." In *Time Sanctified: The Book of Hours in Medieval Art and Life*. Ed. Roger S. Wieck. New York, 1988. Pp. 149–156.
Pollard, Alfred W. *The Illustrations in French Books of Hours, 1486–1500*. London, 1897.
Pollock, Thomas B. *The Litany Appendix, etc: Metrical Litanies by Thomas Benson Pollock*. London, 1871.
Prizer, William. "Music and Ceremonial in the Low Countries: Philip the Fair and the Order of the Golden Fleece." *Early Music History* 5 (1985): 113–153.
Proctor, Francis, and W. H. Frere. *A New History of the Book of Common Prayer*. Rev. ed. London, 1951.
Putter, Ad. "Prudentius and the Late Classical Biblical Epics of Juvencus, Proba, Sedulius, Arator, and Avitus." In *The Oxford History of Classical Reception in English Literature (800–1558)*. 1 vol. Ed. Rita Copeland. Oxford, 2016. Pp. 351–376.
Raby, F. J. E. *A History of Christian-Latin Poetry from the Beginnings to the Close of the Middle Ages*. Oxford, 1927.
Randall, Lilian M. C. *Medieval and Renaissance Manuscripts in the Walters Art Gallery*. 3 vols. Baltimore, 1989–1997.
Reinburg, Virginia. "'For the Use of Women': Women and Books of Hours." *Early Modern Women* 4 (2009): 235–240.
———. *French Books of Hours: Making an Archive of Prayer, c.1400–1600*. Cambridge, 2012.
———. "Oral Rites: Prayer and Talk in Early Modern France." In *Spoken Word and Social Practice: Orality in Europe (1400–1700)*. Ed. Thomas V. Cohen and Lesley K. Twomey. Leiden, 2015. Pp. 375–392.
Remensnyder, Amy G. "Mary, Star of the Multi-Confessional Mediteranean: Ships, Shrines, and Sailors." In *Ein Meer und seine Heiligen: Hagiographie im mittelalterlichen Mediterraneum*. Ed. Nikolas Jaspert, Marco Di Branco, and Christian Alexander Neumann. Paderborn, 2018. Pp. 297–325.
Robertson, Anne Walters. *Guillaume de Machaut and Reims: Context and Meaning in His Musical Works*. Cambridge, 2002.
Rothenberg, David J. *The Flower of Paradise: Marian Devotion and Secular Song in Medieval and Renaissance Music*. Oxford, 2011.
———. "The Most Prudent Virgin and the Wise King: Isaac's *Virgo prudentissima* Compositions in the Imperial Ideology of Maximilian I." *Journal of Musicology* 28 (2011): 34–80.

Rudy, Kathryn M. "Dirty Books: Quantifying Patterns of Use in Medieval Manuscripts Using a Densitometer." *Journal of Historians of Netherlandish Art* 2 (2010): 1–26.

———. *Piety in Pieces: How Medieval Readers Customized Their Manuscripts*. Cambridge, 2016.

Ruini, Cesarino. "Un antico versione dello Stabat Mater in un graduale delle Domenicane bolognesi." In *Deo è lo scrivano ch'el canto à ensegnato: Segni e simboli nella musica al tempo di Iacopone, Atti del Convegno internazionale, Collazzone, 7–8 luglio 2006*. Ed. Ernesto Sergio Mainoldi and Stefania Vitale. Philomusica On-line 9. Rome, 2010.

Sadowski, Witold. *European Litanic Verse: A Different Space-Time*. Berlin, 2018.

Saenger, Paul. "Books of Hours and Reading Habits of the Later Middle Ages." In *The Culture of Print: Power and the Uses of Print in Early Modern Europe*. Ed. Roger Chartier. Princeton, 1989. Pp. 141–173.

———. "Reading in the Later Middle Ages." In *A History of Reading in the West*. Ed. Guglielmo Cavallo, Roger Chartier, and Lydia G. Cochrane. Amherst, 2003. Pp. 120–148.

Schell, Sarah. "The Office of the Dead in England: Image and Music in the Book of Hours and Related Texts, c. 1250—c. 1500." Ph.D. thesis. University of St. Andrews, 2011.

Schildbach, Martin. "Das einstimmige Agnus Dei und seine handschriftliche Überlieferung vom 10. bis zum 16. Jahrhundert." Ph.D. diss. Erlangen-Nürnberg, 1967.

Schiltz, Katelijne. "Gioseffo Zarlino and the 'Miserere' Tradition: A Ferrarese Connection?" *Early Music History* 27 (2008): 181–215.

Schuler, Carol M. "The Seven Sorrows of the Virgin: Popular Culture and Cultic Imagery in Pre-Reformation Europe." *Simiolus: Netherlands Quarterly for the History of Art* 21 (1992): 5–28.

———. "The Sword of Compassion: Images of the Sorrowing Virgin in Late Medieval and Renaissance Art." Ph.D. diss. Columbia University, 1987.

Sheingorn, Pamela. "Performing the Illustrated Manuscript: Great Reckonings in Little Books." In *Visualizing Medieval Performance: Perspectives, Histories, Contexts*. Ed. Elina Gertsman. Burlington, 2008. Pp. 57–82.

Shephard, Tim, Laura Ştefănescu, and Serenella Sessini. "Music, Silence, and the Senses in a Late Fifteenth-Century Book of Hours." *Renaissance Quarterly* 70 (2017): 474–512.

Smith, Kathryn A. *Art, Identity and Devotion in Fourteenth-Century England: Three Women and Their Books of Hours*. London, 2003.

Stäblein, Bruno, ed. *Hymnen: Monumenta monodica medii aevi 1*. Kassel, 1956.

———. "Litanei." In *Die Musik in Geschichte und Gegenwart: Allgemeine Enzyklopädie der Musik. Sachteil*. 10 vols. Ed. Ludwig Finscher. Kassel, 1994. cols. 1364–1368.

Sticca, Sandro. *The Planctus Mariae in the Dramatic Tradition of the Middle Ages*. Trans. Joseph R. Berrigan. Athens, 1988.

Stock, Brian. *The Implications of Literacy: Written Language and Models of Interpretation in the Eleventh and Twelfth Centuries*. Princeton, 1983.

Strohm, Reinhard. "Late-Medieval Sacred Songs: Tradition, Memory, and History." In *Identity and Locality in Early European Music, 1028–1740*. Ed. Jason Stoessel. Burlington, 2009. Pp. 129–148.

———. *Music in Late Medieval Bruges*. Rev. ed. Oxford, 1990.

———. *The Rise of European Music, 1380–1500*. Cambridge, 1993.

———. "Zur Rezeption der frühen Cantus-firmus-Messe im deutsch-sprachigen Bereich." In *Deutsch-englische Musikbeziehungen: Referate des wissenschaftlichen Symposions im Rahmen der Internationalen Orgelwoche 1980 "Musica Britannica"*. Ed. Wulf Konold. Munich, 1985. Pp. 9–38.

Sutherland, Annie. "Performing the Penitential Psalms in the Middle Ages." In *Aspects of the Performative in the Middle Ages*. Ed. Manuele Gragnolati and Almut Suerbaum. Berlin, 2010. Pp. 15–38.

Taft, Robert F. "Christian Liturgical Psalmody: Origins, Development, Decomposition, Collapse." In *Psalms in Community: Jewish and Christian Textual, Liturgical and Artistic Traditions*. Ed. Harold W. Attridge and Margot E. Fassler. Atlanta, 2003. Pp. 7–32.

Teviotdale, Elizabeth C. "Music and Pictures in the Middle Ages." In *Companion to Medieval and Renaissance Music*. Ed. Tess Knighton and David Fallows. London, 1992. Pp. 179–188.

Thelen, Emily S. "The Feast of the Seven Sorrows of the Virgin: Piety, Politics and Plainchant at the Burgundian-Habsburg Court." *Early Music History* 35 (2016): 261–307.
Titze, Ingo R. *Principles of Voice Production*. 2nd ed. Iowa City, 2000.
Van Deusen, Nancy. "Sequence Repertories: A Reappraisal." *Musica Disciplina* 48 (1994): 99–123.
———. "The Use and Significance of the Sequence." *Musica Disciplina* 40 (1986): 5–47.
Van Dijk, S. J. P. "Medieval Terminology and Methods of Psalm Singing." *Musica Disciplina* 6 (1952): 7–26.
Van Orden, Kate. "Children's Voices: Singing and Literacy in Sixteenth-Century France." *Early Music History* 25 (2006): 209–256.
Van Schaik, Martin. *The Harp in the Middle Ages: The Symbolism of a Musical Instrument*. Amsterdam, 1992.
Vauchez, Andre. *Sainthood in the Later Middle Ages*. Trans. Jean Birrell. New York, 1997.
Vellekoop, Kees. *Dies Ire Dies Illa: Studien zur Frühgeschichte einer Sequenz*. Bilthoven, 1978.
Wagner, Peter. *Einführung in die gregorianischen Melodien*. 3 vols. Leipzig, 1911–1912.
Watt, Tessa. *Cheap Print and Popular Piety, 1550–1640*. Cambridge, 1991.
Wieck, Roger S. *Painted Prayers: The Book of Hours in Medieval and Renaissance Art*. New York, 1997.
———, ed. *Time Sanctified: The Book of Hours in Medieval Art and Life*. New York, 1988.
Wijsman, Suzanne. "Silent Sounds: Musical Iconography in a Fifteenth-Century Jewish Prayer Book." In *Resounding Images: Medieval Intersections of Art, Music and Sound*. Ed. Susan Boynton and Diane J. Reilly. Turnhout, 2015. Pp. 313–333.
Williams, Peter. *The Organ in Western Culture, 750–1250*. Cambridge, 1993.
Williamson, Beth. "Sensory Experience in Medieval Devotion: Sound and Vision, Invisibility and Silence." *Speculum* 88 (2013): 1–43.
Wilson, Stephen, ed. *Saints and Their Cults: Studies in Religious Sociology, Folklore, and History*. Cambridge, 1983.
Winston-Allen, Anne. *Stories of the Rose: The Making of the Rosary in the Middle Ages*. University Park, PA, 1997.
Wolinsky, Mary E. "Hocketing and the Imperfect Modes in Relation to Poetic Expression in the Thirteenth Century." *Musica Disciplina* 58 (2013): 393–411.
Wright, Craig M. *Music and Ceremony at Notre Dame of Paris 500–1550*. Cambridge, 1989.
Yuval, Israel Y. "The Other in Us: Liturgica, Poetica, and Polemica." In *Heresy and Identity in Late Antiquity*. Ed. Eduard Iricinschi and Holger Zellentin. Tübingen, 2008. Pp. 365–385.
Zieman, Katherine. *Singing the New Song: Literacy and Liturgy in Late Medieval England*. Philadelphia, 2008.

Index

Abbey of St. Victor 171
abbreviation: of antiphons 44, 48; and "doubled" antiphons 48; of the Pater noster 113–14; vs. recopying 19–20, 44, 129, 213n16; of repetenda 93. *See also* incipits, textual
Adam of St. Victor 171, 210
Adoramus te (antiphon) 59–60
Agnus Dei (Litany of the Saints) 151, 155–6, *158*
Agnus Dei (Mass Ordinary) 201
Agricola, Alexander 77
Aimée (Amadée) de Saluces 114
Albertus Magnus 87
Alcuin of York 121
All Saints, memorials for 183, *184–5*, 188
All Saints, Office and Mass for 209
Alleluia ℣ Post partum virgo 196, *197–8*
Alleluia ℣ Virga iesse 196, *197–8*
alternation, choral 9, 20–4, 36, 64, 130
Amalarius of Metz 49, 142
Ambrosian liturgy 58
Anne, St., suffrage for 178
Anne of Beaujeu 22
Anne of Brittany, Queen of France 168
Ante crucem mater stabat (planctus) 174
antiphonal singing, roots of 22
antiphons 36–61; incipits of 41–9; invitatory 48–53; liturgical sources 37, 60; Marian 53–8; melodic uniformity 40; modes and 38–41; nonliturgical 165–8; Hours of the (Holy) Cross 58–61; Office of the Dead 37, 40–1, **41**, 52–3; Hours of the Holy Spirit 58–61; Office of the Virgin 37–40, **38**, 48–53; relation to psalms 36–7, 49, 52–3; and the Seven Penitential Psalms 130–7; suffrages **163–4**; votive 53. *See also* suffrages
Apollonia, St. 165; suffrage for 165, *166*, 167
Aquinas, Thomas 210
audiation 5–7, 18, 20, 48, 156–7; iconography and 107, *108–9*, 110. *See also* memory, sonic; *mise-en-page*; performance markers
Audivi vocem meam/Beati mortui (versicle-response) 105

Augustine, St. 106
Aurelian of Arles, Rule of 64
Ave Maria gratia plena (invitatory antiphon) 38, 48–53, *50–1*, 110
Ave Maria (prayer) 113
Ave maris stella (Marian hymn) 70–2

Baltimore, Walters Art Museum: MS W.281 ("Malet-Lannoy Hours") 107, *108–9*; MS W.447 127, *128*
Baltzer, Rebecca 39, 70
Barbara, St. 169; suffrage for 168–73, *170*
Baroffio, Giacomo 7, 73
Bata, Ælfric (Anglo-Saxon monk) 129
Beata Apollonia (antiphon) 167
Beata dei genetrix (antiphon) 44, *45–6*, 105
Beata es Maria (responsory) 87, 89, **90**
Beata mater et innupta (antiphon) 32
Beata viscera (Communion) 196, **199**, 201, *207*
Becket, Thomas 173
Beleth, Iohannes 48, 106
"Benedicite omnia opera" (Canticle of the Three Children) 33, **38**
Benedict, St., Rule of 32, 64, 106
Benedicta et venerabilis es (Gradual) 194–5, **195**
Benedicta sit sancta trinitas (Introit) 209
Benedicta tu in mulieribus (antiphon) 38
Benedicta tu in mulieribus (versicle) 105
Benedictus (Canticle of Zechariah) 33, 44
Bethlehem, Lehigh Univ., Spec. Coll., Codex 17 95
Biblia Mariana (Albertus Magnus) 87
Blackburn, Bonnie 167
Bochard family of Vézelay 20
Book of the Three Virtues 3
book ownership 1–4
Book to a Mother 123
books of hours: considered in this study 7–8; contents of 2; development of 1–2; devotions, private, porous boundaries of 7, 159; emulation of the liturgy 9; ethnographic studies of 4; historiography 3–5, 8, 210,

213; performance of 6–7; personalization of 162–3; user experience 9, 19
Bourdichon, Jean (illuminator) 127
Bowles, Edmund 5
breath (inhalation) 20, 22, 25, 158
Brown, Howard Mayer 5, 167, 173

Caesarius of Arles, Rule of 64
Caldwell, Mary Channen 107
call-and-response style 141
canticles 32–3
capitals 20, 22, 53, 64, 79, 81, 93, 96, 129, 159, 200, 201. *See also* color, alternation of; line breaks; *pied-de-mouche*
Carmen paschale (Sedulius) 194
Cassian, John (theologian) 49, 107
Cassiodorus 121
Celi enarrant (Ps. 18) 20, *21*
Charles of Orleans, Count of Angoulême 53
Charles V, King of France 92
"Chasteauneuf Hours." *See* Paris, BnF, n.a.l. MS 3210
Chiu, Remy 159
Christe redemptor omniium/ex Patre (hymn) 69
Christine de Pizan 3
Christmas Day, Mass for 210, *211*
Christopher, St., suffrage for 167
Cibavit eos (Introit) 209
cilicium ("hair shirt") 129
Clamantes et dicentes advenisti (verse) 98
Clark, Gregory 3
Claudius of Besançon, St. 167; suffrage for 167–8
Clement VII (pope) 168
Cohen, Thomas 7
Collationes patrum (John Cassian) 107
Collect (Mass) 113, 180, 181, 189
Colombe, Jean (illuminator) 183, 188
colon 20, 22, 25, 66, 130, 188, 200. *See also* punctuation
color, alternation of 20, *21*, 22, *23*, 129–30. *See also* capitals
Comeau family of Créancey 170
"commendatio" (genre label) 76
Common of Virgins 37
concluding formulas 20
confession 121
Confessions (Augustine) 5
Conseil, Jean 168
contrafacture 171, 175, 210
Converte nos, Deus (versicle) 106
Corpus antiphonalium officii 37
Corpus Christi (feast) 161n37, 171, 193
Corpus Christi, Office and Mass for 209, **209**
Credo (Mass Ordinary) 201
Credo quod redemptor (responsory) 93, *95*
Crocker, Richard 86, 89
cross-references 19–20, 44, 129

David, King 18; and Bathsheba 123, *126*, 127, *128*; depictions of 122–3, *124–6*, 127, *128*; and King Saul 123; Seven Penitential Psalms and 122–9
de Lonhy, Antoine (illuminator) 123, 181
De profundis clamavi (Ps. 129) 20
de Rieux, Marie 132
des Prez, Josquin 69, 174
Deus in adiutorium (versicle) 106–7, 112–13, ***112***
"Deus qui miro ordine" (oration) 181
devotions, intercessory 142
dialogues 10, 105–16; and the Litany 116; participant voices in 116; Pater noster 113–16, ***114***, *115*; salutatory versicles 106–10; sounds of 106, 111–13, 178; in suffrages 175–80, **178–9**
differentia. *See* termination formula
Diffusa est gratia (versicle) 111, ***112***, 178
digitization 213
Dillon, Emma 6, 37
Divine Office, lay emulation of 1, 3, 4–5
Divitis, Antonius 168
"Domine Dominus noster" (Ps. 8) 22, *23*
Domine exaudi/Et clamor (versicle-response) 188
Domine labia mea aperies (versicle) 106, 107, *108–9*, 110
"Domine ne in furore tuo" (Ps. 6) 123, *124–6*, *128*
"Dominus vobiscum" (Mass versicle) 105
Donatus 24
dot of division 25, 53, 58. *See also* punctuation
doxology. *See Gloria patri*
Duffy, Eamon 4
Dum sacrum mysterium (antiphon) 181, *182*
"Dunois Hours." *See* London, British Library, Yates Thompson MS 3
duplex feasts 48
Durand, Guillaume (bishop) 48, 107, 200
Dyer, Joseph 49

Ecce advenit (Introit) 194
Ecclesiasticus, Book of 87
education, primary 17, 121, 175
Egidius of Rome 73
embodied experience 4, 24–5, 52, 80–81, 107, 159
Emitte spiritus/Et renovabis (versicle-response) 60
Ex hoc nunc et usque in seculum (response) 188
Expositio Psalmorum (Cassiodorus) 121

Fabri, Felix (Dominican diarist) 1, 104n24
Fassler, Margot 171, 175
Felix namque es (Offertory) 196, ***199***, 201, *207*
Felix namque es (responsory) 87, 89–92, ***91***
Foley, Edward 105
Fourth Lateran Council 121

"Fuit homo missus" (versicle) 180, *180*
Fulbert of Chartres (bishop) 89, 194
Fulton, Rachel 3, 36, 52, 87

Gallican rite 142, 159
Gaude Barbara beata 168–3, *172*
Gaude dei genetrix (antiphon) 175
Gaude flore virginali (sequence) 173
Gaude Iohannes baptista (sequence) 172
Gaude Maria virgo (tract) 201, *206*
Gaude pia Magdalena (sequence) 172
Gaude virgo gloriosa (prayer) 174
Gaude virgo Katherina (sequence) 172
Gaude virgo mater Christi (sequence) 172–4
Gaudeamus omnes in Domino (Introit) 209
Gelasius I (pope) 142
genres, liturgical 58, 59, 79–80, 164, 167, 188, 201; and vocal texture 6, 37, 53, 64, 86, 105–6
Gloria (Mass Ordinary) 188, 200
Gloria patri 20, 29, *112*
"Gloria tibi Domine" (response) 105
"Golden Legend." *See Legenda aurea* (Jacobus de Voragine)
goliardic meter 72, 76
goliardic songs 79
Gradual Psalms 121–2; in Office of the Virgin 19
Graduale Sacrosanctae Romanae Ecclesiae De Tempore et De Sancti **114**, *194*, **195**, **197**
Gregory I (pope) 142
Gualenghi-d'Este Hours 5, 107

harp, King David's 122–3, *124–6*, 127, *128*
Harrison, Frank Llewellyn 163
"Has horas canonicas" (stanza) 74, 76, 77, 79
Hesbert, René-Jean 37, 132
Hiley, David 29, 162
horae. See books of hours
Hornby, Emma 25
Horologium sapientiae (Henry Suso) 174
Hours of the (Holy) Cross 9, 18, 58–61, 72–6, 107
Hours of the Holy Spirit 9, 18, *57*, 58–61, 76–9, 107
Hugh of St. Victor 24
Hughes, Andrew 22
Hugues of Cluny 181
hymns 64–84; Hours of the (Holy) Cross 72–6; Hours of the Holy Spirit 76–9; melodies of 65–6; in monastic use 64; Office of the Virgin 65–72; performance of 64; Te Deum 79–81. *See also individual hymns*

Iam hiems (antiphon) *38*, 48
illuminations 5, 53, 60–1, 183, 188; as focus of study 3; of instruments *108–9*, 110; of Mary *108*, 110, *176*, 175

implicit memory (psychology) 106, 113
In loco pascue (antiphon) 41, *42–3*, 48
In odorem unguentorum (antiphon) 40
incipit, melodic (*intonatio*) 29
incipits, textual: antiphon 41–9; concluding formulas 20
initials. *See* capitals
Innocent III (pope) 129
instruments, illuminated *108–9*, 110
Inter natos mulierum (antiphon) 164, *165*
Inviolata integra et casta (prose) 92
Isaac, Abbot (Desert Father) 107
Isidore of Seville 6
Isidore of Seville, Rule of 64

Jacobus de Voragine 165, 167, 169
Jacopone da Todi 174
James, St. 183
Jeanne of France 22
Jeanne of Lannoy 110
Job, Book of 92
John, Duke of Berry 7, 152
John of Salisbury 18
John the Baptist 162, 169, 172–4, 180, 183; sequence for 172; suffrage antiphon for 164; versicle-response for **178**, 180, *180*
John the Evangelist 183
Joys of the Virgin 113, 172, 173, 175, 190n39
Jube domne benedicere (versicle) 116

Katherine, St. 172; suffrage for 178
King'oo, Clare Costley 122, 127
Kugel, James 24
Kyrie eleison 114, *115*, 142, 200, *204*

Lady Mass. *See* Mass for the Virgin Mary
Laetamini in Domino/Et gloriamini omnes (dialogue) 183
Lambert, Guillaume (illuminator) 142
lament. *See* planctus
Lassus, Orlande de 122
Lauda Sion salvatorem (sequence) 210, *212*
Laudes crucis attolamus (Adam of St. Victor) 171, *172*, 173, 174, 175
lay devotion 2, 3, 5, 11, 81
Lazarus, suffrage for 181
Legenda aurea (Jacobus de Voragine) 165, 167, 169
Leipzig, Universitätsbibliothek, MS 1494 ("Apel Codex") 73–4, *74*
Leo X (pope) 168
Leroquais, Victor 9
"Letatus sum" (Ps. 121) 44, *47*
Liber quare 48
Liber ymnorum (Notker of St. Gall) 169
Libera me Domine (responsory) 98–103; CAO 7091 98–101, *101*, *102*, 103; CAO 7092 98, **99**

line breaks 74, 157, 171. *See also* capitals
line-fills (*Zeilenfüller*): in the Litany 157–8; and poetic form 74, 129–30, 171, 175. *See also* line breaks
"litanic rhythm" 159
Litanies, Lesser 159
Litany of the Saints 10, 141–2, *143–9*, 150–9; "ab"/"a" petitions 153, *154*; *Agnus Dei* 151, 155–6, *158*; catalog of saints 150; concluding items *156*; embodied experience 159; Kyrie eleison 142, 150, 151; liturgical occasions 142; local devotions and 141; musical models for 153; opening of *153*; "per" petitions 150, 154, *154*; performance cues 157–9; petitions ("deprecations") 150; pitch space 153–7; processions 159, 161n37; rhymed and rhythmical 174; sounds of 152–7; "ut" petitions 151, 154, *155*; versicle-response and 116
literacy: and illiteracy 17, 175; and Latin 2, 4, 17, 121, 175; and orality 6
"Little Office" 11n4. *See also* Office of the Virgin Mary
liturgical dramas 81
liturgical feasts and seasons: Advent 8, 53, 103n4, 193, 208; Advent, Ember Days of 135; after Pentecost 132, 189; All Saints 89, 183, 188; Annunciation 2, 58, 87, 107, *109*, 110; Ascension 159; Ash Wednesday 129, 130; Assumption 32, 37, 89, 92, 110; Christmas 87, 89, 193, *211*; Compassion of Mary 174; Conception of Mary 58, 91; Corpus Christi 171, 193; Cross, feasts for the 59; Easter 142; Holy Thursday 209; Lent 92, 129; Nativity of Mary 37, 58, 89; Pentecost 59, 142; Purification 32, 37, 87, 89, 193, 201, 208; St. Mark, feast of 135, 159
liturgical sources. *See* service books
Lives of St. Colette 18
London, British Library: Add. MS 23935 *112*; Add. MS 27697 114, *115*; Add. MS 35214 *57*, 58; Yates Thompson MS 3 ("Dunois Hours") *186–7*, 188
Lord's Prayer. *See* Pater noster
Louis de Laval 183
Louis of Savoy, Hours of. *See* Paris, BnF, lat. MS 9473
Louis XII, King of France 168
Louise of Savoy 53

Machaut, Guillaume de 193
Magnificat (Canticle of Mary) 32–3, 105, 143
Mak, Bonnie 157
Malet de Berlettes, Thomas 110
"Malet-Lannoy Hours." *See* Baltimore, Walters Art Museum, MS W.281

Margaret, St. 172, 183; suffrages for 180
marginalia 4, 5, 11
Marguerite d'Orléans 123
"Maria mater gratie" (migrant stanza) 66, 68, 69, 70
Marian antiphons 53–8
Marian feasts 32, 58; as source of antiphons 37
Marian hymns 65–72
Martin, St.: liturgy for 179; versicle-response for 179, *179*
Mary Magdalene, St. 172, 183
Mass for the Cross 209
Mass for the Dead 3, 98–9, 208
Mass for the Holy Spirit 208
Mass for the Virgin Mary 11, 173, 193–213, *202–7*; Alleluias 196, *197–8*; Offertory and Communion 196; Ordinary 200, 201; polyphonic settings of 193; Propers 193–6, 199; sounds of 200, 201, 208
Mass Ordinary, lay familiarity with 200
Mass XVIII ordinaries 155
Masses, supplemental, in books of hours 208–10, **209–10**
Master of Flowers (illuminator) 77
Master of the Burgundian Prelates (illuminator) 20
Master of the Hours of Louis of Savoy (illuminator) 44
Matins: iconography of 107, 110; and Lauds 68; Office of the Dead 52–3; Office of the Virgin 48–52; and responsories 86
Maur-des-Fossés, St. Monastery of 111
Maurus, Hrabanus (Carolingian scholar) 159
McKinnon, James 194
measure, sequence. *See* meter, sequence
Memento salutis auctor (Marian hymn) 69–70, *70*
memorials 183–9, 189n1. *See also* suffrages
memory, sonic: bells 81, 201; dialogues 106; organ 81; and *pied-de-mouche* 96; of responsories 86, 91–92
memory aids: color 24; text 5. *See also* script size, differentiation of
mental glance 17
Messe de Notre Dame (Guillaume de Machaut) 193
Metalogicon (John of Salisbury) 18
meter, sequence 169, 171, 173, 174, 175
meter, trochaic 171
metrical litany 159
Meurier, Hubert 3
Michael, St.: oration for 181, *181*; suffrage for 181, *182*
Milanese rite 142
mise-en-page: antiphons 49–55; dialogues 114, 116; hymns 74, 79, 81; Litany of the Saints

157–9; Mass for the Virgin Mary 197, 200, 201, 208; psalms 20, 22, 32; responsories 93, 96, 100–101, 103; Seven Penitential Psalms 129–30, 132, 134; *Stabat mater dolorosa* (sequence) 175–8; suffrage orations 181, 183, 188; suffrages 163, 170–1, 178. *See also* performance markers
monastic devotion 64, 106, 175
Motetti de la corona 168
motetti missales 69
Mouton, Jean 169–70
Mozarabic rite 142
musica mundana 24
musical notation 3, 5, 7, 106, 179

Ne reminiscaris Domine (antiphon) 130–7, *132*, *133–4*, *136–7*; *Parce Domine* extension 135
Neale, John Mason 121
New Haven, Yale Univ., Beinecke Libr.: MS 411 53, *54–5*; MS 435 165, *166*
Night Office. *See* Matins
Nigra sum sed formosa (antiphon) 44, *47*
"Nisi Dominus" (Ps. 126) *47*, 48
Nobis sancti spiritus (hymn for the Holy Spirit) 76–9
Nos autem gloriari oportet (Introit) 209
Notker of St. Gall 6, 169
Notre Dame of Paris (cathedral) 39, 70, 183
"Nunc dimittis" (Canticle of Simeon) 33, 58

Ó Carragáin, Éamonn 155
O desolatorum consolator (antiphon) 167–8
O gloriosa domina (Marian hymn) 68, *70*, 105
Office of the Dead 17; antiphons 37, 40, **41**, 52–3; centrality to books of hours 2–3; Matins 52–3, *97*; Matins responsories **92**; psalms **19**; responsories 92, 98–103; Vespers 105, 114, *115*
Office of the Virgin Mary 17; antiphons 37–40, **38**, 48–53; centrality to books of hours 2; Compline 53, 69; history of 183; hymns 65–72; illuminations of 107; Lauds 68, 105, 183; Marian antiphons 53–8; Matins 48–52, 65, 79, 107, *108–9*; minor hours 69, 70; psalms 18–19, **19**; responsories 87–92; Te Deum 79–81; versicle-response pairs 106–7, 110; Vespers 70–1
Office-Mass pairs 208–9
Officium Parvum Beatae Mariae Virginis. *See* Office of the Virgin Mary
Old Testament, Marian readings of 87
Omne quod dat (antiphon) 105, 114, *115*
orations (*orationes*), suffrage 180–3
"Ora/Ut digni" (versicle-response) 178–9
Owens, Margareth 5

Palestrina, Giovanni Pierluigi da 170, 174
paragraph sign 96
paraph. *See pied-de-mouche*
Parce Domine (antiphon) 135, 137
Paris, Bibl. Mazarine, MS 502 200, *202–3*
Paris, Bibl. Sainte-Geneviève, Ms. 113 *66*
Paris, BnF, Ars.: MS 562 *rés*. 28; MS 616 *rés*. *50–1*, 209–10, **209–10**, *211*, *212*; MS 637 *rés*. *42–3*, *137*; MS 638 *rés*. 77, *78*; MS 644 *rés*. 23; MS 645 *rés*. *21*; MS 1194 *rés*. 123, *125*
Paris, BnF, lat.: MS 920 (Hours of Louis de Laval) 183, *184–5*, 188; MS 1090 **179**; MS 1156B 123, *124*; MS 1157 66, *67*; MS 1160 *45–6*; MS 1170 132, *133*, 135; MS 1181 *176–7*, 175, 188; MS 1184 *97*; MS 1188 93, *94*; MS 1374 *136*; MS 8886 152, *153*, 155, **155**, **156**; MS 9473 ("Hours of Louis of Savoy") 74, *75*, 196, *197–8*; MS 12044 **90**, **112**, **165**; MS 14819 **172**; MS 15181 39, **88**, **91**, **165**; MS 15182 39, **99**, **101**, **132**
Paris, BnF, n.a.l.: MS 1412 **180**; MS 3110 *102*; MS 3111 *204–5*; MS 3117 142, *143–9*; MS 3187 *82–3*; MS 3196 173–4, 191n47; MS 3197 170–1, *170*; MS 3209 181, *182*, 191n68; MS 3210 ("Chasteauneuf Hours") 123, *126*, 130, *131*, *134*; MS 3213 *158*; MS 3229 201, *206–7*, 208–9; MS 3258 44, *47–8*
parody 171
Pater noster 113–16, **114**, *115*
Patris sapientia veritas divina (hymn for the Holy Cross) 72–6, **73–4**, *75*
pauses (*distinctiones*) 34n25
Peccantem me quotidie (responsory) 96, *97*
Penitential Psalms. *See* Seven Penitential Psalms
Penketh, Sandra 4
performance markers: in *Gaude Maria virgo* (tract) 208; in hymns 64; in the Litany 157–9; in the Mass for the Virgin Mary 200, 201, 208; in the memorial for All Saints 188; in *Patris sapientia veritas divina* (hymn) 74; for the repetendum 93–8; in *Salve regina* 58; in suffrages 178. *See also* abbreviation; capitals; color, alternation of; incipits, textual; line breaks; line-fills; *pied-de-mouche*; script size, differentiation of
period 25, 77, 96, 175. *See also* punctuation
Peter of Luxembourg, St. 174
Petrucci, Ottaviano 168
Petrus apostolus (antiphon) 164–5, **165**
Pfintzing, Barbara (Dominican nun) 92
Philadelphia Art Museum, Dept. of Prints, Drawings, and Photographs: MS 1945-65-8 *30–1*; MS 1945-65-13 26

Philip the Fair 77
Philip the Good 77
pied-de-mouche 53, 58, 96–8, 129–30, 135, 208
pilcrow 96
Pius V (pope) 2, 141
Placebo Domino (antiphon) 40
Planchart, Alejandro 171, 173
planctus 174
Play of Daniel 81
polyphonic sources for untraced plainchant 71, 167, 168, 169, 173
"Praise Psalms" 19, 20
prayer, unceasing 107
priming (psychology) 106
Prizer, William 77
processions 53, 81, 92, 137, 159
prostrate psalms 121
"Protege Dominum populum tuum" (oration) *184*, 188
Psalm 50:17. *See Domine labia mea aperies* (versicle)
Psalm 69 106–7, 116. *See also Deus in adiutorium* (versicle)
psalms 17–34; antiphonal singing 22; bipartite form 24; canticles treated as 32–3; choral alternation 20–4, 130; connection with music 18; duplicate 19–20, 44, 129; embodied experience 24–5; groupings 37; intonation of 25, 29; liturgical assignments 18–20; medial distinction and silence 24–5; memorization of 24, 25; modal connection with antiphons 29; in Office of the Dead 19–20, **19**; in Office of the Virgin 18–19, **19**; psalmody 18, 22, 25–9, 38, 49, 81. *See also* Seven Penitential Psalms
Psalms 148–50 ("Praise Psalms") 19, 20
psalters 2, 5, 24, 48, 79; illustrated 121–2; and literacy 17–18
Pulchra es decora (antiphon) 36
punctuation 24, 25, 58, 66, 77, 130, 181. *See also* colon; dot of division; line-fills; period

Quem terra pontus aethera (Marian hymn) 65–66, **66**, *67*, 68, *70*
Quintilian 24

Raby, F. J. E. 171
Ramos de Pareja, Bartolomé 138
Rationale divinorum officiorum (Guillaume Durand) 48
recitation, rhythmical 73, 171
recitation tone 29, 111
"recommendatio" (genre label) 76
Regem cui omnia vivunt (invitatory antiphon) 52–3
Regina caeli (Marian antiphon) 53, 58
Reims Cathedral 3, 92, 193

Reinburg, Virginia 4, 5
Rennes (France) 49
repetendum 86, 93–8, *94*, *95*, *97*, *102*
repetition, signals for. *See pied-de-mouche*
Requiem aeternam (verse) 98
Requiem Mass. *See* Mass for the Dead
responsoria prolixa ("great responsories") 86
responsories 86–103; Office of the Dead 92, **92**, 98–103; Office of the Virgin 87–92; repetendum 86, 93–8, *94*, *95*, *97*, *102*; structure of 86
Rogations 159
Rolle, Richard 122
Roman de Fauvel 87
Rorate caeli (Introit) 208
Rothenberg, David 53, 110
Ruini, Cesarino 174
Rusconi Codex 167

saccadic eye movement 6, 93, 96, 159
Sadowsky, Witold 159
Saenger, Paul 5
Saluces, House of 114
Salve mater dolorosa 174, 191n47
Salve regina (Marian antiphon) 1, 53–8, 92
Salve sancta parens (Introit) 193, 194, **194**
Sancta et immaculata virginitas (responsory) 87–9, **88**, 92–3, *94*
"Sancta Maria succurre miseris" (Fulbert of Chartres) 89, 194, 213n7
Sancte Christofore martir (antiphon) 167
Sancti dei omnes (antiphon) 183, *184*, 191n72
Sanctus (Mass Ordinary) 201
"Sanctus" (Te Deum) 80–1, **80**, *82–3*
"script devices" 7
script size, differentiation of: and musical style 52; in service books 34n5; and vocal texture 6, 37, 53, 64, 103
script size, larger 17, 64, 72, 74, 106, 180
script size, smaller 37, 52, 86, 103, 132, 178
Sedulius (poet) 194
sensorium, inner 5. *See also* audiation
sequences 59, 169; by Adam of St. Victor 171; with "Gaude" salutation 172–4; and lay literacy 175; performance of 171, 190n25; *Stabat mater dolorosa* (sequence) 174–5, *176–7*, 190n44; as suffrage antiphons 168–74
service books: antiphoners 60, 106, 111, 132, 159, 179, 180; breviaries 29, 36, 39, 48, 77, 84n24, 132; graduals 159, 171, 174, 189n7; missals 34n5, 100, 171; ordinals 48; pontificals 152, 155; processionals 152, 159; psalter-hymnals 66; sacramentaries 159, 180
Sessini, Serenella 5, 107

Seven Penitential Psalms 10, 17, 121–39, *124–6, 128*; antiphon for 130–7; David, King, and the 122–9; and devotional life 122, 129; duplicated in books of hours 138; and the *Gloria Patri* 130; modal ethos and 137–8; *Ne reminiscaris Domine* (antiphon) 130–7; performance of 129–30; sounds of 138; vernacular translations 122
Seven Sorrows devotion 174
Sforza, Galeazzo Maria 69
Sheingorn, Pamela 4, 6
Shephard, Tim 5, 107
Sign of the Cross (physical gesture) 107
silence (caesura) 20, 24–5
silent reading 5, 18
Simeon, Canticle of ("Nunc dimittis") 33, 58
singers, illustrated *108–9*, 110
Sistine Chapel 168
Sit nomen Domini benedictum (versicle) 188
"Specie tua" (versicle) 180
Speculum de mysteriis ecclesiae 48
Spiritus Domini replevit (Introit) 208
Stabat mater dolorosa (sequence) 174–5, *176–7*, 190n44
Stäblein, Bruno 66, 68, 69
Ștefănescu, Laura 5, 107
Strohm, Reinhard 81
Sts. Peter and Paul, suffrage for 164–5
Sub tuum praesidium (antiphon) 58
suffrages 10–11, 162–89; antiphons 163–5, **163–4**; antiphons, nonliturgical 165–8; definition 189n1; dialogues 175–80, **178–9**; memorials 183–9; musical models for 163–5; orations 180–3; roster of saints 162–3; sequences as antiphons 168–73; sounds of 171, 179; structure 188; versicle-response 175–80
Summa de ecclesiasticus officiis (Iohannes Beleth) 48
supererogation 121
Suso, Henry 174
Sutherland, Annie 129

Te Deum 79–81, **80**, *82–83*
Te invocamus, te adoramus (antiphon) 164, **165**, *186–7*, 188

termination formula (*differentia*) 29, 36
Teviotdale, Elizabeth 123
texture, vocal 9–11, 37, 64, 86, 105–6, 213; in the Litany 157–9; in the Magnificat 32; in the Mass for the Virgin Mary 208; in orations 181; in the Pater noster 114, 116; in psalms 20, 22; in responsories 93, 96; in suffrages 188
Three Children, Canticle of the ("Benedicite omnia opera") 33
Tobit, Book of 130
tract (Proper) 201
Trent, Bibl. Capitolare, MS BL (Trent 93) *73*
Trent Codices 73
Trinity, Office and Mass for 209
Trinity, suffrage and memorials for 164, 188
Trisagion. See Sanctus (Mass Ordinary); "Sanctus"(Te Deum)
Twomey, Lesley 7

usage, liturgical 8, 32, 106, 209

van Deusen, Nancy 174–5
van Orden, Kate 5, 17
Venantius Fortunatus (bishop) 65
Veni creator spiritus (hymn for Pentecost) 70, 208–9
Veni sancte spiritus (antiphon) 59, 60–1, 77, *78*
Veni sancte spiritus (sequence for Pentecost) 208
"Venite exultemus" (Ps. 94) 48
versicle-response. *See* dialogues
versicles, salutatory 106–10
Vicentino, Nicola 138
votive masses 193

Washington, D.C., Library of Congress, Music Division, MS 36 152
Wieck, Roger 22
Wijsman, Suzanne 123
Williams, Peter 81
Williamson, Beth 5, 6, 24

Zamora, Juan Gil de 138
Zarlino, Gioseffo 138
Zechariah, Canticle of (Benedictus) 33, 44
Zieman, Katherine 6, 18, 37

9780367691325